AMERICAN TEEN DRAMAS

AMERICAN TEEN DRAMAS

FROM SUNNYDALE TO RIVERDALE

JOANNA HAGAN

WHITE OWL
AN IMPRINT OF PEN & SWORD BOOKS LTD.
YORKSHIRE – PHILADELPHIA

First published in Great Britain in 2025 by
PEN AND SWORD WHITE OWL
An imprint of
Pen & Sword Books Ltd
Yorkshire – Philadelphia

ISBN 978 1 03611 393 3

A CIP catalogue record for this book is available from the British Library.

Typeset in Times New Roman 12/16 by
SJmagic DESIGN SERVICES, India.
Printed and bound in the UK by CPI Group (UK) Ltd, Croydon, CR0 4YY.

The Publisher's authorised representative in the EU for product safety is Authorised Rep Compliance Ltd., Ground Floor, 71 Lower Baggot Street, Dublin D02 P593, Ireland.
www.arccompliance.com

For a complete list of Pen & Sword titles please contact

PEN & SWORD BOOKS LIMITED
George House, Units 12 & 13, Beevor Street, Off Pontefract Road,
Barnsley, South Yorkshire, S71 1HN, England
E-mail: enquiries@pen-and-sword.co.uk
Website: www.pen-and-sword.co.uk

or
PEN AND SWORD BOOKS
1950 Lawrence Rd, Havertown, PA 19083, USA
E-mail: uspen-and-sword@casematepublishers.com
Website: www.penandswordbooks.com

Contents

Pre-Credits

Welcome to…

It's around 8pm on a Friday night in Brooklyn. I'm sitting alone, at a small table, in a bar. There's a card on the table that states 'The Rupert Giles Research Assistants.' I am the first of my group to arrive for *Buffy* trivia. I haven't met the other two members of the group yet, although we've exchanged an email to agree on the team's name.

Sasha and Matt arrive, we introduce ourselves, and I admit that yes, I've travelled from England just for this weekend of events. We cram in around the table and settle in for the serious business that is a *Buffy* pub quiz.

I have not travelled this far purely for the quiz. I've travelled this far because I'm attending the *Buffering the Vampire Slayer* prom; a celebration of a show I love, organised by a podcast that loves the show even more. *Buffy the Vampire Slayer* ended in 2003, and *Buffering the Vampire Slayer* – the incredibly popular *Buffy* recap podcast hosted by Kristin Russo and Jenny Owen Youngs – began in 2016. Now, in 2024, both the show and the podcast maintain crowds of adoring fans.

All of the shows in this book, and the fandoms around them, are strange and miraculous. They're shows that were tough sells, shows that don't make sense on the surface. All of these shows got to exist, got to run for a good few years, got to build up audiences that became fandoms and subcultures. Many of them got to become as beloved as *Buffy*, if not more, to crowds of people that found each other through online message boards, or websites like Tumblr, or just by recognising certain t-shirts in public.

Teen dramas make for unique television. When teenagers emerged as a unique audience, and television started being made specifically for them, storytelling on television changed forever. These shows got to be tastemakers, and music and fashion on screen took on a whole new relevance. More importantly, these shows got to be *weird*. Supernatural stories, fantasy and science fiction, stories that pushed boundaries and tried new things became mainstream. More than that, they became part of the zeitgeist.

What makes the teen market so unique? Why are teen dramas the perfect place for creative, off-the-wall television? When teenagers became a unique television audience, they became test subjects. These shows became safe spaces where nothing is completely out of the question. Writers revisiting their youth could explore ideas of identity and relationships and the chaotic ways we adore things when we're young, either literally or through the metaphorical lenses of vampires, folklore, dystopias and surreal diners.

This book contains over twenty-five years of television history. The way television is made, the way shows are written and how long they get to last are all things that have changed massively over that period. This is the story of the shows that got to be made, that got to last, and got to be loved. It's the story of fandoms, and how we love things together. It's the story of how we watch and consume and talk about television, and just how much that's changed.

Warning: there will be spoilers.

Chapter 1

Before Sunnydale

Welcome to Beverly Hills

Before there was *Buffy the Vampire Slayer*, there was *Beverly Hills 90210*. Before The CW network, before The WB and UPN, there was Fox. Before there were teen dramas, there were soap operas and family-friendly programming blocks. The world of teenagers on television, and teenagers watching television, didn't start with *Buffy* by a long shot.

The Fox network launched in October 1986, the first in a long time to challenge the dominant 'big three' networks of ABC, CBS and NBC. When the network, headed up by Jamie Kellner, debuted on air it was a soft launch with a late-night talk show – *The Late Show* – hosted by Joan Rivers. The grander launch of the network came with an expansion into prime time[1] programming in April 1987.

That prime-time line-up, overseen by Fox's entertainment president Garth Ancier, began with just two shows: *Married...with Children* (a sitcom that became one of the longest running shows on the network) and *The Tracey Ullman Show*, a sketch comedy show that introduced *The Simpsons* (now one of the longest running shows of all time) to the world. Slowly and carefully, Fox began to spread its programming over multiple nights, but not too many. The Federal Communications Commission had strict guidelines about

1. Prime time, in the network programming sense, means the hours between 8 and 11 pm on television

what legally constituted a 'network', and by keeping programming under a certain number of hours, Fox remained exempt from network status and a lot of associating rules. Most importantly, Fox was free from the Financial Interest and Syndication Rules, widely known as the 'fin-syn' rules, which prevented networks from owning their own shows. Those rules would be abolished in 1993, changing the world of television dramatically.

By the beginning of the nineties, Fox had established itself as the cool, young, not-like-other-networks network. Fox was particularly popular with the eighteen to forty-nine age range – a demographic that advertisers loved. Ratings for the network began to climb and programming spread across more nights. The American network television season usually begins around September and runs through until May the following year. The 1990/1991 season saw Fox increase their prime-time programming to Thursday nights.

Thursdays were a battleground for the networks. They were particularly popular with advertisers, so every network competed for big Thursday ratings. NBC dominated Thursdays for most of the nineties with their 'Must-See TV' line-up – in the 1990/1991 season *Cheers* at 9pm was a huge draw. Fox countered by showing *The Simpsons* at 8pm and following it up with *Beverly Hills 90210.*

Beverly Hills was a sleeper hit, not a ratings smash right off the bat. The teen-focused soap opera made stars of Shannon Doherty, Tori Spelling and Luke Perry, among others. The show was produced by Darren Star, who would go on to create *Sex and the City* for HBO, and Aaron Spelling – one of the most prolific TV producers of all time and father of Tori Spelling. Aaron Spelling had been working in television since the fifties, with a pedigree that included *The Love Boat*, *Charlie's Angels* and *Dynasty* – the iconic soap opera that came to an end in 1989. With *Dynasty* over, there was room on television for a shiny new soap opera and *Beverly Hills 90210*, with its focus on fish-out-of-water teenagers living newly affluent lives, fit the bill. While the show's first season wasn't a ratings hit, a 'summer season' of eight episodes that aired in July and August 1991, while the other networks were airing reruns, found the show its audience.[2] A more adult-focused spin-off, *Melrose Place*, began in 1992 and kicked off the Beverly Hills cinematic universe that would go on to span multiple shows and decades. *Beverly Hills 90210* made it clear that teenagers were perfect fodder for soap opera storytelling.

As the teenagers in *Beverly Hills* inevitably grew into adults, Fox began looking for another young series to take its place. *Beverly Hills* continued on, running for a decade, but in 1994 a new show starring teenagers became part of Fox's line-up. *Party of Five*, the show about a family of siblings orphaned after their parents die in a car crash, is probably best known now for making a star of Matthew Fox; he would go on to lead the ensemble cast of *Lost* a decade later. At the time it first aired, it was another weak spot in Fox's ratings. It took a Golden Globe win for the show and a passionate letter-writing campaign from fans to keep *Party of Five* on the air during its first couple of seasons, before it found a larger audience.

Party of Five became infamous for its 'very special episodes'; where *Beverly Hills 90210* was pure soap opera, *Party of Five*'s over-dramatic storylines were written to educate its audience on issues of the day. The family in the show was an unlucky one. Through the show's six season run they dealt with substance abuse, domestic abuse, mental health issues, teen pregnancy and eventually a dead dog. While *Party of Five* certainly heaped an unrealistic amount of suffering onto its central family, it was far more grounded in reality than its soap opera predecessors. As a 2014 *Variety* article pointed out, this was one of the shows that 'moved televised stories about and targeted at young

2. This same tactic would come in handy again with another teen soap opera on Fox in 2004.

adults away from the soap-opera genre and helped make the medium safer for the more realistic teenagers we'd meet later.'

While *Party of Five* was still finding its audience in 1994, two new networks were waiting in the wings. The fin-syn rules being abolished meant it now made sense for larger media companies to create their own broadcast networks – they could make and release their own television and keep the profits in-house. Both Warner Bros Entertainment and Paramount both began preparing to launch their own networks, The WB and UPN. Eventually, they would become one single network – The CW – that was best known for airing teen dramas. In 1994, however, they were simply two networks racing to get on the air first. Fox's success had proven that the bigger broadcast networks could be challenged, and both The WB and UPN wanted to be the next challenger. It was a race to get on the air first and get the biggest audience, and both networks officially launched in the same month – The WB on 11 January 1995, and UPN just five days later.

Neither of the networks aimed for teenage audiences at the start. The WB's first night of programming opened with *The Wayans Bros*, a sitcom starring Shawn and Marlon Wayans. UPN began with *Star Trek: Voyager*, the fourth show in the *Star Trek* universe. The *New York Times* pointed out in a review of *Voyager*'s premiere that 'Much will be made of the political correctness of this new venture, not least in that the captain of this ship is a woman.' Some things never change. Both of these new networks were targeting different audiences; The WB was comedy-focused, and targeted African-American audiences, while UPN was looking to trade off the pre-existing *Star Trek* fandom by targeting young male audiences with sci-fi and boyish sitcoms.

This was a huge time of transition for American television – akin to the more recent streaming boom. Premium cable was absorbing more and more viewers, and the networks were fighting to retain their share of that eighteen to forty-nine age range. As a result, more and more prime time shows were aimed at adult markets. At the time, having multiple television sets in the house wasn't common, so parents and their children would often be watching television together during prime time. The hour between eight and nine pm had generally been the domain of family-oriented shows, but now programming in that slot was growing more and more adult in the hopes of appealing to advertisers.

The main broadcast networks had isolated their shows more suitable for family audiences into small programming blocks. In 1995, as The WB and UPN were still finding their feet, ABC had a two hour 'T.G.I.F' line-up on Friday nights that featured coming-of-age teen sitcoms like *Boy Meets World* and *Sabrina the Teenage Witch*, while NBC kept their family shows like *The Fresh Prince of Bel-Air* in the early evening hours of Sundays and Mondays. The WB began to look for ways to capitalise on the demand for shows the whole family could watch together.

Garth Ancier had, at this point, moved from Fox to The WB, and was now head of programming for the new network. He told the *New York Times* in a 1995 interview that 'I found I would go to my college reunions or other fathers, and whenever people heard I worked in television, I'd be instantly surrounded by angry mothers saying "I'm home at 8 with my kids, and there's nothing for us to watch."' The WB began their own kid-friendly Sunday evening programming, with *Pinky and the Brain* – produced by Warner Brothers thanks to the end of the fin-syn rules – becoming a cornerstone, adored by both kids and their parents.

Then The WB began to incorporate hour-long dramas into the schedule alongside new comedies – calling on Aaron Spelling for assistance. Two new Spelling shows debuted on The WB in 1996. The first – *Savannah* – was a soap opera that took inspiration from *Dynasty* and *Gone with the Wind*, and proved to be sadly short-lived. The show stumbled in its second season, but its replacement turned out to be one of the best things that could have happened to the network. The other new Spelling show was *7th Heaven*, which went on to run for ten seasons, making it The WB's longest-running show. *7th Heaven* was another attempt to fulfil the need for family programming, with a show that followed the life of a minister, his wife and their seven children.

The *New York Times* called the first episode of *7th Heaven* 'perfectly pleasant but predictable' – these were the things that made it a success. As with *Party of Five* before it, the show used its young cast to handle 'issues of the week'. Unlike its predecessors, however, *7th Heaven* had a saccharine wholesomeness that made it 'fun' for all the family. This was The WB's first hit, and it was still a show that had one foot firmly planted in soap-opera storytelling. It was a show written for the adults watching it as much as it was for kids or teens. In the mid-nineties, there was still very little television being made specifically for a teen audience. For a whole demographic, television was a barren landscape.

Just as The WB and UPN were getting started, a groundbreaking teen drama was facing cancellation on ABC. *My So-Called Life* has become a cult classic in the years since it aired, and when it was on it was like absolutely nothing else. The show was created by Marshall Herskovitz, Edward Swick and Winnie Holzman. The trio had previously worked together on ABC's *Thirtysomething*, and with *My So-Called Life* they wanted to create something more deeply realistic about teenage life than the soap operas that had come before. In a retrospective piece about the show for *Yahoo Entertainment*, Herskovitz recalled that 'Most shows about teens on television were very exploitative about sexuality and meant to be titillating rather than inside the experience of what it meant to be an adolescent.' *My So-Called Life* was critically acclaimed and celebrated for its realism from the beginning of the show. It launched the careers of both Claire Danes and Jared Leto. It was well-liked because it didn't talk down to its audience, but managed to be painfully relatable; one episode – 'The Zit' – spent an hour comparing the agonising teen issue of a single spot to Kafka's *Metamorphosis*. These were teenagers on television actually getting to be teenagers, warts and all. *My So-Called Life* wasn't glossy or soapy; instead, it was a dive down into the murky depths of adolescence.

Unfortunately, critical acclaim and quality writing weren't enough to keep a show on the air in the early nineties. Ratings were king, and that was an area where *My So-Called Life* suffered. It didn't help that the show was airing on Thursday nights against stiff competition from NBC. The show had rapidly built a die-hard audience, but that audience wasn't big enough. After just nineteen episodes, with the very last airing just weeks after the launch of both The WB and UPN, *My So-Called Life* was cancelled.

When rumours of the cancellation began to spread, fans of the show didn't take them lightly. When the network first began to consider ditching the show, Edward Swick went directly to Bob Iger (then-ABC network president) to fight for it. Marshall Herskovitz, in the *Yahoo* retrospective, recalled Swick telling Iger 'You should keep this show on the air because teenage girls have no voice in our culture, and this show is giving them a voice.' The appeal fell on deaf ears, and the burden of keeping the show alive fell to the fans. In December 1994 ABC announced that *My So-Called Life* would end in January the following year. There was still hope that if ABC could just see the love the viewers had for the show, it might be able to continue.

In the first campaign of its kind, fans came together online to show their support for the show. The internet as an organising and communication tool was still fairly new, so while letter writing campaigns had happened in the past, this was the first time one of these campaigns had been organised online. Entertainment news outlets got involved, publishing pieces encouraging fans to write to Bob Iger and Ted Harbert (ABC's entertainment president) with personal pleas to keep the show on the air. The campaign almost worked; when Ted Harbert saw the overwhelming amount of support for the show he considered resurrecting *My So-Called Life* for a second season. Unfortunately, Claire Danes was reluctant to return. She was the straw that broke the camel's back, and the absence of a lead actress combined with the too-narrow appeal of the show cemented its fate.

My So-Called Life might have ended too soon for the fans, but even the creators of the show have since admitted that this might have been for the best. The show never got the chance to grow stale or repetitive, instead consisting of just a perfect run of nineteen episodes. The show regularly lands on best-of lists, including the WGA's 2013 'Best Written TV Series' and a later list from *Entertainment Weekly* of '25 Greatest TV Shows Ever'. *My So-Called Life* has been cited by multiple teen drama-creators as an inspiration. It's a show that still, thirty years after it came to an end, remains both beloved and discussed. Kristin Russo of *Buffering the Vampire Slayer* and Joanna Robinson from Spotify's *Ringer* podcast network even joined forces to recap all nineteen episodes in 2019 with *The Boiler Room: A My So-Called Life Podcast*. This was a show that was sadly just a couple of years ahead of its time, but it's incredibly present in all of the teen dramas that came after.

Just a couple of years after *My So-Called Life* came to an end, late in 1996, the media was decrying a lack of television aimed at teenagers. The networks were being slow to catch on to the fact that teens were a very viable market. There were obviously the shows created for family audiences, and newer sitcoms with young stars like *Friends* catered to the older end of the teen and young adult spectrum, but that was it. There were the programming blocks like 'T.G.I.F' on ABC but these were largely sitcom focused, and there was nothing with any depth being aimed at teens.

Teenagers were a group of television viewers who were constantly at the forefront of new trends. The eighteen to forty-nine range was golden for advertisers, but teens – with their disposable incomes and lack of responsibilities – were coming in silver. Slowly, more and more television sets were making their way into teenage bedrooms –

freeing them from having to sit through whatever their parents wanted to watch. At the same time, computers were becoming a household staple. The mid-nineties internet boom saw teenagers communicating like never before – and spreading their love for their favourite shows. Anything that targeted this demographic was set up for success. The WB and UPN were both finding this to be true; shows like *Sister Sister* and *Moesha* that starred teen protagonists were both big audience draws, but these too were sitcoms. They were funny, but not totally relatable.

Everything was about to change, however. In March 1997, a new show began on The WB as a mid-season replacement, kicked the doors down and opened up a whole new world of television.

Chapter 2

Buffy the Vampire Slayer

Welcome to Sunnydale

Sunnydale is a small California town, somehow big enough for a high school, a university (complete with secret military labs underneath), an airport, working docks, a convent, numerous cemeteries and shopping malls, a train station, a bus station, a forest big enough to get lost in, a museum prestigious enough to have pieces on loan from the British Museum, a local vineyard, somehow only one coffee shop and two bars, and, of course, a hellmouth.

When *Buffy the Vampire Slayer* came along in 1997, there was nothing quite like it on television. *Buffy* wasn't the first show to tell supernatural stories, the first with a strong female lead or even the first teen show filmed at Torrance High School[1]. *Buffy* still, however, managed to be groundbreaking television. When the show began as a mid-season replacement for *Savannah* it sparked a new era of teen dramas and fandom. The show spawned message boards, fanfiction galore, adoration and even a whole field of academic study. Now, over twenty years after the show's final episode aired, *Buffy the Vampire Slayer* remains an important part of the cultural conversation.

Before there was *Buffy the Vampire Slayer* the TV series, there was *Buffy the Vampire Slayer* the 1992 comedy film. In 1991, Joss Whedon sold the script for the *Buffy* movie to Sandollar Productions – the

1. The working high school used for exterior shots during the first three seasons of the show was also used for *Beverly Hills 90210*.

production company founded by Dolly Parton. Whedon came from a screenwriting background – both his father and his grandfather wrote for television. While he intended to enter the movie business after college, he first began working as a sitcom writer. Movies stayed in the background, until an idea for a character dubbed 'Rhonda, the Immortal Waitress' grew into the script for the original *Buffy*.

It was tough to get major studios interested in making the 1992 movie. It took Fran Rubel Kuzui, who had recently had a hit with *Tokyo Pop*, signing on to direct and Luke Perry being cast as the film's male lead Oliver Pike, to get 20th Century Fox's interest. While Fox was willing to make the film, they wanted it done as fast as possible; with that and Perry's *90210* filming schedule, *Buffy* had to be shot in just five weeks. Kristy Swanson joined the cast as Buffy, and Donald Sutherland signed on to play Buffy's watcher Merrick. While a new writer like Whedon wouldn't usually have much to do with the production of their screenplay, the tight schedule meant that Whedon remained closely involved while the film was being made. That was, until he grew frustrated watching the director change his vision, and hearing Donald Sutherland change his dialogue; then he chose to walk away from the project before the movie was completed.

The *Buffy* movie was neither a critical nor commercial success. It wasn't quite funny enough to be a comedy, nor dark enough to market as horror. It was a movie that seemed destined to languish as a forgotten VHS tape for eternity, until The WB came along.

Gail Berman was head of television development at Sandollar productions when the *Buffy* movie came out in theatres. She'd read the script and thought it would be perfect for a TV series, but after the film performed poorly, she put *Buffy* to one side. When The WB and UPN launched, Berman realised there might be a future home for *Buffy* after all. While most movie contracts have clauses about future TV rights, Fox had neglected to put such a clause in for *Buffy*, so Berman was free to shop the movie around.

When Berman wanted to bring the *Buffy* TV show to life, she contacted Joss Whedon's agent out of contractual obligation and courtesy, giving Whedon the option to pass on the project. Instead, he immediately wanted to be involved. In the book *Season Finale – The Unexpected Rise and Fall of The WB and UPN*, Berman recalls speaking to Whedon for the first time: 'We talked all about the notion of female empowerment and teenage years, and the fact that there were no young female-led series other than *Blossom* on the air.'

Berman and Whedon put together a short reel of scenes from the 1992 movie, interspersed with images that hopefully set the tone for the show that they wanted to make, and began pitching. The Fox network turned the show down, as did NBC, but The WB were immediately interested. Joss Whedon impressed Susanne Daniels (then-president of The WB) by listing everything he didn't yet know about the show. As Daniels recalls in *Season Finale*, 'He didn't know if the show was an hour or a half-hour. He didn't know if it should be more drama than comedy or the other way around, if it should have a laugh track or not.' Whedon was, however, certain of his vision for the show: high school is hell.

The WB said yes to a pilot presentation and casting began immediately. Sarah Michelle Gellar came in to read not for the lead role of Buffy Summers, but for mean-girl Cordelia. Gellar impressed and signed on for the role, but Buffy remained un-cast. Other actresses came in to audition for the lead, including Selma Blair – who would go on to co-star with Gellar in *Cruel Intentions* just a couple of years later – and Charisma Carpenter, who eventually ended up playing Cordelia. Gellar was asked to come back and read for the role, and turned out to be the perfect Buffy Summers. Riff Regan was cast as Willow, Buffy's nerdy best friend, and Nicholas Brendon – who had only been pursuing an acting career for a couple of months – got the role of Xander, the character Whedon considered to be most like himself. Anthony Stewart Head, the veteran British actor best known in America at the time for a series of instant coffee adverts, took the role of Rupert Giles – Buffy's Watcher.

The twenty-five minute pilot presentation was a condensed version of what would eventually become 'Welcome to the Hellmouth' – the show's opening episode. Whedon insisted on directing despite his lack of experience, determined this time to keep control of his creative vision. It was a rough and ready production, but the seeds of the show were there. Next came a rigorous screening process headed up by Susanne Daniels. When she introduced those twenty-five minutes to a room full of executives, she told them that 'There is nothing like *Buffy* on the air right now. There are no female role models like this, and there's no cool and creepy-scary TV shows like this out there.' The network liked what they saw. While The WB initially passed on a full season order, by September 1997 they'd opted for twelve episodes to serve as a mid-season replacement in January.

The network had notes, of course. One major suggestion was to recast Willow. They wanted a cooler, hipper version of the character, and felt Riff Regan wasn't right for the part. She was replaced by Alyson Hannigan, but Whedon insisted on retaining Willow's bookish sensibilities, guessing that she would be a hit with the audience. He wasn't wrong. With newbie actor David Boreanaz cast as the brooding, mysterious love interest Angel, *Buffy the Vampire Slayer* was ready to go.

Buffy opened with a two-part pilot – 'Welcome to the Hellmouth' and 'The Harvest' – which immediately set up the world Whedon wanted to establish. His vision for the show in its earliest seasons was to flip the familiar tropes of horror. In his words, from the season one DVD commentary, he wanted the show to be 'genre-busting'. He wanted to subvert the idea of 'the little blonde girl who goes into the alley and gets killed in every horror movie.' This idea of Buffy as a petite blonde wielding immense power in the twin worlds of demons and high school, capable and tough without sacrificing femininity, was a huge selling point for the show. Whedon took that subversion further with the opening moments of *Buffy*; the first scene of 'Welcome to the Hellmouth' showed what seemed to be an innocent blonde schoolgirl being led astray by her boyfriend, until suddenly the blonde was revealed to be a vampire (specifically Darla, played by Julie Benz, the woman who turned Angel into a vampire), the boyfriend her victim, and the credits kicked in with a howl.

That opening title music, with brief samples of classic horror movie sounds devolving quickly into heavy drums and guitars, sums up the show. No one has time for scary organ music here. It was Alyson Hannigan who turned Joss Whedon on to Nerf Herder – the band behind the *Buffy* theme.

Those opening episodes established key rules of the show. One of those was that no one is safe. By the end of the two-part premiere Jesse – a member of Buffy's new friend group – had been turned into a vampire, then turned to dust with a wooden stake. The role of Jesse was originally written for Danny Strong, who had played a small role in the pilot presentation. Strong, however, struggled in his audition and the part went to Eric Balfour instead, although Strong eventually returned to *Buffy* as recurring character Jonathan. Whedon debated putting Eric Balfour in the opening credits, to make his death even more shocking to the audience, but budget constraints changed his mind[2].

Another rule was to put Willow in peril and pain whenever possible. Whedon refers to Alyson Hannigan in commentary as the 'king of pain'; she was so good at playing fear and hurt that the writers strived to put her there again and again. It was Willow landing in danger in the first episode that led Buffy to a mysterious crypt and allowed the show to set up its first 'Big Bad'. Each season of *Buffy*, while full of standalone 'Monster of the Week' episodes, would have some big villain lurking in the background ready to be confronted in the finale, with an apocalypse on the side. For the first season, it was The Master, played by Mark Metcalfe, who cleverly infused the

2. He would later use the title sequence rug-pull to devastate audiences on both *Buffy* and the spin-off show *Angel*.

ancient vampire with a dry, sardonic wit. *Buffy* helped popularise the idea of 'Big Bads' and overarching storylines than run through each season. Russel T. Davies, current *Doctor Who* showrunner who also spearheaded the revival of the show in 2005, cited *Buffy* as a source of inspiration for his use of recurring villains in his show.

As the first twelve episodes of *Buffy* rolled on, it became clear that this was a show determined to give equal weight to both supernatural and high school drama; a potential date and the threat of an apocalyptic vampire cult are both as important as each other in 'Never Kill a Boy on the First Date'. The show quickly established that Buffy would have more than just vampires to slay, with a cheerleading witch, hyena demons, a possessed computer, a demon-hunting ventriloquist dummy and a girl suffering from an acute case of invisibility all presenting unique challenges during the first season.

Alongside all of that was the burgeoning love story between Buffy and Angel. The vampire cursed with a soul and doomed to regret every evil act of his undead existence falling in love with the one girl in all the world tasked with killing his kind, while Christophe Beck's score swept dramatically through every moment of their tragedy and tension, was stuff that viewers could fall in love with.

That tragic romance provided a catalyst for the events of the season finale 'Prophecy Girl'. When Angel delivers Giles a book that reveals a prophecy that Buffy will soon die, it's only by chance that Buffy overhears the two men in her life discussing her impending death. The scene took place in the school library; a set that both the cast and the crew grew to hate as it was mostly used for long-winded exposition scenes about the various threats to the world. In 'Prophecy Girl', the library was home to one of Sarah Michelle Gellar's most stunningly emotive performances. There's brief delight as Buffy sees the (200-odd year old) boy that she likes, that delight disappearing from her face as she learns of the prophecy and a follow-up of hysterical laughter. Sarah Michelle Gellar swung wildly between hysterics, fear and fury as Buffy confronts these two men and insists that her time as Slayer is done. She tells Giles 'I'm sixteen, I don't want to die' with tear-filled eyes, and the weight of her life as a slayer gets hammered home for the audience.

By the end of the episode she has technically died, for a second, before being revived with CPR and setting off to destroy the big bad and save the world (in a great dress). The first season of *Buffy* ended with the teenagers walking off into the California sunshine. It was the kind of season finale often made at the time; network television shows weren't always guaranteed a second season so finales would be satisfactory, wrapped-up endings, just in case.

The response to the first season of *Buffy* was positive. A review of the season in the *New York Times* called the show a 'critical and cult favorite', noting that there were 'more than 320 websites devoted to her every aspect.' The article didn't provide a source for the hyperbolic figure, but it's true that *Buffy* had sprung up during a new era of online fan obsession. Teenagers no longer simply watched the same shows as their immediate friends; now they could head online after watching an episode of *Buffy* to discuss the show with fellow fans anywhere in the world. Fandom began to reach a whole new level of dissection and discussion. The WB were pleased as well – *Buffy* had brought a slew of new viewers to the network – and ordered a full-length second season.

That second season took the idea of high school as hell and ran with it. In January 1998, the WB were ready to extend programming to Tuesday evenings and an intense two-part storyline on *Buffy* was the perfect thing to launch the new night. The one-two punch of 'Surprise' and 'Innocence', halfway through the story, was a simple story: new antagonists Spike and Drusila (played by James Marsters and Juliet Landau respectively) attempt to assemble an ancient puzzle box demon just in time for Buffy's seventeenth birthday. Somehow, Buffy and Angel fall into bed together while trying to stop them, only for Angel to lose his soul.

Angel becoming the evil 'Angelus' was part of the broader supernatural plot, but it also continued the high school metaphor.

There was Buffy at seventeen, suffering the teenage experience of losing her virginity only for her lover to become someone else overnight. There's a trope in horror of characters being punished for their sexuality, but in *Buffy* that trope was being realised with an intense emotional punishment, not the attack of a random slasher.

The two episodes aired over two nights. The first, 'Surprise', aired in Buffy's original Monday night time slot, with 'Innocence' airing the day after in the show's new Tuesday night position. Not only did this mark a new night for The WB, but the transition from 'Surprise' to 'Innocence' changed the whole tone of the season with the reveal that the new 'big bad' was a character that both the audience and protagonist had come to love.

Buffy might have been one of The WB's biggest shows in 1998, but it couldn't launch a night of programming alone. The second hour on Tuesday night was filled by *Dawson's Creek.* This show was the brainchild of Kevin Williamson, an up-and-coming filmmaker who was riding high off the success of his slasher movie *Scream* when he was approached about making something for TV. The resulting show was semi-autobiographical for Williamson, set in a fictional Massachusetts town and focussed on the titular Dawson (the role that made James Van Der Beek a star), an aspiring, Spielberg-obsessed filmmaker. *Dawson's Creek* became a flagship show for The WB, pitched perfectly at their target teen audience. It was soapy, like *Beverly Hills* before it, but self-aware, with over-eloquent dialogue and knowing winks to the audience.

Dawson's wasn't without controversy. Part of the show's pre-launch publicity had been built around the fact that critics were concerned about the shows 'racy' plotlines – like the high school student sleeping with his teacher – and the teen characters having open and frank conversations about sex. The parents Television Council gave its worst rating of the year to *Dawson's Creek* and its 'almost obsessive focus on premarital sexual activity'.' A 1998 *Chicago Tribune* article pointed out in response that 'it's safe to assume that teens have said, heard and done far worse.' The controversy surrounding the show helped *Dawson's Creek* far more than it hindered it. Of course, it helped that at least none of the teens in Capeside were losing their virginities to vampires.

Buffy couldn't reach that seismic change in its second season without first misdirecting the audience with its two new antagonists, who literally crashed on to the show (and through the 'Welcome to Sunnydale' sign) in the third episode of the season – 'School Hard'. Spike – the bleached blonde Billy Idol lookalike – and Drusilla, his doolally consort, were a refresh for *Buffy* after the first season's looming threat of The Master. Spike's character arc was only supposed to last for five to ten episodes before the character was killed off. He wasn't. Instead, James Marsters continued playing Spike until the end of *Buffy*, and then for a further season on Angel.

Marsters had found instant chemistry with Juliet Landau during his auditions, and as a working actor he wanted to remain on *Buffy* as long as possible. Whedon made it clear to Marsters that Spike was an evil, soulless killer, incapable of love. Marsters completely ignored him, instead playing a depth of tenderness and adoration with Juliet Landau that made fans fall in love with Spike. Joss Whedon and the other writers paid close attention to the fans of the show. Whedon was particularly known for trawling *The Bronze* – a popular *Buffy* message board named for the night club/gig venue on the show – and taking the audience's temperature. It became clear that Spike was a hit, and so the character survived and the show got a little more morally grey.

Before Angel lost his soul, Spike and Drusila were the catalyst for a new character introduction: Kendra, the vampire slayer. In the first ever two-parter on *Buffy* – 'What's My Line' – Kendra was introduced as a new slayer, called to her destiny after Buffy's brief death the previous season. Played by Bianca Lawson, Kendra was a character that suffered from *Buffy*'s difficulties with race. This was a very white show. There were no people of colour starring as main characters, and very few in supporting roles. The show acknowledged the problem out loud in its third season with Mr Trick – a villainous vampire played by K. Todd Freeman – declaring that Sunnydale is 'not a haven for brothers, strictly the Caucasian persuasion here in the Dale.' Nothing changed after that nod to the show's whiteness.

Kendra, unlike Buffy, had known no other life than that of a slayer, having been trained as a 'potential' (a concept explored in the show's final season) since childhood. Kendra was sheltered, unaware of the modern world, and the show found every possible way to other her character and treat her as a foreign concept for comic relief. Her arc on the show was short, just three episodes. She was sent away on a plane at the end of the two-parter, and was brought back only to be unceremoniously killed off in the finale. Between Kendra and the show's cliched depiction of Romani people, the second season was a particularly bad one for Buffy and race, and the show didn't improve much as it went on.

The season finale aired over two weeks in May 1998. The first episode introduced flashbacks to Angel's past, a device that became a regular part of the show. Some of *Buffy*'s most iconic moments took place in the two episodes that made up the finale. In the second half, Buffy was forced to admit the truth about her life as a vampire slayer to her mother. The scene parallelled a coming-out moment as Joyce Summers (played by Kristine Sutherland) asked questions like 'Have you tried not being the slayer?' The layer of queer subtext made the end of the conversation even more heartbreaking as Buffy gets kicked out of her home.

In the final fight between Buffy and Angelus, Buffy's character was summed up in a single word. Her ex-boyfriend descends on her, wielding a sword as he points out that she's lacking friends, weapons and hope. He asks Buffy what she has left and as she catches his sword thrust, she answers 'Me.' On the one hand, it was an incredible display of strength from the tiny blonde protagonist. On the other, it brought up a theme that continued through the show – the prolonged isolation that came along with Buffy's power. Although Angel's soul gets restored, it's too late and Buffy is forced to kill him to prevent the apocalypse, and the episode ends with Buffy leaving Sunnydale. Over six million people watched Buffy take that bus out of town, seemingly for good.

The twin power of *Buffy* and *Dawson's Creek* proved perfect for The WB. That Tuesday double bill made the network number one among teenagers for the season. Both of the shows became powerful lead-ins – shows that had big enough audiences that any new show in a following time slot was almost guaranteed viewers. As *Buffy*'s third season began, the show became a launchpad for *Felicity*, a college drama created by J. J. Abrams, while on Wednesday nights *Dawson's Creek* served as a springboard for *Charmed* – a fantasy drama about three witches living in modern-day San Francisco. Coming-of-age and supernatural stories became The WB's biggest draw as the network continued to grow.

The third season of *Buffy* saw the characters approaching the end of high school. Multiple rankings of *Buffy* seasons put the third at the top, and for good reason. This was, after all, the season of Buffy and Faith; the ship that launched a thousand fanfics. Faith, played by Eliza Dushku, a new slayer and Buffy's antithesis, arrived towards the beginning of the season and immediately became a hit with fans, not least for the underlying tension in her and Buffy's relationship.

Faith wasn't the only new character to arrive in Sunnydale that season. Emma Caulfield joined the cast as Anya – a vengeance demon who creates an alternative, Buffy-free Sunnydale in 'The Wish' and becomes human as a result. Caulfield was best known before *Buffy* for playing Susan Keats in *Beverly Hills 90210*. She was only meant to appear in a few episodes, but like Spike she charmed the audience, and later became a series regular. Also joining the cast was Alexis Denisof as Wesley Wyndam-Pryce – a new watcher for Faith and Buffy after Giles was fired from his role for caring too much about his charge. Wesley was pure comic relief – stuffy and mildly incompetent. According to writer Doug Petrie in the DVD commentary for the episode 'Bad Girls', a script note from Joss Whedon explained that

Wesley 'thinks he's Sean Connery, but in fact he's George Lazenby.' Wesley eventually got to become a rich and complex character on the spin-off *Angel*.

Faith was by far the most impactful character on the season. The show certainly started getting queerer when she arrived. It wasn't until the fourth season of *Buffy* that an actual, textual queer relationship became part of the show, but the sapphic undertones and overtones of Faith and Buffy's relationship were obvious to fans. Whedon never intended this aspect of their story, but admitted it was there after seeing fans intensely discussing the relationship on multiple message boards. The pairing remains a favourite of fans to this day. At the time of writing, popular fanfiction website *Archive of Our Own* has 1555 stories listed under the 'Faith Lehane/Buffy Summers' tag – a respectable number considering the website started over five years after the end of *Buffy*.

The episode 'Bad Girls' and its follow up 'Consequences' brought the Buffy and Faith relationship to a head. The first of the two episodes saw Faith tempting Buffy into a darker side of slaying, and featured an iconic moment of the two slayers dancing, post-kill, at The Bronze. That dance even became an animation reference for an episode of the *X-Men: Evolution* cartoon, with Rogue and Kitty Pryde recreating it move for move. Faith was in the show to answer the question 'What if Buffy didn't have friends, family and a support network in her life?' The show took that as far as it could with Faith accidentally killing a human at the end of 'Bad Girls', insisting she doesn't care, and in 'Consequences' joining forces with the season's big bad – Sunnydale's evil Mayor Wilkins (played wonderfully by Harry Groener).

In the third season of *Buffy* the big finale-confrontation consisted of the Mayor turning into a giant snake during high school graduation, and the high school being demolished with explosives. There was some other stuff about Buffy and Faith and a coma and putting demons to bed, but really it was all about blowing up the snake. And, the end of high school.

First, of course, there had to be a prom episode; something that became a staple of teen dramas, although usually without the hellhounds. The episode saw Buffy and Angel breaking up (to set up Angel's spin-off), but more importantly it saw Buffy resigning herself to loneliness again as she sends her friends to prom while staying behind to fight demons. The episode ended with Buffy entering the dance just in time to receive a special 'class protector' award from her fellow students; finally making her feel less alone by acknowledging all that she'd done to save their lives. It was a gentle closure before an explosive finale.

That final episode ended up being heavily delayed. In April 1999, just a month before the two-part finale was due to air, the Columbine High School massacre took place in Colorado. At the time it was the deadliest mass shooting at a high school in US history, and the media reaction was understandably intense and emotional. Two episodes of *Buffy* were pushed back as a result. 'Earshot', an episode which implied that a student (Jonathan, played by Danny Strong) was planning a shooting at the high school, was due to air in April and instead pushed back until September, airing just before the beginning of the next season. While the first half of the finale aired as planned, 'Graduation Day – Part Two' was pushed back due to the depiction of students armed with weapons, instead airing two months later in July 1999. Despite the delay between the episodes, the third season finale was a success; it closed the door firmly on the high school lives of the core characters.

A common issue in teen dramas is the awkward transition to college for both the characters and the shows. In *Buffy*, that transition became a way to explore all kinds of growing up and finding one's place. Admittedly, the same old hellmouth was still there, but in the fourth season of *Buffy* there was also a shiny new underground lab and a secret military organisation to serve as the show's big bad.

Multiple characters left *Buffy* after the third season. Angel spun off to Los Angeles, and Charisma Carpenter as Cordelia followed suit. Willow's werewolf love interest Oz, played by Seth Green, also stepped away from the show; the actor was frustrated about his character being relegated to the sidelines, and wanted time to pursue other opportunities. New characters filled in the gaps. For Buffy's love interest, that meant Marc Blucas joining the show as all-American secret soldier Riley Finn. The character wasn't particularly well-received by the fandom. Blucas was even warned by Joss Whedon that the audience weren't going to like him – it was going to take longer than a three-month break between seasons for the viewers to get over Buffy and Angel. Riley was never the most beloved of Buffy's boyfriends, by the audience or Buffy herself, but his character was an essential part of moving Buffy past the relationship that defined her high school years.

Taking Cordelia out of the equation left a big space to fill. In an interview for the hit recap podcast *Buffering the Vampire Slayer*, James Marsters recalled that Cordelia was the character who would tell Buffy 'You're stupid and we're all going to die.' When Whedon was debating who could fill Cordelia's shoes, it was Sarah Michelle Gellar who pointed out that Spike was the most obvious choice. He, alongside Emma Caulfield's character Anya, became the blunt voices of sarcasm and reason that the show needed. Spike, given a chip in his brain that prevented him from harming humans by those secret soldiers, became a character that Joss could play with, undercutting his bad-boy cool with a Hawaiian shirt and a comic-relief girlfriend in the form of high school mean girl-turned-vampire Harmony (played by Mercedes McNab) before eventually giving him a much more nuanced story.

The loss of Oz from the cast gave the writers room to experiment with Willow's character. The high school seasons had featured Willow's first forays into witchcraft, and in college Willow's relationship to magic and her sexuality became two sides of the same coin. The eventual relationship between Willow and Tara became one of the first committed same-sex relationships on mainstream television. It was built slowly, first implied in witchcraft scenes before being made clear by the text.

The first episode to introduce Amber Benson as Tara is one of *Buffy*'s most famous for an entirely different reason. 'Hush', the tenth episode of the fourth season, is an episode with almost no dialogue. For around thirty minutes of the episode, the characters were completely voiceless thanks to terrifying demons 'The Gentlemen'. Whedon was struck by the idea to do a speechless episode after noticing that while *Buffy* was often praised for its dialogue, his directing style had become formulaic. The demons in the episode are almost incidental to the theme of talking getting in the way of real communication. It took losing their voices for the different characters to confirm feelings for each other, and this became the episode that took Buffy and Riley's relationship to a new level both by having them kiss for the first time and, in the end, revealing their secret lives to each other.

When Tara was first introduced in *Buffy*, she was only supposed to be part of Willow's experimentation with magic and Amber Benson was at first only cast for a couple of episodes. Both Benson and Alyson Hannigan assumed that the relationship between their characters was completely platonic, even as the crew kept pointing out their chemistry. It was only when Joss Whedon took the pair to one side and told them 'By the way, you guys are going to be lady friends now,' as Benson recalled in a 2010 interview with *AfterEllen*, that the pair realised they were definitely playing a romance.

It took until the nineteenth episode of the season for the relationship to be definitively acknowledged on the show, during a coming-out scene between Willow and Buffy that bore no relation to Buffy's heartbreaking slayer coming-out in season two. Instead, it was a moment of brief misunderstanding between the pair followed by complete and easy acceptance. Part of the relationship took so long to be realised on screen at all was the limitations put on the show for what *could* be shown between the two women. Everything had to be implied carefully though spells and blown-out candles.

The final episode of the fourth season – 'Restless' – was by far the least subtle about the lesbian relationship. It was also a massive departure from other *Buffy* season finales. The season's 'Big Bad' Adam, a demon-human-cyborg created in those aforementioned underground labs, was defeated in the season's penultimate episode 'Primeval'. Instead of a grand battle to save the world the finale showed an extended series of dream sequences that served as character studies with a healthy dose of foreshadowing for the next season.

For Willow, that means painting a Sappho poem on her lover's back before facing her insecurities through a surreal performance of *Death of a Salesman*. For Xander, it meant facing up to his directionless existence via an ice cream truck, an overly titillating male-fantasy version of Willow and Tara (although they still couldn't be shown kissing on screen) and a tribute to *Apocalypse Now* featuring Armin Shimerman returning as Principal Snyder. For Giles, the dream explored his father-figure role in Buffy's life as he escorts Buffy through a hellmouth-themed funfair. The antagonist of the dream sequence took the form of the First Slayer – Sineya, referred to as 'The Primitive' and made non-verbal and violent in another not-great depiction of a non-white character. Buffy's dream saw her confronting and eventually walking away from the figure and the episode ended undramatically.

'Restless' was an off-the-wall episode of *Buffy*, and it was a creative risk to end a season on a series of trippy dreams, but it worked; the episode regularly crops up on *Buffy* 'Best-Episode' lists. Not only did the episode push the show's boundaries, it also picked up threads of foreshadowing scattered throughout the show. In a dream sequence in the third season finale, Faith told Buffy 'Little Miss Muffet counting down from 7-3-0' (the number of days in two years). In another Faith dream, from the fourth season, she reminds Buffy that 'Little sis is coming.' In 'Restless', Tara tells Buffy to 'Be back before Dawn.' *Buffy* was setting up for an incredibly bold move.

The opening episode of *Buffy*'s fifth season was pure fun – it brought the legendary Count Dracula to Sunnydale and set a tone that the rest of the season would thoroughly subvert. The end of the episode introduced Dawn – Buffy's never-seen-before younger sister. Fans of the show love to gently gaslight new viewers when Dawn arrives – 'What do you mean you don't remember her?' – but at the time the reveal was shocking. Dawn wasn't a long-lost-sister being introduced in a soap opera twist, she was a mystical key sent to Buffy by monks and given human form to ensure her protection, rewriting the history of the show in the process. The story was convoluted, ridiculous and brave. It was by coincidence, fate or luck that Michelle Trachtenberg – star of *Harriet the Spy* – happened to be visiting the *Buffy* set during the filming of 'Restless', which led to her being cast as Dawn. While Dawn was a divisive character for fans who had grown used to an only-child Buffy, she was also beloved. When Michelle Trachtenberg passed away at just thirty-nine years old in 2025, the outpouring of adoration from fans who had grown up watching her in shows like *Buffy* and *Gossip Girl* was a testament to how fantastic she was in these roles. This new big-sister role for Buffy meant the nature of family being deeply explored in the fifth season of the show, and pushed *Buffy* into a new kind of maturity.

The biggest part of that push came with the death of Buffy's mother in the sixteenth episode of the season – 'The Body'. This was another episode that toyed with the format of the show, this time by removing all non-diegetic sound. It was the masterful depiction of grief, however, that made this episode one of the show's very best. With 'The Body', Whedon wanted to explore 'the almost boredom of the first few hours' after a big loss.

The episode opened with the final moments of the previous week's instalment – Buffy arriving home to find her mother on the sofa, and something wrong – before going into the opening credits and following that with a short flashback to the group celebrating Thanksgiving to give the rest of the credits something to appear over so that the rest of the episode wouldn't have to share screen space.

This was followed up with an incredible, almost three-minute take that followed Sarah Michelle Gellar with a hand-held camera as she went through the immediate panic of finding her mother's body and contacting the paramedics. The rest of the episode continued with hard reactions to Joyce's death. There's a quiet distance in the scene where Buffy tells Dawn – the conversation is unheard, shot from the other side of a window. A scene with Willow, Tara, Xander and Anya showed some of the tiniest minutiae of grief. Whedon used his own experience of desperately trying to pick the correct tie to wear to a friend's funeral to inform Willow's panicked search for the right clothes to wear. Anya then delivers a speech on grief that despite her new-to-humanity perspective was one of the most relatable parts of the episode; she frustratedly cries that 'Joyce will never have any more fruit punch, ever, and she'll never have eggs, or yawn, or brush her hair, not ever, and no one will explain to me why.'

'The Body' was also the first episode in which Tara and Willow actually kissed on screen. This was the first kiss between two women in a committed relationship on American network television. The WB reportedly pushed against the kiss. According to Whedon, speaking at a *Buffy* event at the Paley festival in 2010, the network felt they had enough gay characters on screen already[3]. Whedon claimed to have told the network 'We're going to do this thing. It's true to character. It's what we're going to do,' and threatened to quit entirely if the kiss couldn't be in the show. Whedon was determined not to have a big 'they kiss' episode, the sort of 'very special episode' that would crop up in *Buffy*'s teen soap predecessors, and instead wanted to show Willow and Tara acting as any other couple would. The kiss was as quietly groundbreaking as the rest of the episode.

3. The WB did already have a gay character – Jack McPhee on *Dawson's Creek*.

The critical response to 'The Body' was overwhelmingly positive. A *Guardian* review of the episode called it 'ingenious' and insisted that 'the allegation that the drama is just another schmaltzy American teen show – *Dawson's Creek* with fangs – is refuted.' A *Salon* piece called that evening's *Buffy* and *Angel* double bill a 'sublime two-hour package of passionately original storytelling' and said that 'there hasn't been a finer hour of drama on TV this year than "The Body".' There was a feeling in many of these reviews, and reviews of the show in general, that *Buffy* deserved to be given more critical consideration. That *Salon* piece complained of snobs who dismiss *Buffy* as 'cheesy kid stuff', while a *New York Times* piece published near the beginning of the fifth season complained that *Buffy* 'has yet to be taken seriously – to be removed from the status of cult entertainment.' *Buffy* never made a splash at the Emmy awards, winning just two awards (for makeup and for score) throughout its entire seven-year run. That lack of recognition was part of what the critics were picking up on. Episodes like 'The Body' never received awards consideration, but they're the reason *Buffy* has kept its cult status over twenty years after its final episodes aired.

The season five finale was arguably a better end to *Buffy* than the show's actual final episode. 'The Gift', which was also the 100th episode of *Buffy*, certainly had a feeling of finality to it. The fifth season came to a head when the blonde bombshell hell god Glory (played by Claire Kramer, who had co-starred with Eliza Dushku in teen cheerleading classic *Bring it On* the previous year) kidnapped Dawn and began to enact her plan of opening a gateway to her hell dimension. The 'previously on' for the episode sped through all ninety-nine previous instalments of the show before landing on Buffy, in an alley, saving someone from a vampire who's somehow never heard of The Slayer. Everything in the episode was set up not just by the foreshadowing, but by five years of the show.

An epic battle ensued in the episode as Buffy tried to save her sister. Everything seemed in vain, as Dawn finds herself bleeding and opening up the hell dimension thanks to the malicious 'Doc' – played by Broadway legend Joel Gray, *Cabaret*'s original master of ceremonies. Rips in reality form, hell spills forth and the limitations of the CGI budget were made obvious. The themes of family and blood also become obvious as Buffy sacrifices herself, leaping from a tower to save Dawn. The episode ended on a shot of Buffy's grave; a headstone etched with the words 'She saved the world. A lot.' A 2008 *Entertainment Weekly* piece named the episode one of 'TV's Best Season Finales Ever', citing that epitaph as summing up 'all seven years of [*Buffy*'s] greatness.' 'The Gift' was an epic end to the season, and it felt like the end of the show. There's a common misconception that it almost was.

When The WB opted to air *Buffy*, the network signed a five-year licensing contract with 20th Century Fox (who were producing the show). Late in 1998, during the third season, Sandy Grushow (president of 20th Century Fox) tried to begin early negotiations with Jamie Kellner, head of The WB, to extend that contract. Kellner refused to discuss things early, and a chain of events began that ended with *Buffy* leaving The WB at the end of its fifth season.

In 2001, an unusually public fight between Jamie Kellner and 20th Century Fox took place. The WB and Fox thought fair offers weren't being made on either side. An *Entertainment Weekly* piece in March 2001 quoted Kellner as saying 'Our audience is a younger audience. Maybe what we should do is not stay with the same show for many years and refresh our line up.' Joss Whedon took that personally, and encouraged Fox to find a new home for *Buffy*. A deal was struck with UPN; the network had been foundering compared to The WB and needed a big hit. News of the deal broke in April 2001, and Joss Whedon told *Variety* that 'I've been dumped by my fat old ex, and Prince Charming has come and swept me off my feet.' Buffy's sister show *Angel* still had another year contracted at The WB, meaning the two shows were now going to air on separate networks. Many people make the assumption that 'The Gift' was so final because the future of the show was in jeopardy – but when the episode was written there was no real risk that the show wouldn't continue.

As *Buffy* moved to UPN, the show also experienced a major tonal shift. This had little to do with the network switch, and plenty to do with the continued use of the supernatural as a metaphor for growing up. Where the fifth season had focused on family ties, the sixth saw the characters reaching the 'depression' stage of adulthood, and the season is often ranked as the worst of *Buffy*. In a 2018 piece for *Vanity Fair* titled 'How *Buffy the Vampire Slayer*'s Most Hated Season Became Its Most Important', critic Joanna Robinson cited two fan nicknames for the season: 'Season Sex' and 'Season Sucks'.

There was one big, gloriously technicolour bright spot in the season, and that was the seventh episode 'Once More with Feeling'. The idea of a musical episode was completely new when *Buffy* did it, but 'Once' was groundbreaking, and brought the idea into the mainstream. Joss Whedon claimed in the DVD commentary for the episode that he had wanted to make a musical all his life, and the idea had been simmering for some time before it finally happened. He knew some of the cast members could sing thanks to gatherings at his house, and Tony Head had already sung on the show in a couple of season four episodes, but a musical was a far grander prospect than anything *Buffy* had attempted before. Whedon spent time during the season break working on songs for the musical episode with his then-wife Kai Cole (who wasn't credited in the episode), arriving to start work on the sixth season with a script and a CD full of music. This was going to be more than just a gimmick episode – it also needed to drive the season forward.

The force behind the sudden singing, in-universe, was the demon Sweet – played by the sadly deceased Hinton Battle, who also assisted with choreography for the episode – who causes musical numbers to happen around him that make people spontaneously combust, eventually. Sweet was, really, just a catalyst to force hard truths from the characters.

The cast worked intensely to prepare for the episode, learning choreography and complex numbers. Michelle Trachtenberg, who had a background in ballet, requested a dance sequence instead of a singing part. Her limited role in the episode meant that she was put front and centre in the preceding episode – 'All The Way' – to allow the rest of the cast time to rehearse. Anthony Stewart Head had a musical theatre background that included a starring role as Frank N. Furter in a West End revival of *The Rocky Horror Show* and James Marsters had some experience performing in a rock band, but this episode was a new experience for the rest of the cast.

The songs in the episode played with various genres. Buffy's opening number 'Going Through the Motions' was pure Disney, even featuring her bursting through a cloud of vampire dust in a visual reference to Ariel's song 'Part of Your World' in *The Little Mermaid.* Whedon knew that Amber Benson had an amazing voice, and wrote her a challenging ballad called 'Under Your Spell' that featured one of the most overtly sexual scenes between Tara and Willow in the show; Willow making Tara levitate while Tara sings 'You make me com… plete.' Xander and Anya performed a Fred and Ginger-style duet – 'I'll Never Tell' – that foreshadowed their devastating wedding later in the season, and Spike delivered a punchy rock song called 'Rest in Peace'. The episode was full of winks at musical theatre. Janitors danced with brooms in the background, Giles mentions police taking 'Witness arias' and both Marti Noxon and David Fury – writers and producers on the show – briefly appeared to sing miniature musical numbers. The episode was glorious and ridiculous until it wasn't; things took a dark turn in the final act with Buffy admitting that she was in heaven before being resurrected by her friends at the beginning of the season.

The musical episode was the high point, tonally, of the sixth season. It ended with curtains closing on a kiss between Buffy and Spike, beginning a relationship that becomes one of the hardest parts to watch on the show. The following episode began as a comedy of errors after one of Willow's spells goes awry and erases everyone's memory, and ended with heartbreak as Willow's overuse of magic sends Tara packing, while Giles leaves for England for the rest of the season. The latter plot point is often criticised for being wildly out of character, and it was. Giles left largely because Tony Head didn't want to extend his five-year contract into a full sixth year, and wanted to take a break from the show to spend time with his family. The episode – 'Tabula Rasa' – ended with Michelle Branch appearing at The Bronze to sing 'Goodbye to You', a song guaranteed to make any *Buffy* fan sob.

The core villains of the sixth season were a major shift for *Buffy*. Each season's villain had so far been something demonic. In the sixth season, three young human men – Andrew, Warren and Jonathan – became the main antagonists. Warren, played by Adam Busch, had been introduced in the previous season as the guy who built himself a robot girlfriend. Jonathan was a recurring character finally given a major role, and Andrew – played by Tom Lenk – was a new character. The Trio were, at their core, nerds; immature boys playing super villains. For most of the season they were treated as a non-threatening joke, but as the show built to the finale a harsh truth was exposed via the Trio – toxic masculinity is a terrifying villain. Their actions, especially late in the season, were described in Joanna Robinson's *Vanity Fair* piece as 'a frightening look into the entitled, misogynistic rhetoric that rose to the surface during the gamergate culture wars of 2014, and has seemingly infiltrated everything since.'

The other villains of the season were depression, and Joss Whedon. Buffy's struggles in a harsh human world led to a twisted, violent sexual relationship with Spike. Dawn became a kleptomaniac. Xander leaves Anya at the altar. Willow struggles with magic and eventually becomes the true monster of the season. That journey for Willow has led to some of the hardest parts of *Buffy*'s legacy.

In the sixth season Willow's relationship with witchcraft went from a metaphor for queerness to a metaphor for addiction. Willow struggles, driving away those she loves. There was a traditional rock-bottom moment, matched with Buffy's attempt to end her toxic relationship, but as the season wound towards its end things seemed on the up. Willow and Tara reconcile, with Tara outlining all the things they needed to work on before asking 'Can we skip it? Can you just be kissing me now?'

Happiness couldn't last for long. The episode 'Seeing Red' is one of the most controversial in *Buffy* for two big reasons. The first of those, Spike's attempt to sexually assault Buffy, was written to try and drive home an awful truth to viewers; a vampire without a soul could never be truly good. Whedon had grown frustrated that fans loved Buffy and Spike together, and wanted to open viewers' eyes to the fact that this relationship couldn't be healthy. Filming that scene was a hard day for the actors. James Marsters, speaking to *Buffering the Vampire Slayer*, recalled telling one of the writers 'You don't understand what you put us through sometimes', and spoke of becoming depressed after filming the episode.

Seeing the hero of a show like *Buffy* go through this was immensely tough on the viewers. Buffy was more than just a main character; she was a rare feminine superhero. Seeing someone that strong, inspiring and powerful still end up in such a horrifically vulnerable position is a hard thing to deal with, and it arguably wasn't even the worst part of the episode.

That honour instead goes to the final moments. At the end of the episode, Warren enters the garden of the Summers house, intending to shoot Buffy as revenge for thwarting one of the Trio's schemes, while upstairs Willow and Tara don clothes for the first time since reuniting. One bullet gets Buffy, and upstairs a spray of blood hits Willow. Tara, bleeding from the chest thanks to a second bullet, notices, says 'Your shirt' and collapses to the ground, dead.

'Bury Your Gays' is a long-standing and long-criticised trope. The website *TV Tropes* offers this definition: 'The presentation of deaths of LGBT characters where these characters are nominally able to be viewed as *more expendable* than their heterosexual counterparts.' On the one hand, Tara wasn't killed off because being a lesbian made her expendable, she was killed off so that Willow could become a villain. On the other hand, ending one of the very rare queer relationships on television at the time with a stray bullet was gut-wrenching. *The Kitten Board* was a popular message board at the time, devoted to Willow and Tara's relationship, with most of the members being queer women themselves. A post titled 'The Lesbian Cliché FAQ' from 2002 went into great detail about the problem of 'The Dead/Evil Lesbian Cliché'. A summary at the end of the post explained that 'Joss Whedon and the writers are Not Homophobic, but have perpetuated a hurtful lesbian cliché with the death of Tara and the resulting Vengeance Willow storyline.' The post gathered multiple quotes from Buffy writers that revealed the real issue – the people making the show knew that Tara's death would contribute to a harmful cliché, but they did it anyway. To make the decision worse, this is the only episode of *Buffy* to feature Amber Benson in the opening credits. The relationship between Willow and Tara was a historical part of queer television, but with 'Seeing Red' that history ended on a sour note.

The season ended with Willow determined to get revenge and destroy the world. Buffy, for once, wasn't the one to save it. While she was trapped underground, it fell to Xander to talk Willow off the ledge with a speech about a yellow crayon, a story from their shared childhood. 'Grave' was the only *Buffy* season finale not written by Joss Whedon – who was busy working on his new show *Firefly* – but he did write Xander's speech, giving his self-insert the big hero moment. Buffy's final action in the episode was to crawl out of the earth, mirroring her climb out of her grave at the beginning of the season. It was tough for Sarah Michelle Gellar to play Buffy as hopeful again after everything the show had put her through. In a 2010 Paley Center panel, Marti Noxon remembered Gellar telling her that 'I've lost the hero completely in all this exploration.'

For one final season, however, that hero had to return more powerful than ever. Buffy's opening line in the seventh season – 'It's about power', came to be the throughline of *Buffy*'s last episodes. The decision to end the show with the seventh season was very natural. The deal with UPN was coming to an end, and Sarah Michelle Gellar felt it was the right time to move on. It was, and still is, very rare for a show to end on its creator's terms rather than on the whim of its network, and with season seven *Buffy* went out with a bang.

The final season featured Sunnydale High rebuilt over the hellmouth, and the 'First Evil' (first introduced in the third season episode 'Amends'), attempting to destroy the slayer line and open the hellmouth for good. The First was able to appear as any dead person, which led to an excellent sequence at the end of the opening episode as the previous season's big bads morphed into one another, counting down from Warren to The Master, before The First manifested as Buffy and repeated that mission statement – 'It's about power.'

The first few episodes of the season misdirected the audience with classic 'Monster of the Week' episodes. 'Selfless', the fifth episode, showed a series of flashbacks to Anya's past and revisited the previous season's musical, giving Anya one more number. The sixth episode, 'Him', was a tribute to the early high school years of the show, with Dawn (and then Buffy, Anya and Willow) falling for a quarterback with an enchanted jacket. Then, in the seventh episode, the momentum kicked in with some of the very best writing on *Buffy*.

'Conversations with Dead People' told four distinct stories, and it took four distinct writers to do it. Joss Whedon took charge of Buffy's story, in which she got some much-needed therapy from an old high school classmate-turned-vampire. Drew Goddard had the story of Andrew and Jonathan returning to Sunnydale. Jane Espenson had Dawn's story, a tribute to classic horror that saw Dawn fighting off a poltergeist and apparently seeing a vision of her dead mother. It was Willow's story, written by Marti Noxon, that revealed what 'From Beneath You it Devours' – a refrain running through the season – meant. Willow is visited by a dead high schooler, Cassie (played by Azura Skye, who brings this book full circle by later appearing in *Riverdale*), who claims to be delivering a message from Tara. The conversation slowly turns sinister as Cassie tries to convince Willow to end her life, eventually revealing that she is The First, trying to take out one of Buffy's allies.

There were hopes that Amber Benson could return for the episode. Benson turned the opportunity down, citing a scheduling conflict. She later admitted, speaking to Evan Ross Katz for his book *Into Every Generation a Slayer is Born,* that she didn't entirely trust what would happen with her character. Benson 'felt like people had already been really hurt by this', and believed that playing Tara as a villain would be harmful.

From this episode, the season raced forward, dealing with a newly ensouled and insane Spike, the new high school principal (Robin Wood, played by D. B. Woodside) revealing himself to be the son of a slayer that Spike killed, the Watcher's council being blown up and an influx of potential slayers from around the world. There was Lalaine (who had previously starred in the tween sitcom *Lizzie McGuire*), Rachel Bilson (who would go on to star in *The O.C.*[4]) and Felicia Day (actress, writer and nerd-verse darling) joining the *Buffy* cast, to name just a few.

As the season drove on and events escalated, Faith returned thanks to a crossover with *Angel*. The episode that brought her back to Sunnydale – 'Dirty Girls' – also introduced Nathan Fillion (who had led Whedon's *Firefly* before its untimely cancellation) as Caleb, a nasty preacher who became the mouthpiece for everything *Buffy* stood against. Deus Ex Machina was in play as Buffy acquired a handy mystical scythe meant for the slayer. Then, there was the arrival of Angel himself with a soaring kiss at the end of the penultimate episode that was pure fan service, along with the delivery of a mystical necklace that could destroy the hellmouth for good.

It's impossible to ignore the importance of sticking the landing when it comes to a show's legacy. For seven years, *Buffy* had been

---

4. *The O.C.* serves as a nexus point for this book – almost every other show in here can be connected to *The O.C.* in a maximum of two steps.

exploring the idea of power in the hands of an unlikely blonde hero, saving the life of the little blonde girl that usually dies in the alley. The final episode took everything *Buffy* had explored: the isolation that comes with power, the potential for corruption, dominating patriarchal monsters (whether in the form of the Watcher's Council or demons), and turned it all on its head. Willow uses the scythe to change what it means to be a slayer, giving every potential there is or ever will be that power. The fight is taken directly to The First and its army of suddenly not-too-overpowered über-vampires; there were plenty of plot holes at the end, but Whedon has since admitted in interviews that those were less important than the message he wanted to deliver.

The plot really isn't as important as the speech at the core of the episode. As Willow's spell takes place, the episode flashed back to a speech that began earlier in the episode. Buffy tells her assembled troops: 'My power should be *our* power.' A montage of women standing up and finding strength plays as Buffy continues, ending on a question: 'Slayers, every one of us. Make your choice. Are you ready to be strong?' That power that had been an isolating force in the show was suddenly something shared. It was a colossal and impactful ending to a show that had been a source of inspiration and strength to millions of viewers.

The finally-destroyed hellmouth led to one hell of a final shot for the show. A school bus full of slayers and the show's surviving heroes (Anya having been unceremoniously killed off during the finale in one of the worst character deaths on the show) makes it out of Sunnydale just in time for the entire town to collapse into nothing, the hellmouth gone. The 'Welcome to Sunnydale' sign falls. While Buffy's friends contemplate what comes next, she simply looks at the horizon and smiles. Whedon called the finale 'closure, not closing', insisting that while this was an ending, the story lived on.

One of the places the story continued was in the fifth and final season of *Angel*, which aired the following season. By remaining on

The WB when *Buffy* went to UPN, *Angel* had begun to stand on its own and build a unique audience. Unlike *Buffy*, Whedon had no plans to end *Angel* going into the final season; he felt it was starting to pick up momentum, and assumed that The WB would definitely extend the show's five-year contract. The cancellation news broke in February 2004, blindsiding Whedon and the rest of his team. Whedon took to *The Bronze* to confirm the news, telling fans that 'my heart is breaking' and that 'I don't think The WB is doing the right thing.' Writer and producer David Fury later admitted in an interview that Whedon had pushed The WB for an early pick-up, wanting confirmation before the end of the season that the show would continue. By forcing the network into an early decision, it's possible that he indirectly caused the surprise cancellation. A fan campaign for the show's renewal began, pushing for the show to be renewed or picked up by UPN. Fans wrote emails, sent letters, organised themed blood drives and paid for a mobile billboard to travel around studios and networks, but to no avail.

Both *Angel* and *Buffy* did continue, however, in a series of comics published by Dark Horse and written by Joss Whedon, beginning in 2007. The new medium, and the fact that there were no actors to pay, meant the continuation could be bigger, bolder and more batshit. The comics initially garnered a positive reaction, but fans have since turned away from the stories. While Whedon has insisted that they're a fully canon continuation, many *Buffy* fans are happy to ignore the events of the comics.

The legacy of *Buffy* goes far beyond comic books. There's an entire academic field of *Buffy* studies. The first academic conference dedicated to *Buffy* – 'Blood, Text and Fears' – took place at the University of East Anglia in 2002, and academic study of the show continues into the present day. Along with scholarly interest, both the fandom and professional TV-lovers continue to celebrate *Buffy*. The show consistently turns up in lists ranking best television shows. It landed second in *Entertainment Weekly*'s 2021 list 'The 50 Best Teen

Shows of All Time', and forty-ninth in the WGA's 2013 list 'The 101 Best Written TV Series of All Time'. In 2016, it was thirty-eighth in *Rolling Stone*'s '100 Greatest TV Shows of All Time', although it fell to seventy-seven in a similar *Rolling Stone* list from 2022. Multiple podcasts have sprung up recapping and reengaging with the show, not just *Buffering the Vampire Slayer* (who have begun recapping the show for a second time), but *Slayerfest 98* and *Still Pretty*, to name just a couple. There are still active message boards, fan spaces online and more – this is a show that still engages fans decades after it ended.

There's nuance needed in discussions about the show now. Joss Whedon made a name for himself making a 'feminist' television show. In 2017 his ex-wife Kai Cole published a piece for *The Wrap* that called Whedon 'a hypocrite preaching feminist ideals.' In the piece, Cole details a pattern of infidelity from Whedon that ran throughout their marriage and – according to Cole – began with an affair on the set of *Buffy*. Cole discusses being diagnosed with Complex PTSD as a result of her marriage to Whedon, and states 'I want the people who worship him to know he is human, and the organizations giving him awards for his feminist work, to think twice in the future about honoring a man who does not practice what he preaches.'

In 2020, there were further controversies around Whedon's actions on the set of *Justice League*. Then, in February 2021, Charisma Carpenter released a lengthy statement, saying that Whedon had 'abused his power on numerous occasions while working together on the sets of Buffy the Vampire Slayer and Angel.' Multiple *Buffy* stars came forward to support Carpenter, corroborating her statement and distancing themselves from Whedon, with some acknowledging their own issues on set. Michelle Trachtenberg stated on Instagram that 'There was a rule saying that [Whedon]'s not allowed in a room with Michelle again.' Whedon himself stayed quiet on the subject until 2022, when he was profiled in *New York Magazine*. In the piece, he acknowledged his past infidelity on the *Buffy* set, but denied many of the allegations against him.

In 1967, Roland Barthes put forward in his essay 'The Death of the Author' an argument that the meaning of a text is determined by the reader, not the writer. Now, in the wake of the 'Me Too' movement and a long-needed reckoning concerning abuses of power in the entertainment industry, 'Death of the Author' has ironically taken on a meaning different from Barthes' intention. Now, people consider authors dead to them while still enjoying the work of problematic creators.

It's a struggle to conflate the feminist ideals of *Buffy* with the idea of an alleged abuser being the show's creator, but the show remains exactly what it is. *Buffy* belongs to its fans now more than it belongs to Whedon. Watching the show with this new context, however, some issues become more obvious. The disappointing fate of Cordelia, the gleeful tone in which Whedon discusses putting his characters in pain and Xander's misogynistic characteristics all bear looking at in a new light.

In 2018, news broke that a reboot of *Buffy* was in the works at 20th Century Fox, with Joss Whedon and Gail Berman attached as executive producers. However, as the allegations against Whedon mounted, news of the reboot dried to a trickle. In 2022, in an interview with the *Hollywood Reporter*'s *Top 5* podcast, Gail Berman said the reboot was 'on pause.'

Buffy did get a sequel of sorts in 2023. *Slayers: A Buffyverse Story* was a nine-part audio drama created for Audible. The show, co-written by Amber Benson and Christopher Golden, takes place a decade after the end of the TV show, largely in an alternate universe. Benson obviously has a long running relationship with *Buffy*, and Christopher Golden has had a storied writing career that includes *Buffy* novels and the non-fiction *Watcher's Guide* companion books. *Slayers* got the nod from Whedon, but beyond that he had no involvement in the production. Charisma Carpenter, James Marsters, Emma Caulfield, Juliet Landau, Anthony Stewart Head and Amber Benson all reprised their roles from the show, with Laya DeLeon Hayes joining as a new slayer. *Slayers* put the power back in the hands of beloved characters.

Christopher Golden tweeted that *Slayers* was 'about creating a story that would showcase our favorite characters and do better by some of them than the show had done.' By taking the *Buffy*verse out of its creator's hands, *Slayers* delivered a redemption fans had been hoping for.

While, sadly, *Slayers* was cancelled after a single season, fans rejoiced in 2025 when the news broke that a *Buffy* reboot was on the verge of a pilot order from Hulu. The most exciting part of the news for *Buffy*-lovers was that Sarah Michelle Gellar herself would be returning to the role, alongside Chloe Zhao directing and Nora and Lilla Zuckerman joining the writers room. A theme appeared in both the comments on Gellar's Instagram post and elsewhere across the internet – in our current political climate, *Buffy* was needed now more than ever.

The importance of *Buffy the Vampire Slayer* can't be denied. It was a show that changed what teen dramas could be. It pushed boundaries and inspired people to find their own power. Even now, more and more people are discovering the show and falling in love with it for the first time. A 2023 *Slate* review of *Slayers* pointed out that 'A new kind of Buffy fandom has grown, epitomized by the popular recap podcast *Buffering the Vampire Slayer*, which focuses on supporting the actors who spoke out, loving the characters, and living up to the ideals the show represents.' *Buffy* is a show that is still loved, endlessly watched and most importantly talked about. Without *Buffy* we might not have gotten the rest of the shows in this book. *Buffy the Vampire Slayer* changed the world. Or, at least, the world of television.

Chapter 3

Gilmore Girls

Welcome to Stars Hollow

A selection of pristine, candy-coloured houses and shops surround a lush, green town square crowned with a bright white gazebo. It's the platonic ideal of a small town in New England. The *Seinfeld* gang found the bucolic setting appalling when they were rerouted into that odd little town during the sitcom's final episode. This is Stars Hollow.

I should be clear, at this point, that the *Seinfeld* finale, which aired in 1998, was not a crossover with *Gilmore Girls*. At that point in television history, the square that would become the centre of Stars Hollow was just a set lying around at Warner Brothers. It took the hard work of Amy Sherman-Palladino and her husband Daniel Palladino to take that generic set, populate it, and create the home of *Gilmore Girls*.

The Palladinos met while working on the nineties sitcom *Roseanne*. Amy Sherman-Palladino, known as much for her penchant for huge feathered hats and punk aesthetic as for her writing skills, met with Susanne Daniels in the late nineties to pitch potential new shows for The WB. She came armed with multiple ideas for half-hour comedies – the area of television where she'd been honing her skills – all tailored to the network's youthful demographic and centred on strong female characters. As the meeting drew to a close Amy dropped an afterthought of an idea – a show about a mother and her teenage daughter who were more like best friends than parent and child. Daniels jumped on the idea immediately, recalling in *Season Finale* that Amy expanded the afterthought, pitching a teenage character that wouldn't be stunningly beautiful, or a 'mousy loner' waiting for Prince Charming. Daniels surprised Sherman Palladino with the suggestion that the show could have hour-long episodes, rather than half-hour.[1] Amy was concerned that her comedy talents were in question, but she took on the challenge.

Beyond the mother-daughter concept, Sherman-Palladino had no idea what this show was. She didn't know who the main characters were, who their friends were, what the mother did for a living, where the daughter went to school or even where they lived – small town or big city? She was leaning towards a big city until she took a vacation to see Mark Twain's house. Staying in a tiny, charming inn in a small town (Washington, Connecticut, specifically) where the locals all greeted each other by name and helped themselves to coffee in the local diner, *Gilmore Girls* fell into place for Sherman-Palladino. She wanted to play with the ideas of class divide, which meant there needed to be an affluent area and a big city close by. Hartford in Connecticut became the nearby metropolis, and Stars Hollow was born.

The setting informed the premise of the show. *Gilmore Girls* became the story of Lorelai Gilmore and her daughter Rory. Lorelai – the daughter of wealthy, old-money parents – got pregnant at sixteen and ran away from home when her daughter was a baby. At the beginning of the show, Rory is almost sixteen herself, and the pilot saw Lorelai returning to her old home and asking her parents for the money to send Rory to an elite private school in the hopes of eventually getting an Ivy League education.

In the early days of *Gilmore Girls* Amy Sherman-Palladino had to wrestle with comparisons to the hit teen shows of the time. In an interview with the *New York Times* around the show's fifth season, she recalled regular notes like 'On *Dawson's Creek* we do things this way.' *Gilmore Girls* quickly found its own niche, however. Rory was

1. In network television, that would make the show a drama rather than a sitcom.

in no way comparable to the female leads of *Dawson's*, she was very much the character Sherman-Palladino had envisioned in that first meeting. Neither was Lorelai the classic hands-on-hips, lips-pursed mother of these other shows; she was just sixteen years older than her daughter and still getting her life together.

The 1999/2000 season, the season before *Gilmore Girls* began, was a big time of transition for television. Sitcoms and dramas had dominated prime time for the last decade, but things were shifting. The biggest shock of that season was ABC's *Who Wants to Be a Millionaire*, which came to dominate the ratings and spawned a slew of copycat quiz shows across network television. Amidst this new trend, The WB continued to offer a solid slate of teen dramas. The newest addition in 1999 was *Roswell*, based loosely on the *Roswell High* young adult book series, a high school drama featuring secret aliens. Described as *Dawson's Creek* meets *X-Files* by critics, *Roswell* was a sleeper hit that quietly built a network of devoted fans.

In the 2000/2001 season, as *Gilmore Girls* began, the big four networks were jumping on the new reality television trend. When *Survivor* started on CBS and began to dominate in ratings, the network went to war with NBC on Thursday nights – putting their new reality hit up against *Friends* in the schedule. With those battles waging, *Gilmore Girls* ran the risk of getting lost in the shuffle in its Thursday time slot. Instead, being put in the schedule in a potentially ignored slot, and clearly being ignored by its network, the show managed to find its feet. The unique comedy, rich characters and critical acclaim certainly helped the show find its audience, but *Gilmore Girls* early popularity can be attributed in large part to the central relationship of the show. The mother and daughter story had more than just teenage appeal; there was a built-in adult audience too. Mothers and daughters began watching the show together, finding common ground in that core relationship of the eponymous Gilmore girls.

Casting that mother and daughter, along with the rest of the show, was a challenge. The pilot had a tight time frame; according to casting director Jill Anthony the whole thing had to come together in just four weeks, rather than the six to ten weeks a show like this would normally have been given. Amy Sherman-Palladino wanted funny, and she wanted fast talking. Despite Lauren Graham already being attached to NBC sitcom *M.Y.O.B*, the casting directors insistently pursued her. The sitcom was clearly going nowhere, and Graham was a rare actress that had the necessary screwball comedy skills to play Lorelai Gilmore. In a 2002 interview with the *Daily Texan*, Sherman-Palladino said of Lauren Graham 'The fact that you had someone that talented running around Hollywood, not found yet, was the biggest coup in the world.' Graham was well known among her peers, among casting directors and producers, but she was yet to land a starring role, and she was the perfect Lorelai.

Alexis Bledel had absolutely no acting experience before being cast on *Gilmore Girls*. She was an N.Y.U student with a few modelling jobs under her belt, just breaking into the industry, and was suffering from a nasty flu on the day of her network screen test. She'd impressed so much in prior auditions, however, that her illness and obvious lack of enthusiasm didn't get in the way, and Rory Gilmore became her big break.

The old-money Gilmore grandparents fell quickly into place. Sherman-Palladino wanted veteran stage and screen star Edward Herrmann to play Richard Gilmore, but assumed he wouldn't be interested in this silly little television show. As it turned out, he was more than happy to meet with the casting directors, read for the part and make the role his. Kelly Bishop, another stage veteran and a contemporary of Herrmann's, was cast as the acerbic Emily Gilmore after her first audition, and she and Herrmann went on to build a close, although completely platonic, relationship that mirrored their on-screen marriage.

Outside of the core family, Stars Hollow was fleshed out with richly detailed residents. Alex Borstein was cast in the pilot as Lorelai's best friend and eventual business partner Sookie St James, but her contract with *MADtv* wouldn't let her take on the role long-term. Instead, the casting team found then-unknown Melissa McCarthy, who reshot

Borstein's pilot scenes, played the role for the entirety of the show's run, and went on to become a household name. Borstein did appear as a couple of minor characters during the show's run; she played the furious harpist Drella in the first season and was almost unrecognisable as stylist Miss Celine in a few episodes further down the line.

While Borstein had to be recast, her husband did end up with a long-running role on the show. Borstein's voice work as Lois on *Family Guy* led to both herself and her husband Jackson Douglas becoming friendly with the Palladinos. In an interview with *Vanity Fair*, Douglas recalled hitting it off with Amy, who offered to write him a small part in *Gilmore Girls*. Originally, his character, Jackson Belleville, was only meant to be in the show for a few episodes; 'I was just gonna be the vegetable guy – just some comic relief,' he told *Vanity Fair*. The chemistry between his vegetable farmer character and McCarthy's chef Sookie kept his character on the show for all seven seasons. This kind of organic chemistry on the show wasn't unique to the pair, and other couples emerged naturally as the show progressed.

Originally the diner owner Luke Danes was written to be a woman, and a very minor background character. A network note that the pilot was too 'female-centric' led to 'Daisy's Diner' becoming 'Luke's Diner' and a different gender in the casting call. Scott Patterson was in a foul mood the day he attended his audition for the role, having been struggling for a few years to find success as an actor and with concerns that this script was just too good for him. After seeing Patterson in action, the casting team stopped seeing other actors and offered him the role that day. Luke was a small part of the show, to begin with, but just a few episodes into shooting *Gilmore Girls* Sherman-Palladino noticed the palpable tension between Luke and Lorelai and the chemistry between the actors, and Luke was quickly upgraded to be a major part of the show.

The minor weirdos that filled Stars Hollow became the foundation of *Gilmore Girls*' unique sense of humour. Amy Sherman-Palladino often, when coming across actors she found funny, would make them a regular part of the world just so she could keep writing for them. Sally Struthers and Liz Torres as Babette and Miss Patty enriched the show as bawdy broads, while Michael Winters was almost unintentionally hilarious as Taylor Doose, the terrifying gavel-wielding overlord of Stars Hollow town meetings. Liza Weil originally auditioned to play Rory, and while she wasn't quite right for the part Sherman-Palladino felt she was a 'master comedienne' and created the role of Rory's best frenemy Paris just for her.

One of the biggest small roles in *Gilmore Girls* was Kirk Gleason, played by Sean Gunn. Now best known for his appearances in Marvel's *Guardians of the Galaxy* movies (directed by his brother, James Gunn), Sean Gunn's first appearance on *Gilmore Girls* was in the second episode – 'The Lorelai's First Day at Chilton' – as Mick, a DSL installer. For the next episode, the show needed a swan delivery guy and Sherman-Palladino liked the idea of using the same actor again. It became an homage to her father, a jobbing actor and writer who would get a different hat and name every week. Mick became Kirk, a comic-relief character who during the show worked at almost every business in Stars Hollow.

The one place that remained free of Kirk in Stars Hollow was Sophie's music shop, introduced in the second season. Sophie was played by none other than the absolutely iconic singer-songwriter Carole King. King had, however, been a part of *Gilmore Girls* from the very first episode. The show's main title theme 'Where You Lead' is one of King's most famous songs. Originally written for her 1971 album 'Tapestry', by the time *Gilmore Girls* was taking shape King had stopped performing the song in concert as she felt that its message of a woman following a man wasn't something she wanted to promote. Amy Sherman-Palladino wanted something 'classic' for the show's theme, as she told *Entertainment Weekly* in a 2015 interview, and approached King about using the original 'Where You Lead'. She didn't really believe that her unknown show would get permission from the legendary Carole King, but she had to try.

King loved the mother and daughter focus of the show, and offered to record a more relevant version of 'Where You Lead'. She approached her co-writer Toni Stern and they tweaked the lyrics to suit a mother-daughter relationship. Then, King recorded the new version of the song with her daughter Louise Goffin. In that same *Entertainment Weekly* piece, Amy Sherman-Palladino called it 'the greatest theme song in the world.'

Music had a vital role in *Gilmore Girls*. There was no official Music Supervisor on the show – it was something Amy Sherman-Palladino wanted to do for herself. She didn't want a score that worked like a sitcom laugh track, instructing the audience how to feel throughout every moment of the show. She was a big fan of the musician Sam Phillips, and had used a couple of her songs in the pilot. It was Daniel Palladino who suggested that Phillips might be willing to get more involved in the show. This was another long shot, but Phillips agreed to work on the score, and provided not just beautiful music, but a series of signature vocal cues (the show's 'la-la-la's') that became part of the fabric of *Gilmore Girls*. Sherman Palladino, in a 2010 interview with *Outsmart*, spoke on the importance of that score, how those vocal moments 'felt like an extension of [Rory and Lorelai's] thoughts,' and how it 'elevated the show'. The score, like the casting and the distinctness of Stars Hollow, was another detail that could never be too small in making *Gilmore Girls* a fully realised and unique world.

Phillips' song 'Reflecting Light' soundtracked one of the most beloved romantic moments on the show, when Luke and Lorelai danced together for the first time, and returned in the revival to underscore their wedding. Phillips also made a cameo appearance in the sixth season finale – 'Partings' – as a busker. The idea of live music on the streets of Stars Hollow was a part of the show from the beginning. The town troubadour, played by Grant Lee Phillips, regularly appeared on street corners singing both his own songs and covers during scene transitions. The first season finale 'Love, Daisies and Troubadours' saw Grant Lee Phillips in competition with

Dave (Gruber) Allen – who had starred in NBC's very short-lived teen drama *Freaks and Geeks* the previous year – as the two fought over the title of official town troubadour. In the sixth season finale, Phillip's troubadour character set off on tour with Neil Young and sparked an infestation of buskers in the town.

That episode was a culmination of the music that had been shaping the show for years. Each busker performance was a great little cameo; alongside the returning Dave Allen and the appearance of Sam Phillips came other guest appearances from musicians that the show's creators loved. Sparks, Yo La Tengo and Sonic Youth[2], among others, all appear as street performers. Yo La Tengo's song 'My Little Corner of the World' had bracketed the show's first season – a cover version appeared at the end of the pilot and the original played at the end of 'Love, Daisies and Troubadours.' Sonic Youth's Kim Gordon and Thurston Moore included their daughter, Coco in their appearance. Daniel Palladino even appeared in the episode, singing his self-penned ditty 'A Beaver Ate My Thumb'.

It wasn't confirmed, when 'Partings' came together, that the episode would be the Palladinos' last on the show, but it was an episode that summed up much of the hard work that had gone into the show over the previous few years. The series of ridiculous musical cameos were surreal, nonsensical and in the world of *Gilmore Girls*, completely believable.

Unlike other teen dramas of the time, *Gilmore Girls* didn't use a venue in the show to bring in regular live music performances. Instead, much of the music on the show came from headphones, speakers, and characters sharing music they cared about. Where *Buffy* had The Bronze, *Gilmore Girls* had mixtapes and burnt CDs. There were a couple of big concerts in the show – The Bangles in the first

2. If I had a pound for every time Sonic Youth, in the 2000s, appeared in a teen drama with the word 'Girl' in the title, I'd have two pounds. Which isn't a lot, but it's weird that it happened twice. (See next chapter.)

season and an appearance from The Shins[3] in the season four spring break episode, but much of the live music on *Gilmore Girls* came from the show's in-house band 'Hep Alien'.

The character of Lane Kim – Rory's best friend, played by Keiko Agena – was inspired by Amy Sherman-Palladino's friend (and *Gilmore Girls* producer) Helen Pai. Lane – a Korean-American raised in Stars Hollow as a Seventh-Day Adventist – had the biggest teen rebellion storyline on the show. She was a music geek who loved everything her mother hated, and her character got some of the show's best soundtrack moments. In the third season Lane, who secretly began learning to play drums at Sophie's music shop, puts out a 'drummer seeks rock band' advert. Her first draft of the advert comes in at about three pages long, citing a long alphabetical list of musical influences including The Adolescents, The Adverts, Agent Orange and Ash, with AC/DC, The Animals and A-Ha already cut for space. The scene ended with Lane's announcement that she's going to have to 'crank The Ramones' to make cuts, followed by a blast of 'I Wanna Be Sedated' from behind a closed door. Eventually, the advert leads Lane to Dave Rygalski – played by Adam Brody – who invites her to join his band. Dave Rygalski was named after Helen Pai's musician husband – the real Dave Rygalski appeared in Daniel Palladino's busking group in 'Partings'. The relationship between Lane and Dave went on, with both him and their bandmates pretending to be a Christian music group to work around Lane's strict household, and the pair eventually have their first kiss to David Bowie's 'The Man Who Sold the World'.

The relationship proved short-lived when Dave moved to California for college at the end of the third season – an in-show reference to Adam Brody leaving *Gilmore Girls* to star in *The O.C.*[4] Sebastian

3. Who got their start in the mid-nineties touring with Cibo Matto – one of the early bands to appear at The Bronze on *Buffy*.

4. Alright, this was an easy link.

Bach, famous for being a rock and roll pretty boy and the front man of Skid Row, joined the show as Dave's replacement Gil, and Lane went on to get together with the band's frontman Zack – played by Todd Lowe. While Bach was an entertaining addition to the show's cast, the Lane-and-Zack romance wasn't popular with fans. The band Hep Alien (an anagram of Helen Pai) was an essential part of both the show and Lane's story of rebellion and acceptance, but her character settled down into a 'married-with-kids' life in the show's final season that felt like a cop-out, less than Lane Kim deserved. Then again, there was a *lot* about the final season of *Gilmore Girls* that fans didn't love.

That fandom formed quickly when *Gilmore Girls* began. It was the writing – the blend of sitcom, drama, screwball comedy and a hint of surrealism – that built a world viewers could fall in love with. The number of references to David Lynch's surreal classic *Twin Peaks* alone helped the show always feel slightly to the left of the real world. A 2015 *New York Times* piece that looked at *Gilmore Girls*' ongoing fandom in light of the popular recap podcast *Gilmore Guys* called the world of the show a place that 'resembles our own, but everyone is just a little quicker, a little livelier and a little more real than real life.'

When *Gilmore Girls* began, teen shows tended to fit in one of two boxes: there was the supernatural, sci-fi and fantasy storytelling of shows like *Buffy* and *Roswell*, and then there was the soapy world of shows like *Dawson's Creek*. The latter shows were full of precocious, unrealistic teenagers that irritated Paul Feig enough to make him create *Freaks and Geeks*, which was a show that didn't quite fit in either box but also ran on a network completely unwilling to give it a chance to find its audience, instead consigning it to the same early-cancellation/cult classic bin as *My So-Called Life*. *Gilmore Girls*, on the other hand, was also unique from its peers but appeared on The WB – a network far more willing to give a new show a chance.

These shows were all, to varying degrees, in conversation with each other. *Dawson's Creek* had become such a ubiquitous part of pop culture that its contemporaries would regularly drop nods to Joey,

Dawson and Pacey. *Gilmore Girls* didn't just reference the shows it shared a network with though; it referenced *everything*. Classic cinema, music from all over the previous century, writers, comics, politicians, reporters, television – nothing was too sacred or too obscure, and the show had the cameos to back these references up. The *Twin Peaks* nods included asking if the character Sherry seemed like a 'diner girl' – Sherry was played by Mädchen Amick, who had previously appeared in *Twin Peaks* as diner waitress Shelly Johnson. Renowned American writer Norman Mailer wasn't just referenced, but appeared in a single episode as a plot vehicle to deliver the news of Sookie's pregnancy. Former Secretary of State Madeleine Albright appeared as herself in a dream sequence on Rory's twenty-first birthday, and musical icon Paul Anka appeared in a different dream sequence, one based on Lorelai's dog (also named Paul Anka).

Alongside those cameos was a constant stream of movie quotes and quips, mentions of old comedians and nods to books, poetry and plays galore. The pilot episode opened with The La's 'There She Goes' and in just the first ten minutes referenced Jack Kerouac, RuPaul, a missing Macy Gray CD and Eminem. Around the ninth episode an executive at The WB finally complained, insisting no one would understand a reference to Oscar Levant. Amy Sherman-Palladino claimed in her 2002 *Daily Texan* interview that her response was 'Well, tough. He was in *An American in Paris*, rent a tape.' Sherman-Palladino wanted to reference anything and everything, and she didn't patronise her audience – expecting them to keep up. Generally, they did, and they loved it.

Gilmore Girls was also full of smaller roles that make the show feel like a time capsule. A pre-*Mad Men* Jon Hamm appeared for a single episode as a potential love interest for Lorelai, Danny Pudi had a recurring role as a member of Yale's newspaper staff long before his appearance on *Community*, a young Seth McFarlane appeared towards the end of the show's second season as a business school graduate furious at the existence of rich people, and Nick Offerman appeared twice on the show, delivering a skin-crawling, awkward and hilarious performance as Jackson's cousin Beau.

One of Amy Sherman-Palladino's favourite bits of casting was Danny Strong (of *Buffy* fame) appearing as Doyle, Rory's editor at the *Yale Daily News*. In a rare bit of DVD commentary, she mentions her 'obsessive *Buffy* days' when Strong appears on screen in the season five episode 'You Jump, I Jump, Jack'. A few episodes later, when Paris heads out for a late-night speed-dating session, Rory asks if she's going to meet Spike and Drusilla; not the show's only *Buffy* reference, but notable considering it was that episode that saw Paris and Doyle get together.

It wasn't just the referential nature of the show that made *Gilmore Girls* stand out – it was the dialogue itself. *Gilmore Girls* is famous for fast-paced, rapid-fire conversations. The scripts for the show were often around eighty pages long; the typical length for an hour-long drama is around half that. In a 2005 interview with the *AV Club*, Amy Sherman-Palladino talked about having a final pass over every script to maintain the tone of the show. She said that 'it's important to feel like the same show every week, because it is so verbal. It's not about car crashes or vampires or monsters or suspense. It's really about people talking to each other and the way they talk to each other, which is very specific.' While the show did have a full writing staff, including *Buffy* alum Jane Espenson and Jenji Kohan who went on to create *Weeds* and *Orange is the New Black*, it was essential that the Palladinos had the final say on every script, no matter how much that added to their workload. The references and rapid dialogue created a world that locked the characters into each other – existing in *Gilmore Girls* meant speaking a different language.

The fast-talking nature of the show also allowed the stories to be told in a unique way. *Gilmore Girls* wasn't a show full of big action moments. Car crashes, heart attacks, weddings, plot twists and huge fights – these were things that took place off-screen. Instead, the show was concerned with the aftermath – talking through these events and examining the how and why, rather than showing the moments themselves.

All of this required a pared-back shooting style compared to some of the show's peers. Sherman-Palladino stuck to her sitcom roots with simple master shots, leaving the camera on her characters for an extended period of time rather than going for stylised, dramatic cuts. The shooting style was theatrical, flowing and choreographed. It maintained the sense of pace and rhythm set by the dialogue. Sherman-Palladino summed up her attitude to shooting in a 2005 *New York Times* interview: 'These television shows that have fourteen shots of somebody looking at each other with the wind blowing through their hair drive me insane. Who's got that kind of time? We got that the girl was pretty when she walked in the door.' *Gilmore Girls* was never a show to linger on a dramatic entrance. At its heart, this was a screwball comedy akin to the classics of the genre.

Many of those classic comedies were stories that played with class – a theme central to *Gilmore Girls*. Class was always something underlying and occasionally unrealistic in teen dramas – consider the wealthy lifestyles in *Beverly Hills* or Xander's wildly different home life compared to his friends on *Buffy* – and eventually class-based fish-out-of-water stories became commonplace in teen shows, but on *Gilmore Girls* it was at the forefront of the story. The show saw Rory finding herself drawn to the upper-middle class lifestyle that Lorelai had run away from, with Rory even 'coming out' at a debutante ball in the second season. As *Gilmore Girls* went on, the characters' relationships to class and privilege became a catalyst for much of its drama.

Every teen drama needs a moment of rebellion for the protagonist, and for Rory that rebellion was embracing the privileges available to her and rejecting her mother's self-sufficient ideals. At the end of the fifth season, Rory opted to drop out of Yale and move in with her wealthy grandparents as a response to being told she didn't have potential as a journalist after an internship working under her boyfriend's newspaper magnate father. A 2023 piece in the (real) *Yale*

Daily News headlined 'Rory Gilmore Should've Gone to Harvard' offered a unique perspective on the storyline. The piece suggested that by staying at Yale and close, physically, to her teenage life, Rory had never experienced the 'reality check' that going to a university far away from home, full of high-achievers just like her, could deliver. As a result, she simply wasn't prepared for rejection, for being told that she didn't have the potential she'd been regularly informed she possessed by the bucket load throughout the show. As a result, she copes with professional rejection by stealing a yacht, dropping out of university and briefly becoming a miniature version of her grandmother as she takes on the life that her mother rejected. It's a rare teenage rebellion that comes with both community service and finger sandwiches, but in the upside-down world of *Gilmore Girls* it worked, even if it made Rory hard to root for.

The show's transition to college for Rory, and the writer's decision to send her to Yale rather than Harvard, is a great example of this struggle for teen shows. Most of these shows start in high school with sixteen-year-old protagonists, allowing for at least three years of storytelling among locker-filled hallways. After that, the shows have to wrestle with the awkward college years. That core sense of space in *Gilmore Girls* – the quirky Stars Hollow juxtaposed with the stuffy world of the grandparent Gilmores – was compromised when the plot required Rory to be elsewhere. This meant that, despite spending three years focusing on Rory's dream of going to Harvard, she had to go to Yale instead. A final plot twist putting Paris at the same school as Rory allowed the show to keep building on the momentum of Rory's private school friendship from the previous seasons.

Buffy dealt with the college problem by inventing convoluted reasons to keep the bulk of the cast in Sunnydale – or shipped off to the spin-off in L.A. *Dawson's Creek* famously suffered when its characters began to scatter for college. *Felicity* was a hit with teens but began with high school graduation and its title character heading off to college, allowing the story to remain static. In a lot of these shows, the awkward college years require the kind of writing that gives the audience an inadvertent peek behind the curtain; seeing storylines that were just there to maintain the status quo.

Although *Gilmore Girls* had been steadily building up a devoted audience throughout its run, that transitional fourth season wasn't the most popular. In her 2005 *New York Times* interview, Amy Sherman-Palladino responded to a question about the show being off its game by acknowledging that it was a different show without Rory living at home, mentioning that they also 'didn't have our boys; we didn't have a love interest.' The most controversial choice of the season was to give Rory a love interest just for the last few episodes of the season, reuniting her with her ex-boyfriend Dean and ending the season as she loses her virginity to him, despite his marriage to Lindsey (played by Arielle Kebbel, who would later go on to star in *The Vampire Diaries*). It was another rare rebellion on the show, the previously perfect protagonist making a colossal mistake and dealing with it by going to Europe with her grandmother.

As the fandom grew, so did the shipping wars. *Gilmore Girls* was popular in the early days of internet discussion. While debates over who the main characters should be with never reached the dizzying heights of later hit shows, the arguments were there. For Lorelai, ending up with Luke was obvious, and even her almost-reunions with Rory's father Chris – played by David Sutcliffe – were clearly just stumbling blocks for the relationship. While Luke and Lorelai Ross-and-Racheled their way through the show's first four seasons, Rory was torn between perfect first boyfriend Dean (played by Jared Padalecki) and Milo Ventimiglia's bad-boy Jess. The latter left the show at the end of the third season with the penultimate episode – 'Here Comes the Son' – serving as a backdoor pilot for a planned spin-off, *Windward Circle*, focused on Jess, which The WB opted not to pick up. The fifth season of the show introduced a new team for fans to join when Matt Czuchry joined the cast as Logan Huntzberger, a love interest that represented the world of privilege and wealth that both Lorelai and, to an extent, the show viewed as 'The Dark Side'.

Both Rory and Logan's relationship and Luke and Lorelai's transition to romance began at weddings. For Luke and Lorelai, it was his sister's wedding where they waltzed to 'Reflecting Light' that sparked them into finally becoming more than friends. The early episodes of the fifth season rapidly established them as a couple, while Rory realised that her relationship with Dean was a non-starter and began to instead fall for rich-boy Logan.

Rory and Lorelai's respective relationships came to two very different boiling points in 'Wedding Bell Blues' – the show's 100th episode. Reaching 100 episodes was a massive milestone for a show on network television. This was the magic syndication number; the point where a show would start being licensed for reruns on small networks, creating a new income stream for the creators of the show and the studio behind it. *Gilmore Girls* celebrated reaching the magic number with the vow renewal/second wedding of Emily and Richard, after the pair had spent much of the fifth season separated. The episode was shot almost entirely on location at the Wilshire Ebell Theatre – which served as the wedding venue – a rare move away from the standard sets of the show.

As Rory and Logan finally moved into romantic territory in the episode, Emily's machinations saw Chris sabotaging Luke and Lorelai's relationship. The episode reset both Luke and Lorelai, and Lorelai's relationship with her mother – firmly estranging the latter pair. There was always a worry, in bringing Luke and Lorelai together, that the show risked stagnating without the tension between them. Amy Sherman-Palladino only wanted them to pair up if she could see storylines ahead, and temporarily splitting the two of them up was one of those storylines. *Entertainment Weekly* called the 100th episode 'one of the greatest of the entire series', celebrating its 'off the charts' pacing and 'pitch perfect' details. It was a hit with viewers, and one of the show's most-watched episodes. Some shows ran a risk of becoming stale parodies of themselves if they went on too long, but *Gilmore Girls* wasn't one of them.

Gilmore Girls wasn't necessarily as groundbreaking or boundary-pushing on the surface as say, *Buffy*, but the show told big stories beautifully. The 100th episode was an incredible demonstration of what the show could be at its best, as a part of a television season that ended in a bang. Remember, this was the show that had to fight during its first season against *Friends* at the height of its popularity. While *Gilmore Girls* never came close to *Friends* in ratings, it held its own on the air. When the fifth season of the show came to an end, it was during an explosive couple of weeks on television. Sweeps is the time period where networks come under the scrutiny of potential advertisers and do their best to attract huge audiences. The sweeps month at the end of the 2004/2005 television season was rife with shows going for huge cliffhangers. *Desperate Housewives* had hostage situations, Claire's baby on *Lost* had been kidnapped by a mad French woman and *One Tree Hill* had a long-lost parent and attempted arson. *Gilmore Girls*, comparatively, ended on a quieter note, but one that resonated loudly with its fans when Lorelai, in a moment of turmoil, blurted out 'Luke, will you marry me?'

While *Gilmore Girls* had been quietly growing its audience, television had been growing more turbulent. Reality TV had risen, with UPN expanding its programming into more than just sci-fi and wrestling with *America's Next Top Model*, *American Idol* on Fox dominating ratings and *Survivor* becoming a massive hit. The WB and its teen drama slate had a lot to compete with.

Some shows fared better than others. *Roswell* had struggled to find a consistent tone and consistent audience. The WB cancelled the show at the end of its second season, but UPN opted to pick it up alongside *Buffy*. Despite having the vampire slayer as a lead-in, and fan campaigns to keep the show on the air (which involved sending bottles of tabasco sauce to network executives), the show was cancelled for good at the end of its third season in 2002.

In that 2004/2005 season, UPN finally aired a teen drama that was theirs from the beginning rather than rescued from another network.

Veronica Mars was a mystery drama inspired by classic film noir, and starred Kristen Bell as Veronica – a high school student moonlighting as a private detective. It was another of those shows that failed to do anything impressive in the ratings, but instead became a critical darling with a loyal fan base.

That loyal fan base was key in keeping *Veronica Mars* on the air on two separate occasions. The second of those was in 2013 when Rob Thomas – the show's creator – and Kristen Bell, launched a campaign on the crowdfunding site Kickstarter to make a movie that would wrap up the show's storyline after its cancellation in 2008. The first occasion was in 2006, when the network *Veronica Mars* aired on had its future in doubt.

The WB and UPN had been competing from the moment the networks launched, and it had become clear by 2006 after a decade of fighting for viewers that neither network could, alone, become a fifth that ranked up there with the 'big four'. Discussions of a merger between the two networks had been ongoing for years and eventually, in January 2006, the announcement came – the current season would be the last for both UPN and The WB. The parent companies of the networks joined forces and The CW was born, picking up the pieces of programming from its predecessors in the process. A new primetime schedule was being formed from each network's most popular shows, and *Veronica Mars* viewers were worried that their beloved mystery wouldn't make the cut.

This was a time when TV bloggers had become a huge part of television fandom. Writers and directors would go directly to blogs and their comment sections to interact with fans and address complaints 'all in an effort to keep the lines of communication open with the people who kept the cult fires burning' as a 2006 piece from *Sign On San Diego* put it. Veronica Mars fans at *MarsInvestigations.net* created 'Veronica Mars: The College Years' postcards to send to network executives, and the fan campaign helped to get the show on to The CW's line up, along with *America's Next Top Model* and

Everybody Hates Chris from UPN, and *Smallville and Gilmore Girls* from The WB, among others.

The first season of *Gilmore Girls* on The CW proved to be the show's last, and it was a very different season of television from the six that came before. When the show was picked up for its seventh year, Amy Sherman-Palladino and Daniel Palladino weren't part of the deal. They had to negotiate separately with the new network. After six years on the show writing, directing and overseeing every episode the pair were, understandably, exhausted. When the show was being renewed for a seventh season, the pair were pushing for a two-year deal with the network, as well as the opportunity to bring in new writing, directing and producing staff. What took place was, in Amy's words to *Vulture* five years after the fact, 'a botched negotiation.' The result was Amy Sherman-Palladino and her husband leaving the show before its final season.

Fans had been critical of some of the storylines in the sixth season. Rory's decision to drop out of school, while temporary, seemed wildly out of character. Once Rory's life settled down Lorelai's went off the rails, and the introduction of a daughter Luke had previously been unaware of – April, played by Vanessa Marano – drove a wedge between him and Lorelai that saw her turning back to Chris in the season finale. All of the stories that started in that controversial season were there for Amy and Dan to pick up in the next, but thanks to that botched negotiation they fell into the hands of someone else – David Rosenthal, previously an executive producer on the show.

The finale season of *Gilmore Girls* wasn't well-received. Viewers felt the loss of the Palladinos as the dialogue started to slow down and sputter like a car running out of petrol. In an *Entertainment Weekly* review in 2007, Ken Tucker summed up the feelings of the once-devoted fans: 'The current Sherman-Palladino-less, death-blow season was more accurately *Gilmore Ghosts*, as the exhausted actors bumped into the furniture searching for their departed souls and smart punchlines.' Tucker rated the first six seasons an 'A' but the final a

'C'. Many fans, and the show still has a long and enduring fandom, went on to insist that the final episodes simply weren't their ending, as they weren't what the show's creator intended.

The final episode certainly set the show in its specific era, with Rory setting off to follow and report on Barack Obama on the campaign bus as he sought the democratic nomination. The final shot of the show played on audience nostalgia, mirroring the end of the pilot episode with mother and daughter in a gently lit diner window. The final words of the show – 'I guess so' carried little impact, and they definitely weren't what Amy Sherman-Palladino had planned.

The show's creator had admitted as early as 2006 that she knew what she wanted the final four words of the show to be. In a *TV Guide* interview given immediately after the news broke that the Palladinos wouldn't be returning for the show's seventh season, Daniel joked that those last four words were 'sitting in a safe-deposit box in Switzerland.' Those four words seemed lost forever and became a rallying cry for curious fans, but Amy Sherman-Palladino kept quiet, never taking them out of the box after the show ended.

In the years after the conclusion of *Gilmore Girls*, the show's cult classic status only grew. Like many shows, it had a major resurgence when it landed on Netflix. That same year, 2014, the hit recap podcast *Gilmore Guys* launched and further increased fan fervour. In 2015 a four-part revival of the show called *Gilmore Girls: A Year in the Life* was announced, produced by Netflix with Amy and Daniel at the helm. Lauren Graham, in a 2015 *TV Line* interview, credited the 'enthusiasm and joy' of the fans as the driving factor in making the revival happen. Fan speculation was rife after the announcement; there were plenty of questions that the viewers wanted answered. Who would Rory be with? Would Luke and Lorelai still be together? Will it end with *those* four words?

The revival was an exercise in millennial nostalgia. The revival and reboot trend on television was already underway when the announcement of *A Year in the Life* came; Showtime had promised a return to *Twin Peaks*, Netflix had already revived *Arrested Development* and Fox was working to bring back *The X-Files*. These reboots and sequels are safe bets for networks and streaming services struggling for viewers – nostalgia is an easy sell. For *Gilmore Girls*, however, there was another level – fans didn't just want more of the show, they wanted Amy Sherman-Palladino's ending.

The four feature-length episodes were a clever mix of fan service and genuinely good storytelling. Almost all of the original cast came back, some in major roles and some in smaller cameos. One notable absence was Edward Herrmann, who sadly had passed away in 2014, but the show made his presence felt with moving depictions of grief. Luke and Lorelai got married in the fourth episode, while Rory spent the revival living a scattered, chaotic and distinctly millennial existence as she struggled with the media industry of the late 2010's. Alexis Bledel had told fans she was 'Team No One' when asked who she thought Rory should have ended up with, and while the revival saw her character having a failed relationship with a forgettable boyfriend, an affair with Logan and a one-night stand with a Wookiee, she ended the four episodes alone. Almost. Barring an unfortunate series of musical numbers, the revival was a hit with critics and fans, although some found it hard to see a version of Rory that wasn't sailing through life quite as easily as she had in the original show.

Then there were those four words, in the final minutes of 'Fall', the last episode of the miniseries.

'Mom?'

'Yeah?'

'I'm pregnant.'

Amy Sherman-Palladino had always wanted to bring *Gilmore Girls* full circle, giving Rory an alternative version of her mother's story. With the revival, she finally got her wish. The critical response to the last four words was mixed, with *Slate* even running two side-by-side pieces that alternately called the last four words 'perfect' and 'a disappointment'. Fans clung, for a while, to the idea that this meant a future series could be in the works, a *Gilmore Girls: The Next Generation*. At the time of writing, no such show has been announced.

Much like its peers, especially *Buffy*, *Gilmore Girls* was beloved by its audience, and by critics, but never impressed either in ratings or with awards bodies. The show was only nominated for a single Emmy throughout its run, which it won; 'Outstanding Makeup for a Series' in 2004 for the episode 'The Festival of Living Art'. As early as 2001, the *New York Times* was pointing out that The WB as a whole was being snubbed by awards bodies. *Gilmore Girls* has, however, been listed in numerous 'best TV show' lists at outlets like *Time* and *Entertainment Weekly*.

After *Gilmore Girls*, Amy Sherman-Palladino went on to create the short-lived but much-loved *Bunheads*, but it was in 2017 with *The Marvelous Mrs Maisel* – a period comedy about a housewife-turned-comedienne in 1950's New York that starred a handful of *Gilmore Girls* alumni, including Alex Borstein in a lead role – that she finally got the acclaim she so clearly deserved. *Mrs Maisel*, throughout its five-season run, won the Emmys, Golden Globes and Critics Choice awards that Amy Sherman-Palladino should have been winning since the early 2000's.

Gilmore Girls broke the mould so quietly you would be forgiven for not hearing the crack. This wasn't a show that changed what television could be, but it changed what television was. The show was so much more than the sum of its parts. Its aesthetic, dialogue, references and classic comedy stylings; all of those things came into something beyond deserving of the cult classic title.

Beyond anything else, *Gilmore Girls* is a fantasy. Not the kind with vampires or aliens, but the kind where the world is a little softer and easier to live in. The world of the show is safe, a cosy Stars Hollow filled with seasonal festivals and steaming cups of coffee. Somewhere, in that safe fantasy, *Gilmore Girls* changed television without anyone really noticing.

Chapter 4

The O.C.

Welcome to The O.C.

Newport Beach is a coastal city in Orange County, California. It's a sun-kissed, opulent place; full of gated communities and wealth disparity. In 2003 the city became home, on screen, to the teen soap opera *The O.C.* The show, which ran for four seasons from 2003 to 2007, turned this wealthy city into another teen-drama small town – a place where everyone knew each other a little too well.

The O.C. was, according to its creator Josh Schwartz, a show that walked the line 'between melodrama, an operatic level of melodrama, and also this character-based romantic comedy,' as he told *Rolling Stone* critic Alan Sepinwall in 2007. The location was perfect for a story about a boy from the wrong side of the tracks. The teen actors were all beautiful, the music and fashion and pop culture nods were achingly hip for their time, the storylines were a perfect mix of camp, comedy and high drama, and it was produced by Warner Brothers television. It was perfect for The WB. It aired, for all four of its rollercoaster seasons, on Fox.

The show was conceived when Josh Shwartz came together with Stephanie Savage and Joseph 'McG' McGinty Nichol – the pair behind production company Wonderland Sound and Vision – to create something for Warner Bros. McG had grown up as an awkward, nerdy kid in Orange County, and was looking for ideas for a show set in that world. He had nothing more specific in mind – it could have been a cop show, or a soap about sexy real estate agents. Josh Schwartz was newly working in television, trying to sell pilot scripts, had never had a single job writing on a TV show and was familiar with Orange County stereotypes thanks to his time at the University of Southern California. In 2002, while McG was directing *Charlie's Angels: Full Throttle*, Stephanie Savage brought Schwartz to McG's trailer, and Schwartz began to pitch. The bones of a show emerged: *Newport Beach*, the story of a rich white boy and his star-crossed relationship with a Latinx gardener's daughter.

The trio pitched *Newport Beach* to Warner Bros, who expressed interest but wanted the central premise completely retooled. The company already had two (now barely-remembered) dramas in the works that featured relationships with similar class and racial divides. It was back to the drawing board.

Newport Beach became the story of Ryan Atwood, a boy from Chino – a less affluent and more diverse city north of Newport – dragged into the world of the wealthy. There needed to be someone to do the dragging, and so began Gail Berman's involvement with *The O.C.* When Berman was honoured for Alliance for Children's Rights – a charity that provided legal advocates for children in foster care, Schwartz and Savage were inspired to make Sandy Cohen (Sandy Needleman in early versions of the pilot script) a lawyer who advocates for Ryan and eventually takes him in.

Gail Berman was, by 2002, head of the Fox network. With *Party of Five* over and done with, Fox was looking at getting back to its *Beverly Hills* roots just as *The O.C.* started coming together. Having tried to move away from teen dramas and focus more on adult programming, Fox under Berman's leadership had noticed The WB quietly taking a chunk of the network's audience. While The WB was doing well with teens, the network was struggling to work with its parent company – Warner Bros very rarely gave its best shows to its own network, despite the end of the fin-syn rules. Despite *The O.C.* being a perfect fit for The WB, Peter Roth – the head of the production company at the time – wanted the show to get a chance on one of the 'big four'. Gail Berman at Fox fell in love with the concept when the show was pitched, and The WB simply couldn't compete.

In *Welcome to the OC* – an oral history of the show by Alan Sepinwall released in 2023 to celebrate the show's twentieth anniversary – Josh Schwartz called his show a 'trojan horse'. Elaborating in an interview with the *New York Times*, he explained that 'the horse is a glossy nighttime soap in the tradition of *Beverly Hills 90210* with bikinis and bonfires and fistfights at galas. The soldiers inside were our characters.' While the plots were soapy and ridiculous, the characters drove *The O.C.* and captivated the audience with a winking knowledge that all of this was a bit silly, until it wasn't.

Josh Schwartz was just twenty-seven when work began on the show in earnest – incredibly young to be running his first network television show. Fox insisted on bringing in a more seasoned producer to support him, with Bob DeLaurentis eventually taking on the role. Schwartz's youth, however, had an unexpected effect on the show. Being closer in age to his young actors than most showrunners, he was able to spend time with them on a social level and allowed them to shape the characters that they were playing. Casting director Patrick Rush had spent time in the teen-drama ecosystem, and he signed on to help find those young actors.

Ben McKenzie took the role of Ryan Atwood, the brooding boy from Chino. Among others to audition for the role were a young Chris Pine, Garret Hedlund (who turned down the part to play Patroclus in the Brad Pitt movie *Troy*), and Chad Michael Murray, who was fresh off a short run on *Gilmore Girls* playing a sulking teenager, and who opted to brood in a hoodie on a new show on The WB instead. McKenzie, however, was perfect for the part. Rush spotted him outside the casting office before his audition, smoking a cigarette in the California sun, and immediately knew that this was their Ryan. As the show began, Schwartz realised that McKenzie could be surprisingly funny, and his quick and quiet wit became part of the character, making Ryan much more than just a bad boy.

Mischa Barton was one of the first actors to be cast on the show, and she was just fifteen when she won the role of tragic love interest Marissa Cooper. Barton was neck-and-neck with Olivia Wilde during the casting process, but Wilde was a little too tough to play a character who so desperately needed to be rescued. She did, however, join the cast for a short while in the second season. Barton was already well-known by the time she was cast on the show due to her role in *The Sixth Sense* and her successful modelling career. Sixteen by the time the pilot began filming, she was by far the youngest of the 'teen' cast, and the quietest on set. Marissa was a difficult character for Barton to grab hold of – a popular girl with a drinking problem who needed to inspire sympathy from the audience – but Marissa's music tastes came directly from Barton herself. In the second episode of the show, 'The Model Home', Marissa lists off the punk bands she's been listening to, appalling Seth Cohen when he realises the two have a lot in common. The dialogue was taken almost verbatim from a conversation Schwartz had overheard between Barton and Adam Brody.

Seth Cohen was something of a self-insert for Josh Schwartz, and almost wasn't a part of the show. He was the character the network had the most notes on; Fox executives struggled with the idea of an awkward nerd as the co-lead of the show. The original Seth Needleman was irritating and one-dimensional, apparently, hurtful critiques for Schwartz considering his relationship to the character. At this point in the writing process, due to Fox's plans for a tight time frame between green-lighting the show and putting it on the air, more writers were already coming on board. Allan Heinberg was one of the writers, and as the team started discussing how to turn Seth into the character the network wanted, he got Schwartz's music tastes, Heinberg's love of comics and a passion for sailing that made him stand out from the classic nerd stereotype.

When Adam Brody arrived at his audition, he asked to read for Ryan instead of Seth. Patrick Rush gave Brody the chance, and while

Brody's request didn't pay off, Rush was so certain that he was perfect for Seth, he sent him straight on to audition in front of the producers. Which he did, without knowing a single line of the script. It took a lot of convincing from Rush, and a second audition for Brody, but eventually he landed the role and swapped Stars Hollow for sunny California.

Marissa's best friend, Summer Roberts, was originally going to be a small guest role. Rachel Bilson only needed a few auditions to get the part, despite looking nothing like the sun-kissed blonde originally imagined as the character. It only took a few episodes for Summer to be upgraded to a major part of the show. Bilson charmed with her delivery of lines like 'oxycontin is gnarly', and her ability to make the room laugh made Summer the second female lead of the show.

The first and last characters to be officially cast were both parents of the core teens. Peter Gallagher already had a long history of both screen work and Broadway stardom, and was one of the names on the initial list that Stephanie Savage and Josh Schwartz gave Patrick Rush when trying to find Sandy Cohen. Gallagher was offered the role with very little auditioning required – just a test at Fox which included Gail Berman (who was familiar with his Broadway work) asking him to sing. His performance of 'Hey Big Spender' landed him the part – the first actor to join the cast.

Melinda Clarke was, like Rachel Bilson, originally only cast as a guest star in the role of Julie Cooper – Marissa's mother – but she saw the potential for much more in the role. Unfortunately, she was already committed to *Battlestar Galactica*. It took some begging to get out of her contract and on to *The O.C.* instead. Clarke was technically too young to play a woman with a teenage daughter, but Clarke knew she was perfect for the part, especially having grown up in Orange County herself. As with Bilson, there were certain lines in early episodes that Clarke delivered so well they cemented her role on the show. Her dramatic revelation about her youngest daughter's pony, 'China has alopecia', was borderline Emmy-worthy.

A lot of teen dramas struggle to find the balance between the younger cast members and adult storylines. Networks didn't trust teen characters to hold an audience's attention alone, and in *The O.C.* it was the parents that got some of the soapiest stories. Rounding out the adult cast were Kelly Rowan as Sandy's wife Kirsten and Tate Donovan – the eighties heartthrob who had more recently appeared in a short run on *Friends* as one of Rachel's love interests – as Jimmy Cooper, Marissa's father. The cast member with the most soap opera credibility was Alan Dale, who appeared as Caleb Nichol – Kisten's terrifyingly capitalist father. The New Zealand-born Dale had spent eight years on the Australian soap opera *Neighbours* before moving his acting career to the States, so he was no stranger to *The O.C.*'s ridiculous melodrama.

The O.C. was rare in successfully finding that balance between teen and adult storylines. A 2003 *New York Times* piece on the role of parents in teen shows celebrated the show for putting in parental characters 'who are more than plot devices, if less than full human beings – a position that may be closer to the true teens-eye view.'

That *New York Times* article came out just in time for *The O.C.* to return to the air after the show's initial seven episode run and six-week hiatus. Fox had learned from *Beverly Hills* and premiered the show in the summer, effectively running a seven-episode mini-season without competition from other networks, before pausing *The O.C.* for baseball seasons and bringing it back in October. This was why there was such a tight schedule for the pilot being made, but it also allowed the first few episodes of the show to be filmed in a vacuum, with no critical or audience response.

When the response to those seven episodes did come, it was overwhelmingly positive. *The O.C.* rapidly became the most popular drama among teens and young adults. The *New York Post* called the pilot 'as good as TV soap gets,' the *Seattle Post-Intelligencer* called the show 'perfect TV teen bait' and a *Variety* piece from 2004 celebrated the entire first season and the show's potential longevity as more than just another soap opera, comparing the 'ingredients that give the show a much longer shelf-life' to the 'jaw-dropping plot-twists and cleavage' used by most TV soaps. Schwartz's trojan horse had clearly worked.

The O.C. began during an interesting time for television. Both *Dawson's Creek* and *Buffy* had come to an end just a few months before. In fact, Fox's other big new drama for the season was *Tru Calling*, a supernatural story starring Eliza Dushku that would prove to be sadly short-lived. The decline of sitcoms and dramas and the rise of reality TV were in full effect. Just as *The O.C.* began, *Friends* and *Frasier* were airing their final seasons – two of the last great sitcoms of the nineties. These teen shows were still a new market, and while *The O.C.* landed on Fox, The WB had found a new drama to replace the audience-grabbing *Dawson's Creek*: *One Tree Hill*, a high school drama featuring basketball, betrayal and the brooding Chad Michael Murray.

The way television was criticised, reviewed and discussed had also changed. Fans had been using the internet to gather together and discuss their favourite shows since the nineties, but more critical viewing had remained the work of writers for established publications. Slowly, that started to shift in the early 2000's, as the internet became a place for people who loathed as well as loved to get vocal. One of the first big online discussion forums that focused largely on critiquing what was on the air was *Television Without Pity*, a site that wouldn't have existed without *Dawson's Creek*.

In 1998 Sarah D. Bunting and Tara Ariano (who first met on a *Beverly Hills 90210* message board), along with Ariano's web designer husband David T. Cole, created the website *Dawson's Wrap* – *Television Without Pity*'s predecessor. The website was a home for vitriolic recaps of *Dawson's Creek*. One of the most infamous moments of *Dawson's* happened at the end of the third season when a long-running love triangle concluded with Dawson telling Joey she should go to Pacey before bursting into tears. The resulting shot of

James Van Der Beek's twisted crying face became one of the first GIFs to go viral, and lives on as a meme today. *Television Without Pity* described Dawson's tears as 'the most hideously misguided man-crying scene since Luke Skywalker learned the truth about his father in *Empire Strikes Back*.'

The hate-watch recaps of *Dawson's Creek* did so well that the website expanded, adding a broader handful of network shows to their offering, and eventually in 2002 taking on the *TWOP* name with the tagline 'Spare the snark, spoil the networks.' The site's blend of criticism and running commentary on the hit shows of the moment changed not just the world of TV criticism – the site was described in a 2021 *Vox* piece as the place 'where the rest of the internet learned to talk about television' – but also how showrunners and writers approached their work.

It became standard to keep an eye on online feedback, and *Television Without Pity* became one of the loudest voices. Sarah D. Bunting admitted in a 2002 *New York Times* interview that 'there's no way for us to prove we had a direct impact, but we spent three years taking the *Dawson's* writers to task, and in the wake of our criticism, the character became almost bearable.' Characters were tweaked based on criticism and reactions were rapid when it came to this instantly available feedback, and producers and writers couldn't get enough. Then, there was Josh Schwartz.

Josh Schwartz was one of the youngest and least-experienced showrunners in history when he was working on the first season of *The O.C.* He had an overwhelming amount of work on his plate, and on top of that he was accessing feedback on the show in real time. *The O.C.* was a phenomenon in its first season, but constantly being caught between network and audience demands inevitably changed how Schwartz shaped the show.

Thanks to that summer premiere, the first season of *The O.C.* was twenty-seven episodes long. The downside to such a long season was the need to keep the story and the action constantly moving forward, and in those twenty-seven episodes Schwartz and his team burned through the plot like wildfire.

The final episode of that summer mini-season ended on a cliffhanger when Marissa overdosed in a Tijuana back-alley. As the season picked back up, it saw Marissa's father lose his career, declare bankruptcy and almost open a restaurant with Sandy, while dating Kirsten's younger sister Hayley after his divorce from Julie. Meanwhile, Seth was caught in a love triangle with Summer and Anna (played by Samaire Armstrong); the convoluted romance involved cotillion, comic books, toy horses, an actual Wonder Woman costume and eventually Anna's unceremonious departure for Pittsburgh. There was a substance abuse storyline for Marissa that led to a stalker storyline, with Taylor Handley playing the unhinged Oliver Trask. There was a redemption arc for Marissa's ex-boyfriend Luke, who cheated on her in Tijuana but became less intolerable after discovering his father was secretly gay. He went on to sleep with Marissa's mother. There was a visit back to Ryan's hometown that led to the introduction (and eventual pregnancy) of past flame Theresa – played by Navi Rawat. There was a trip to L.A. thanks to fictional show-within-the-show *The Valley* (which existed entirely so Schwartz could make fun of his own soapy storylines) that featured Paris Hilton playing herself, discussing her P.H.D. on magical realism in literature. There was eventually a romance between Julie Cooper and Caleb Nichol that saw the two married in the season finale (after a bachelor party episode shot on location in Las Vegas), making Marissa Ryan's step-foster-aunt. The finale had Ryan moving back to Chino, apparently for good, to support Theresa and the baby that may or may not have been his (the other paternity candidate being her ex-fiancé Eddie – played by Eric Balfour of *Buffy* pilot fame), Marissa miserable in a new mansion, and Seth setting sail for Tahiti. The first season of *The O.C.* was a *lot*, and the audience loved it.

When the second season came around, Josh Schwartz knew that *The O.C.* needed to slow down and spend some time with its characters.

Fresh faces were introduced throughout the season, but their stories were mostly short-lived. For financial reasons (Tate Donovan was an expensive cast member) Jimmy Cooper was written off to go and do something with boats in Hawaii. Shannon Lucio joined the cast at the beginning of the season as Lindsay, a potential new girlfriend for Ryan who came from a class strata closer to his. Lindsay was revealed to be Caleb's illegitimate daughter (and therefore Ryan's foster-aunt) and was written off the show a couple of episodes later.

The early episodes of the season also saw Marissa dating the family gardener – DJ, played by Nick Gonzalez – in a parallel to the original *Newport Beach* pitch. This was another short-lived romance. *Desperate Housewives*, ABC's hit drama with a similar elevated-soap-opera tone, began in 2004 as *The O.C.* was entering its second season, and featured a similar romance with Eva Longoria and Jesse Metcalfe. While the stories were written indcpendently of each other, they were too close for Schwartz's comfort, and DJ made a rapid exit.

A short-lived character who was far more successful with critics and fans in the show's second season was Alex – played by Olivia Wilde. Alex was introduced as the manager of a new location – The Bait Shop – which became a huge vehicle for bringing more and more music into the show. She was also a new love interest for Marissa. While the word 'bisexual' was never said on screen, a relationship between two women both shown to be attracted to their own gender and others was still a step forward for representation, but the storyline quickly became tangled in network interference.

Earlier in 2004, during the Super Bowl halftime show, Justin Timberlake accidentally ripped off part of Janet Jackson's top and exposed her nipple to millions on live television. It was a moment that changed television regulation, and even led to government hearings about broadcast standards and Gail Berman herself having to speak before Congress (despite the incident airing on CBS, not Fox). Every network began to pull back on potential controversies in the wake of the pearl-clutching public outcry. The casual intimacy between two women that eventually became the norm on *Buffy* was once again too risqué for prime time. Marissa and Alex were still allowed to kiss on the screen, but that kiss couldn't be overly titillating.

The promotion for the episode that saw the two getting together pushed the kiss as a shocking, scintillating plot twist. Critics took a cynical view of the promotion, with the *New York Times* nodding to the long history of sweeps week lesbian stunts. In the episode itself, the kiss was cut down to almost nothing on screen. After just six episodes, the Alex and Marissa relationship came to an end, largely due to network interference, and Olivia Wilde left the show with the rare queer storyline abandoned to the ether.

The O.C. was often self-referential, using *The Valley* to mock anything about the show that the online commenters were picking up on in an attempt to reassure the audience that the show wasn't taking itself seriously. There were nods to network interference aplenty in the *Atomic County* storyline, which saw Seth and Zack – Seth's rival for Summer's affections, played by Michael Cassidy – create a graphic novel inspired by their lives in Orange County. The storyline featured hipster marketing executives demanding less irony and more sports drinks. It was pointed, and completely unsubtle.

The graphic novel storyline culminated in a cameo from George Lucas – creator of *Star Wars* – playing himself, interested in adapting the graphic novel into a movie. This was around the time of the *Star Wars* prequel trilogy, and an ad filmed to air during the episode's broadcast had Adam Brody promoting the third film in the trilogy – *Revenge of the Sith.* Brody filmed the promo spot begrudgingly; he shared the popular opinion that the first two films in the trilogy weren't so great. *Atomic County* did spin off into a short series of animated 'mobisodes' – cartoons designed specifically to be viewed on cell phones and new video iPods – in one of the many attempts for networks to jump on the latest technology for consuming media.

The addition to the second season that worked best was the return of Ryan's older brother Trey. Trey was arrested alongside his younger brother in the pilot of the show and remained in prison until late in the second season. Trey, played by Logan Marshall-Green who replaced Bradley Stryker in the role, joined the Cohen household in the seventeenth episode of the season, and became a reinvigorating antagonist for the final eight episodes. Schwartz had constantly been keeping an eye on the *Television Without Pity* recaps as the show was airing, trying to find what worked, and with Trey he had finally found a story that gave the show a new burst of energy. Trey and Ryan gave the network the big dramatic moments they were demanding while delivering smaller character beats that the audience loved.

The second season of *The O.C.* had been up and down in terms of quality compared to the first, but its finale is the show's most memorable. Things came to a head with a funeral for Caleb Nichol after his heart attack in the penultimate episode (which saw him collapsing into a swimming pool in slow motion while Coldplay's 'Fix You' played), Kirsten going to rehab and the most iconic moment of the show – Marissa shooting Trey.

Critics didn't enjoy the second season of the show quite as much as they did the first, but *The O.C.* had managed to build a loyal fanbase, even if it wasn't doing so well in the ratings. The third season of the show, on the other hand, was and is broadly considered to be its worst.

The third season did have a few high points; Julie Cooper returning to her trailer park roots, the introduction of Autumn Reese as Taylor Townsend (a character written to be a short-lived villain who rapidly became one of the brightest parts of the show), and Willa Holland joining the cast as an aged-up Kaitlin Cooper (Marissa's younger sister, who was played by a pre-stardom Shailene Woodley in the first season before the character was shipped off to boarding school).

There were multiple reasons for the season being so lacklustre, but a lot of blame can be placed on the network. There had been a change at Fox – Gail Berman had left the network to run Paramount Pictures and her replacement, Peter Liguori, was pushing for *The O.C.* to be broader, soapier and easier to promote. One of the network's early notes was a request to include a 'femme fatale' character to the adult's storylines. Jeri Ryan, of *Star Trek: Voyager* fame, appeared in the show as a con woman Kirsten meets in rehab, in a forgettable storyline that wasted a talented actor.

Many of the stars of *The O.C.* were facing burnout and a growing disinterest in the show. Making network television was demanding work with a tough, year-filling schedule; it dominated the actor's lives and didn't allow them much freedom to pursue other interests or career opportunities. Tate Donavan returned as Jimmy Cooper for the first few episodes of the season and made his directorial debut on the eighth episode – 'The Game Plan'. He recalled, when appearing on Melinda Clarke and Rachel Bilson's 2021 recap podcast *Welcome to the OC Bitches*, how frustrating it was to work with actors that were sick of making television instead of pursuing potential movie careers. Adam Brody's apathy in particular was so reflected in his performance that the writers added a subplot about Seth smoking marijuana to explain his lazy delivery. Of course, on network television, drug use had to come with consequences, and Seth's pot-smoking led to some inadvertent arson in the conclusion to a long, incomprehensible storyline about Sandy Cohen playing businessman.

One of the most hated storylines of the season saw Marissa going to public school and getting caught up in the lives of her new surfer friends, introducing Ryan Donowho as Johnny, a baffling not-quite-love-interest who dragged the story into a quagmire of angst that it struggled to rise from for the rest of the season. It was a story that never really had a plan. There was an Oliver-like fixation on Marissa, and eventually Johnny was killed off by drunkenly falling off a cliff. The story dominated the show while dragging the tone down, killing the humour that had made *The O.C.* stand out as something more than its soapy counterparts.

As the third season wound towards its end, the network interference became uglier and more insistent. Fox said that the show needed to do something big to be saved from cancellation. Specifically, the network wanted a major character death; Schwartz had to kill off one of the core cast. Some of the actors were so bored with being on the show that they might have been happy to face an untimely end, but Mischa Barton wasn't necessarily one of them. Marissa Cooper, however, was such a tragic character that killing her off made the most sense. Also, on plenty of the snarky television boards that the writers were paying attention to, she just wasn't a popular character. Sara Morrison, one of the *Television Without Pity* freelancers responsible for recapping *The O.C.* recalled in Alan Sepinwall's book that 'everyone hated Marissa. Just hated, hated, hated, hated, hated.'

The writers had considered a car crash for Marissa back in season one before going with the back-alley overdose. They returned to the idea for season three. Originally the plan was for Ryan and Marissa to drive off a bridge, and have Ryan fail to save Marissa. The plan changed, thanks in part to *One Tree Hill* ending its third season on an almost identical storyline.[1] Instead, the third season finale saw Marissa and Ryan driven off the road by Marissa's ex-boyfriend Volchuk – a villain played by Cam Gigandet and the only holdover from the surf storyline – followed by Marissa's death in the ensuing fiery wreck.

Dramatic promos aired on Fox in the lead up to the season finale, warning the audience that one of these beloved characters was going to meet their end. Unfortunately, the audience learned exactly which character it was before the episode aired. In an *Access Hollywood* interview, Mischa Barton accidentally revealed her character's fate a week early.

There was an unexpected outcome to Marissa's death; the viewers were distraught. It turned out that while Marissa had plenty of

1. In *One Tree Hill*, the car was a limo stolen after a wedding, driven by the groom's uncle with the high school cheerleader he'd had an inadvertent affair with before learning her real age in the passenger seat. Also, someone was pregnant.

critics, there were even more fans that absolutely adored her, who demonstrated their grief to writers previously unaware of the Marissa fandom with long blog posts and fan art depicting Marissa Cooper ascending to heaven on angelic wings. The twin pressures of the network and *The O.C*'s critics had taken the show to a place from which it couldn't return.

The final season of *The O.C.* began with a sixteen-episode order from Fox. While Schwartz had some hopes that the network might up that to a full season, it was clear that *The O.C.* was coming to an end. Fox under Peter Liguori was losing interest in the show and starting to move in a different direction to attract audiences. With that network apathy, and after the heaviness of the third season, the tone of the show changed for the better in its last episodes. Stephanie Savage became the dominant voice in the writer's room, and insisted on the show embracing what worked; less angst, more laughs, and enjoying the freedom that came with a lack of oversight.

Summer's father, who had had a brief romance with Julie Cooper in the third season, was dispatched off the show and sent to work at the fictional, 'quirky' Seattle Grace hospital in a nod to *Grey's Anatomy* – the ABC medical drama that was thoroughly trouncing *The O.C.* in the ratings. Julie Cooper was caught in a love triangle between Ryan's no-longer-absent father Frank, played by Kevin Sorbo of *Hercules* fame, and Bullit – an oil magnate played by the hilarious character actor Gary Grubbs. An environmental activism storyline for Summer led to Chris Pratt joining the show as Che, one of her fellow students at Brown university.[2] Ryan, after a brief career in cage fighting, fell in love with Taylor Townsend and helped her extricate herself from an accidental French marriage. The Chrismukkah – A portmanteau

2. J. J. Philbin, a writer on *The O.C.* then suggested Pratt to her husband Mike Schur when he was casting a new sitcom for NBC: *Parks and Recreation*, which Pratt went on to star in for seven seasons.

of Christmas and Hannukah that become one of *The O.C*'s most enduring traditions – episode was a tribute to *It's a Wonderful Life*, with an extended dream sequence that showed what Newport would be like if the Cohens had never taken Ryan in. Eventually, everything ended with an earthquake.

Fox didn't officially give word that the fourth season of the show would be its last until the writers were a few episodes in, but no one was surprised. The most disappointing part of that shortened episode order was that the finale would be the show's ninety-sixth episode – just four shy of the magic syndication number. The critical response to the final season was, however, appreciative of the show moving back to its meta, self-mocking roots. It was a strange, sad end for a once-huge show with such a massive cultural footprint, and while there were many factors that led to the show's demise, it makes sense to ultimately lay the blame on Fox. On a smaller network, like The WB, with less pressure to pull in huge audience numbers, things might have been different. *One Tree Hill*, for comparison, lasted nine seasons, first on The WB and then on The CW. Whether lasting that long would have been a good thing is anyone's guess. Once *The O.C.* did come to an end, in February 2007, it didn't take long for Josh Schwartz to return to the world of affluent teenagers.

The Upper East Side is the most affluent neighbourhood in New York City. It's an opulent place, full of museums and stunning architecture left over from the Gilded Age. In 2007, the Upper East Side became home, on screen, to the shiny new teen soap opera *Gossip Girl*. The show, which ran for seven seasons from 2007 to 2012, managed to turn this Manhattan neighbourhood into another teen-drama small town – a place where everyone is interconnected and knows each other a little too well.

Sound familiar?

The O.C. and *Gossip Girl* have a lot in common, the most obvious being the creative hands of Josh Schwartz and Stephanie Savage. In late 2006, with an end to *The O.C.* in sight, Schwartz was already hard at work on two new shows. One, *Chuck*, was an action comedy for NBC starring Zachary Levi in the title role – a Schwartz self-insert nerd turned secret agent. The other was an adaptation of Cecily Von Ziegesar's popular teen book series *Gossip Girl* for The CW.

Gossip Girl followed the lives of ultra-rich, ultra-privileged teenagers. Schwartz was sceptical about the project at first, telling the *Boston Globe* in 2006 that 'I don't want to do "The O.C – N.YC."' He went on to add, however, that he thought 'the books were smart. The characters are worldly in a way that Orange County kids aren't.' The shared DNA was there, and the two shows had plenty in common, but *Gossip Girl* managed to be a distinct show that wasn't overshadowed by its predecessor. *Gossip Girl* began just a few months after *The O.C.* ended and immediately dived into that self-aware teen soap tone that had made Schwartz's first show such a hit.

Running like a common thread between both shows was that other teen drama – *One Tree Hill*. This was a soap without the self-consciousness, and had been all camp and drama (and basketball) from its opening episode. *One Tree Hill* began in 2003, just a month after *The O.C*, and ended in April 2012, just a few months before the end of *Gossip Girl*. When looking at any one of these three shows, it's difficult to understand the impact without comparing it to the other two. That almost-decade of television; four seasons of *The O.C*, six seasons of *Gossip Girl* and nine seasons of *One Tree Hill*, was a defining era of teen dramas.

Gossip Girl was originally intended to be a movie adapted from the books, with Amy Sherman-Palladino at one point attached to the project. The film, however, never panned out, and the rights to the books became available again just as The CW merger was about to take place. The new network needed a signature series to define its brand identity, and *Gossip Girl* fit the bill perfectly. Peter Roth at Warner Bros knew Savage and Schwartz well thanks to *The O.C.* and considered them the 'only choice' to produce the show, as he told the *Hollywood Reporter* in 2012. Blake Lively and Leighton Meester signed on to play the two female leads, Serena Van Der Woodsen and Blair Waldorf, and Penn Badgely joined the cast as Dan Humphrey – a blend of Schwartz's Seth Cohen tendencies and Ryan Atwood's wrong side of the tracks back story; the wrong side of the tracks in this context meant Brooklyn and no trust fund.

Unsurprisingly, critics immediately compared *Gossip Girl* to *The O.C.* when the pilot aired. The comparisons weren't all generous. The *AV Club* review of the episode said it played 'a little like a discarded *O.C.* script with the names changed and CW's demographic-clubbing factored in.' Quickly, however, *Gossip Girl* began to stand on its own. That same reviewer, just seven episodes later, changed his tune to glowing praise, saying in a review of 'Victor/Victrola' that 'Every episode since the pilot has been a night-and-day improvement, a weekly celebration/parody of conspicuous consumption and spectacularly cruel adolescent back-biting', raising the show's grade from a 'C' to an 'A-'.

The show itself was centred on the titular Gossip Girl – an anonymous gossip site that tracked the lives of the show's 'Manhattan elite' teen cast. Gossip Girl served as a narrator for the series, voiced by Kristen Bell. Much like *The O.C.*, the built-in class system in the show proved perfect for soapy storylines.

By comparison, *One Tree Hill* began as a much quieter story, focusing its early episodes on a basketball rivalry between estranged half-brothers Lucas (Chad Michael Murray's character) and Nathan (played by James Lafferty). By the end of the show's first season, however, there had been drugs, abusive parenting, a teen marriage, a car accident and near-death experience, a love triangle that came to define the high school seasons of the show and eventually a cliffhanger heart attack. *One Tree Hill* certainly earned its soap opera credentials.

The Trojan horse nature of *The O.C.* allowed the show to be gently mocking and self-referential from the start. *Gossip Girl* was similar, staying far away from realism in favour of melodramatic storytelling so over-the-top that even the most serious stories had a comedic undertone. The show, using its fictional gossip site, was always ready to mock itself. The readers of Gossip Girl, in the show's universe, became an audience surrogate, as opinionated on the lives they were consuming as the fans of the show debating who Serena should date on Tumblr. Later in the series, Dan Humphrey writes a book fictionalising the lives of his peers, taking them to another level of soap opera. This was the show reminding the audience 'look how much worse it could be', while nodding to its book series roots. The show did, however, have a lot of realism in its location. It was almost entirely shot in New York City, all on location, using real hotels and restaurants in a way that hadn't been seen on the small screen since *Sex and the City*. Against that realistic backdrop, the hilarity of the melodrama was heightened even further. *One Tree Hill*, on the other hand, struggled to strike that kind of knowing tone.

These shows were all constantly in conversation with pop culture. Teen dramas were often heavily laden with nods to music, movies and fashion. *The O.C.* took this a step further, not just referencing culture, but making it. Seth Cohen had an inarguable influence on comic book popularity; no longer just the province of nerds, Cohen helped make comics cool at a time when Superhero cinema was just on the rise. *The O.C.* even referenced the famous inverted, rain-soaked kiss from 2002's *Spider-Man* in a season two episode. *Gossip Girl*'s biggest influence, on the other hand, was in fashion. The show became a lifestyle magazine that inspired its teen audience, and designers and couture houses clamoured to dress the Upper East Side teens.

References to classics were there, as well. *Gossip Girl* episodes were all named for famous films and novels. The show regularly paid homage to Audrey Hepburn's filmography, classic noir movies and even featured a sequence in which Blake Lively lip-synced to 'Diamonds are a Girl's Best Friend' from the 1953 film *Gentlemen Prefer Blondes*, dressed as Marilyn Monroe, in full pink finery. *One Tree Hill* used a school dance storyline to spend an entire episode paying tribute to the work of the late, great John Hughes, and filled one episode with a film-noir dream sequence that took all of the characters back to the 1940's.

Not only did the shows make references, but they in turn were referenced. The memes that grew out of these shows quickly escaped their original containment to become part of online culture. *Dawson's Creek* and the crying GIF did it first, of course, but the cultural impact of Marissa shooting Trey while Imogen Heap's song 'Hide and Seek' played was massive.

Josh Schwartz heard 'Hide and Seek' for the first time just as he was beginning work on *The O.C*'s second season and immediately asked Alex Patsavas, the show's music supervisor, to reach out to Imogen Heap – who was a fairly unknown artist at the time – and reserve the song for the season finale. The song was used twice during the episode. First the opening verses played over Caleb's funeral and then, in the final scene, as Marissa pulled the trigger, the familiar chorus of 'Mmm, what'd you say?' began. The scene had an immediate impact, skyrocketing the song to the top of the charts and exploding Imogen Heap's career. Two years later, the memeification was complete when *Saturday Night Live* used the song and parodied the shooting in the infamous 'Dear Sister' sketch, which featured multiple gunshots and that chorus kicking in over and over again.

In 2009, Jason Derulo sampled 'Hide and Seek' on his debut single 'Watcha Say'. Also in 2009, the third season *Gossip Girl* episode 'The Treasure of Serena Madre' aired. The climax of the Thanksgiving episode saw characters gathered around the dining table, revealing each other's secrets in a ramping up of ridiculous revelations. The scene was soundtracked by the Jason Derulo song in an homage to the original 'Hide and Seek' moment – a nod to the showrunner's legacy and a scene that became a meme in its own right.

As with the teen dramas that came before and after, music was a huge part of these shows. This was another area in which *The O.C.* became a tastemaker. The familiar strains of the opening theme song – 'California' by Phantom Planet – were as much a part of the show as Chanel accessories and punch-ups on the pier, and the song became a huge hit for the previously little-known band.

In the second season, with the introduction of the Bait Shop, live acts became a standard on the show. Death Cab for Cutie were one of Adam Brody's favourite bands and so became a favourite of Seth's, and they were just one of many bands to appear in that second season. They struggled, however, with becoming known as an 'O.C. Band' – they'd been building a loyal following for years before being referenced on the show at all, and yet their success was being attributed to a fictional character. Some bands refused to appear or have their music on the show at all, not wanting to be considered sellouts or associated with a high school drama. Arcade Fire, Arctic Monkeys and Clap Your Hands Say Yeah all turned Alex Patsavas down.

Some bands, however, were more than happy to experience the 'O.C. Effect'. The Killers appeared at the Bait Shop just a few months after releasing their debut album 'Hot Fuss', and the performance helped make their now-iconic song Mr Brightside a hit. Capitol Records gave Schwartz and Patsavas first refusal on any song from the latest Coldplay album, and were surprised when Schwartz requested 'Fix You'. Originally, the song wasn't even intended to be a single. When *The O.C.* needed some filler for 'The Mallpisode', Patsavas was able to negotiate debuting five new songs from Beck, leading to some dubbing it 'The Beckisode'. This was a very different music industry to now, and *The O.C.* was instrumental in making television the best place to debut new music in the early 2000's.

One Tree Hill also introduced a music venue – Tric – in its second season, and the show had its own array of musical guests, including an appearance from Fall Out Boy which led to a mercifully short story arc in which one of the teenage characters dated Pete Wentz, the band's twenty-odd-year-old bassist. The show cast singer-songwriter Bethany Joy Lenz as Hayley James-Scott, and built a fictional music career for the character. When the character on the show went on tour with The Wreckers, the real Bethany went on a One Tree Hill tour with the Michelle Branch and Jessica Harp duo, along with Gavin DeGraw (whose song 'I Don't Wanna Be' was the show's main title track). One storyline saw the characters putting together a benefit and associated CD to raise money for cancer charities. The CD – 'Friends with Benefit' – came out for real in 2006. The story brought multiple bands to the show in a single, music-packed episode, including Audioslave, Jack's Mannequin and Jimmy Eat World, as well as Fall Out Boy. Where *The O.C.* was influencing its audience, however, *One Tree Hill*'s music – beyond the original creations for the show – was largely a reflection of what its audience were already listening to.

By the time *Gossip Girl* came around, television had stopped being such a useful marketing avenue for music. The music on *Gossip Girl* was largely interstitial, and live performances were far rarer, although Lady Gaga and Robyn both made notable appearances. The show was airing at a point in time just a little bit further away from the nineties than its predecessors, which meant Dan's father Rufus Humphrey – played by Matthew Settle, and the closest thing the show had to Sandy Cohen, though he was sadly comparatively lacking in the eyebrow department – could plausibly be a forgotten nineties indie rock star. Those nineties connections led not just to a lot of references to Serena's uptight mother Lily (played by Kelly Rutherford, who had previously auditioned for the role of Kirsten Cohen) having a sexual history with Trent Reznor of Nine Inch Nails, but eventually to Sonic Youth appearing on the show and performing 'Star Power' at Rufus and Lily's Wedding.[3]

That wedding was just one of many event episodes that appeared across these shows. *Buffy* used a 'Monster of the Week' concept. *The O.C.* and *Gossip Girl* has 'Black-tie Fundraiser/Benefit/Gala/ Any Excuse for Champagne and Canapes' of the week. The weekly

3. There's the other pound.

event episode became a staple of teen dramas. In *One Tree Hill* the setting was more likely to be a basketball game or a gig, but the idea remained the same – get everyone in one room, dress them up, heighten the emotions and let carnage reign.

There were some particular stand-outs. *The O.C.* and *Gossip Girl* both featured cotillion/debutante ball events, as did *Gilmore Girls*; coming-out parties were another way to demonstrate the massive class divides in these shows. Prom episodes are a classic of the genre, the formally-dressed coming-of-age ritual being a perfect backdrop for melodrama. *Gossip Girl*, in particular, used its prom episode to feature a backdoor pilot for an eighties prequel to the show – *Valley Girls*, starring Krysten Ritter and Brittany Snow – that was never picked up.

Of course, these event episodes were easy for the networks to promote, allowing for big 'Next time on' trailers promising all sorts of scandal. This was the cause of so much of *The O.C.*'s struggles, especially in the third season; the network's push for promotable events overshadowed the stories the show was trying to sell. One of the most obvious examples being not a black-tie event, but that eventually censored kiss between Olivia Wilde and Mischa Barton.

That kiss might have been written off as a sweeps stunt, but these shows all took their own stabs at queer stories with varying degrees of success. Just a month before Alex and Marissa kissed on the beach, on *One Tree Hill*, Daniella Alonso's character Anna quietly admitted her bisexuality and attempted to kiss Hilarie Burton's Peyton in a moment that absolutely didn't shock the viewers, who had overwhelmingly seen it coming. Just a few episodes later, Anna was written off the show, having never managed to become a selling point. By the time *Gossip Girl* was on the air, queer storylines were neither shocking nor particularly promotable. When Serena's younger brother Eric (played by Connor Paolo) was forced out of the closet by the show's best villain – Georgina Sparks, played by a scenery-chewing Michelle Trachtenberg who was almost unrecognisable from her *Buffy* days – it wasn't even the main storyline in the episode.

There was only so much shocking trailers could do to interest viewers, and eventually falling ratings lead to cancellation. The end of *The O.C.* came about at a time when Peter Liguori wanted to change Fox's image, and only wanted shows that could pull in huge audiences. *The O.C.* did well in the ratings, but not well enough. *Gossip Girl*, on the other hand, was never a hit in the ratings, but like *One Tree Hill* the show benefited from being on a smaller network that had lower expectations.

Gossip Girl largely struggled in the ratings due to the nature of its release. When the final season of *The O.C.* was airing, Fox experimented with releasing episodes in advance on Myspace. The CW tried a similar approach with *Gossip Girl*, releasing episodes online on the network's website before they debuted on the network. The show was definitely being watched, but not in a way that counted for Nielsen ratings. In fact, *Gossip Girl* was a show that tech companies loved, especially as it was on in a time when the way audiences consumed media was changing so rapidly. The show featured heavy product placement for cell phone companies and even Microsoft. *Buffy* was the first show to use 'google' as a verb because Google was new technology at the time. *Gossip Girl* was one of the first shows to use 'bing' (referring to the Microsoft-owned search engine) as a verb because no one was using Bing without being paid to reference it.

By the end of *Gossip Girl*, in 2012, the ratings had fallen further and the fan base had started to diminish. *The Atlantic*, in a 2012 article, suggested that the show's declining popularity was due to the 2008 financial crisis, calling *Gossip Girl*'s 'over-the-top decadence… culturally dead.' The article suggested that in the wake of global recession, there was less interest in watching the lives of the über-rich. By the end of *Gossip Girl*'s 121 episode run, its cultural relevance had certainly waned. The driving force of the finale was Gossip Girl's identity – she was eventually revealed to be Dan Humphrey in a plot twist that baffled the audience and placed the episode in the canon of finales that viewers wish they could forget, ranking number eight in the *AV Club*'s 2023 list of the ten worst TV finales of all time.

One Tree Hill, on the other hand, ended quietly. This was a show that had grown astonishingly ridiculous throughout its years. In its sixth season, the writers wanted to test how silly they could get before an edict came from on high to stop it. Even a golden retriever eating a heart meant for a transplant for the show's villain, in the opening ten minutes of an episode, as a B-plot, wasn't too far.

It's possible that *One Tree Hill* dragged on slightly too long. The show was very successful in getting over the awkward college slump by putting in a time jump, skipping ahead five years immediately after high school graduation to pick up with the characters living their post-college lives. Two of the show's main stars – Chad Michael Murray and Hilarie Burton – left the show at the end of that sixth season, and yet the show continued on for three more years. *One Tree Hill* was a great show, a classic of the teen genre, at its peak. As it limped into its ninth year with an incomprehensible story about one of the main characters being kidnapped after a basketball recruitment gone awry in Eastern Europe, it hadn't so much jumped the shark as found itself floundering in the waves, waiting for death. Had *One Tree Hill* ended sooner, instead of dragging on until the actors and writers on the show could take no more, it might be remembered differently, but as it is the show has never had quite the same cultural legacy as its peers.

One Tree Hill's legacy was further tarnished when, in 2017, an open letter came out written by multiple women who worked on the show, accusing creator Mark Schwahn of sexual harassment. *One Tree Hill* lives on, however. Much like fans and the stars themselves have reclaimed *Buffy* from its potentially problematic creator, *One Tree Hill* is clearly still loved and celebrated by its audience and actors. There are multiple podcasts recapping the show, from fans (like *Always and Forever*, hosted by Jeremy Rodriguez and Kaitlyn Ilinitch) and the stars themselves (*Drama Queens*, hosted by Bethany

Joy Lenz, Hilarie Burton and Sophia Bush, who played Brooke Davis, began in 2021).

These three shows all aired in the days before recapping television via podcast was a cultural and critical norm. This was a time when a good critical response was essential, and all of these shows were, at various times, given the hyperbolic title of 'greatest' teen drama around. To some fans, it wasn't hyperbole but truth. The venues where viewers talked about these shows changed in those nine years; moving from devoted message boards to the snarky wilds of *Television Without Pity* to new social media sites as fans debated the Lucas/Peyton/Brooke love triangle, the future of Seth and Summer and the horrifying possibility of a Dan and Blair relationship.

The cultural footprint of these shows was huge. All three were in continuous conversation with a media landscape that saw huge changes. These shows, with their complicated low points and storied legacies, represent such a specific time on television; a time when creators could take outlandish risks. The whole idea of teen dramas on television began with soap operas, but these shows demonstrated that the best could be that and so much more.

Chapter 5

Supernatural

Welcome to Every Small Town in America

There's a diner, a motel, and hopefully there'll be a seedy bar with a few pool tables in the back. The houses are largely identical. On the outskirts there's an abandoned building; a farmhouse, a factory, maybe an insane asylum. There's a local legend, there's something in the woods, something's lurking on the edges. The sheriff's department has a drawer full of cold cases. The diner sells pie. This could be any small town in America.

Or so, at least, *Supernatural* would have you believe. Where many of the shows in this book were built around a specific place – a small town, or a neighbourhood that approximated one – *Supernatural* was different. The show wasn't set in a specific place, but on the road that runs through hundreds of different yet oh-so-familiar places.

Supernatural told the story of two brothers in a '67 Chevrolet Impala, road-tripping from small town to small town fighting horrific creatures from American folklore. That's how it began, at least. Over the fifteen years that the show was on the air it remained a story of folklore, but also became one of family and intense fandom; one underscored by an impressive amount of classic rock.

The show was created by Eric Kripke, whose obsession with urban legends began in childhood. Stories like 'The Hook Man' – the grisly tale of teenagers hanging out at a local lover's lane being killed by a madman with a hook for a hand – sound silly, but they're a part of the fabric of American folklore. Kripke said, in the foreword to the *Supernatural* Season One Companion book, that America has 'a folklore as rich as any world mythology, as American as jazz or baseball, and few people know it.' These stories whispered around campfires, discussed in hushed tones at sleepovers or quietly told then loudly mocked in bars are ubiquitous, from Hook Man to Bloody Mary to cursed scarecrows to haunted asylums; although they're rarely considered folklore in the classic sense. Like myths and legends from around the world, these stories speak to cultural fears and common terrors. This was the foundation of the story Kripke was envisioning, the story that came to be *Supernatural*.

At first, Kripke's vision was a movie that combined all of these legends into one place. Then, he wanted to make an anthology series. By the time Kripke had the chance to pitch a show at Warner Bros, the concept had changed again. Kripke's early film career had started well – two simultaneous screenings at film festivals had earned him a two-picture deal at DreamWorks. Those two pictures came to nothing, however. Kripke had been selling himself as a comedy writer and became trapped in production purgatory. To blow off steam, he wrote *Boogeyman*, a horror script that he never expected to make it to screen. The script fell into the path of acclaimed horror (and *Spider-Man*) director Sam Raimi, and the resulting film made it to number one at the box office in 2005. Before *Boogeyman* Kripke had spent some time developing and writing on the short-lived *Tarzan* for The WB; only eight episodes of the modern adaptation of the Tarzan story every made it to air, but that relationship with The WB gave Kripke a relationship to Warner Bros and was paramount to the development of *Supernatural*.

Kripke's initial idea grew into a story of journalists travelling around America and reporting on urban legends, with the protagonists purely there as a vehicle to get the audience in and out of weekly mini-horror movies. Around 2004, when Kripke was pitching to Warner Bros, the market was perfect for this kind of genre television. *Buffy* had kicked off a new wave of fantasy and horror back in the nineties, while bigger and more 'grown-up' shows full of complex mythology like ABC's *Lost* were proving that this kind of television definitely had an audience. Warner Bros, however, weren't fans of Kripke's journalist premise. He was asked if he had anything else to offer, and he did. A couple of sentences, scrawled in his notebook, written on a whim the previous day. 'One way you could do this show would be two guys on a road trip, cruising the country. *Route 66* style. Brothers?'

The idea sparked something, and *Supernatural* began to come together. McG's company Wonderland Sound and Vision got involved, thanks to Peter Johnson, president of TV at the company, who had previously heard an early pitch for *Supernatural* while working at Fox. McG signed on as an executive producer.[1] The show was shopped around to various networks but it was The WB that made the most sense and the strongest case, and the pilot began to come together.

Kripke's first draft of the pilot had to be heavily reworked. It was overly expositional, with one of the brothers fully unaware of the existence of anything supernatural, having to be convinced throughout the episode that all manner of things were real. The script was laden down with back story, and it took a long series of brainstorming sessions for Kripke and Johnson to streamline the story. Changing the brother's history and making it so they were raised on the road by their father and learned to fight demons from childhood – making them 'blue collar exterminators' in Kripke's words – meant the show could dive directly into the action. Kripke locked himself away over Christmas and pulled together a script that really worked. The pilot did everything it had to; it set up Sam and Dean Winchester as gunslingers rolling into town, dealing with the bad guys (who were rarely 'guys' as such) and driving off into the sunset. It was David Nutter signing on to direct, however, that got *Supernatural* green-lit. Nutter had gotten his start directing on *The X-Files*, and had become

1. There's the link to *The O.C.*

known as *the* pilot director, having worked on the opening episodes of *Roswell*, *Smallville*, *Without a Trace* and many more.

Supernatural shared more than just a director with *The X-Files* – there was plenty of common DNA between the two shows. From the start, *Supernatural* was pitched as a more fantastical version of its sci-fi predecessor. Both shows were shot in British Columbia, lending a similar woodsy, rain-soaked aesthetic; they also shared a deep sense of underlying mystery and mythology. Kim Manners, a regular director on *The X-Files*, was producing director on *Supernatural* from the show's beginning in 2005 until he passed away from lung cancer in 2009, during production on *Supernatural*'s fourth season.[2]

Another essential part of *Supernatural* from its early beginnings was Robert Singer. When the pilot was picked up and the show went to series, Warner Bros felt like Kripke needed someone with a little more experience in the industry to keep the show on its feet. Singer was in a similar role, originally, to Bob DeLaurentis on *The O.C*, the voice of experience supporting a new showrunner. The writer's room for *Supernatural* became a wealth of talent. After Eric Kripke stepped down from his showrunner role at the end of the show's fifth season, members of that writer's room worked their way up to taking charge of the show. First there was Sera Gamble, then Jeremy Carver, and finally Andrew Dabb, who co-ran the final four seasons of the show alongside Robert Singer.

Then there were the stars of the show: Sam and Dean Winchester, who proved surprisingly easy to cast. The names were inspired by Sal and Dean of *On The Road*, the classic Jack Kerouac novel. Originally, their surname was going to be Harrison, after Harrison Ford – the actor famous for playing Indiana Jones and Han Solo and the inspiration for Dean's devil-may-care (and he really did) swagger. Kripke was set on

2. The credits of the fourth season episode 'Death Takes a Holiday' honoured Manners, dedicating the entire season to him, and no one else was given the job title of 'Producing Director' for the show's entire run.

the boys hailing from Lawrence, Kansas, due to the nearby famously haunted Stull cemetery. As there was already a Sam Harrison living in Kansas, there couldn't be a Sam Harrison in the show. Their surname became Winchester in a reference to the Winchester Mystery House, a famously myth-filled mansion in California.

Jensen Ackles was already starring in *Smallville* on The WB when he was offered the opportunity to audition for *Supernatural*. Originally, he was asked to read for the role of Sam, but Dean as a character immediately resonated with him, and Ackles proved to have exactly the kind of Han Solo swagger that Kripke was looking for. Jared Padalecki came in to audition for Sam off the back of his five years on *Gilmore Girls* – a show that Kripke's wife loved. Padalecki already knew both David Nutter and McG from previous work and, just like Ackles, he became the first choice for his part. The chemistry between the pair was so obvious from the outset that no one else was even brought in to audition. David Nutter recalled in the season one companion that 'Never have I done a show where the actors clicked so well together.'

There was one more role to be cast before filming could commence; no road trip story would be complete without a car. Kripke knew that the car needed to be distinct, a signature of the show, and that it had to be a classic. He wanted a 'muscle car', as he told the *Daily Telegraph* in a 2007 interview, originally imagining a '65 Mustang. His neighbour, who regularly restored classic cars, suggested a '67 Impala instead because 'you can put a body in the trunk.' The impala was a 'rottweiler of a car,' according to Kripke. It was big, intimidating and had ample room for weaponry. Dubbed 'Baby' by Dean, the car became one of the most consistent throughlines of the show.

Another consistent part of the show was the music. *Supernatural* was fully scored, with composers Christopher Lennertz and Jay Gruska alternating episodes and creating a score that sounded straight out of a classic horror movie. Alongside that, the show was full of classic rock – all Kripke's idea. He had to fight, early on, to include the music – even threatening to quit over it. One of the largest budgetary constraints that *Supernatural* faced, even more than the expense of staging an apocalypse, was the cost of the songs.

Usually, the music would be blasting from the Impala's speakers. In the pilot episode, Sam criticised Dean for his collection of cassette tapes, listing off 'Black Sabbath, Motörhead, Metallica' and calling it 'the greatest hits of mullet rock'. The response – 'Driver picks the music, passenger shuts his cakehole' – became a running joke on the show. Throughout *Supernatural* there were some obvious musical choices – 'Don't Fear the Reaper' got a particularly clanging drop in the first season and AC/DC turned up in predictable places, but Kripke was right to stand his ground. There could have been no *Supernatural* without the soundtrack of screaming guitars streaming from rolled-down windows as Sam and Dean sped in and out of town.

The songs in the show, especially in the first season, came straight out of Eric Kripke's collection. One of the most important inclusions was the song 'Carry on Wayward Son' by Kansas, originally released 19 November 1976.[3] The penultimate episode of the first season contained a recap, 'The Road So Far', set to the song. It was a hit with fans, far more so than Triumph's 'Fight the Good Fight', which was used for the recap that opened the season finale. From the second season onwards, 'Carry On' was used in every finale's 'Road So Far' segment, and it became the show's unofficial theme song. The lyrics in the chorus, offering peace and rest, grew remarkably more and more poignant as the show went on.

The *Supernatural* pilot aired on 13 September 2005, to an audience of almost six million people. The reviews were broadly positive, although one *New York Times* reviewer called the pilot 'predictable', complaining about the show reverting to a 'WB family drama' part-way through. The WB had cultivated a specific reputation that *Supernatural*, in the beginning, couldn't quite get away from. Kripke,

---

3. This date will be relevant later, I promise.

however, wasn't worried. For most of the first season the show aired on Tuesday nights, directly after the *Gilmore Girls* (at the time in its sixth season). When Kripke was asked if he minded the time slot in an interview with the *Toledo Free Press*, he pointed out that '65 to 70 percent of horror movie ticket buyers are young women, so it's the same market.' While it might have seemed initially that *Supernatural* was going to bring in a similar young male audience to the one that UPN had attracted with *Star Trek* and The WB had tried to build with *One Tree Hill*, it seemed the show wasn't as easily gendered.

Some reactions to the pilot were incredibly favourable. A *Television Without Pity* recap even called *Supernatural* 'the best. WB. Show. *Ever*!' after the pilot aired. That remark deserves full context, however. The recapper was blogging their viewing experience live, and spent much of the episode lamenting that Jessica, Sam's pretty blonde girlfriend, seemed destined to become the centre of a love triangle between the two brothers. When Jessica instead died in the final moments of the episode, in exactly the same manner as the boy's mother during the flashback at the beginning of the pilot (pinned to the ceiling, bleeding horribly and also on fire), the recapper Damian almost exploded with the delight at the idea of the show killing its potential Joey Potter (the centre of *Dawson's Creek*'s painful love triangle). In the pilot, killing off the love interest and making the show truly centred on the relationship between the brothers was a smart bit of storytelling, although the way the show treated women bore more scrutiny as it went on.

Supernatural had a very 'Monster of the Week' format in the beginning, with Sam and Dean largely being catalysts for the weekly horror movie. Much like in the show's spiritual predecessor *Buffy*, the lore rapidly began to deepen. The incredible chemistry between Ackles and Padalecki made the brotherly relationship much more compelling than the monsters of it all. In a 2010 interview with the *Chicago Tribune*, Kripke acknowledged that the first half of the season was a 'little repetitive', but that it picked up after sending the brothers back to their home town for the first time. He recalled around the fourth or fifth episode, watching with Bob Singer and realising 'God, these two guys and their chemistry is so much more interesting than the horror movies we're showing.'

The tagline of 'Saving people. Hunting things. The family business,' stated by Dean in the second episode of the show, never stopped being part of *Supernatural*'s DNA, but the family did become more of a focus than the business. By the end of the first season the boys were reunited with their father – John, played by Jeffrey Dean Morgan[4] – and chasing down the demon that killed their mother so many years before. This began a huge shift for a show that had its beginnings in anthology storytelling, one that compelled viewers to keep returning week after week, year after year.

Bringing in viewers in the earliest days of the show meant marketing, and plenty of it; it wasn't enough to hope that channel hoppers would land on the network at the right time. In 2005 *LA Times* released a piece examining the rise of 'Super Fans': television obsessives that couldn't help spreading the world about shows that they loved. These fans – the types who would encourage their friends to watch, chat about TV online and organically generate buzz for shows – were the audiences that the networks craved. Lewis Goldstein, co-president of marketing for The WB at the time, told the *LA Times* that these people 'are the fuse that lights the firecracker, and really sets things on fire.' At the time *Supernatural* began in 2005, The WB was struggling – the show's first season on the air was the last before the CW merger. The network targeted young horror fans by installing mirrors in nightclubs that showed an image of a woman pinned to the ceiling – the mother's death from the pilot – and distributing *Supernatural* coffee cup sleeves that revealed the same image when heated to cafes across America.

4. Who previously appeared in a small role in *The O.C.* and is married to *One Tree Hill* star Hilarie Burton.

Releasing the show online, as with *Gossip Girl*, was a huge part of the marketing strategy; that's where the target audiences were spending their time. The first episode released on *Yahoo!* a week before debuting on television, and *Supernatural* was one of the earliest shows available to purchase on iTunes after video support was added to the platform in 2006.

These early forms of online distribution – especially those iTunes sales – were a major catalyst for the 2007 writers strike – the 100-day WGA strike that shut down production across Hollywood. *Supernatural*, with its fifteen-year run, is one of the very few shows to have been affected by multiple major events that impacted television production. The 2007 strike cut the third season of the show short – reducing it to just sixteen episodes. The show's fifteenth and final season also faced a major production interruption in 2020 due to the Covid-19 pandemic. It's a truly rare show that's able to run for such a long time, through major events like these; especially considering that the 2007 strike caused an abrupt end to many shows at the time. The 2023 Hollywood labour disputes had a similar effect, and were a major factor in *The Winchesters* – the inevitable *Supernatural* prequel spin-off – not being renewed for a second season. *Supernatural*, however, existed in a perfect storm that gave the show almost unheard-of longevity.

Part of that storm was that surge in popularity of genre television. During *Supernatural*'s early years, articles and think pieces asking why television was suddenly embracing the weird and wonderful worlds of sci-fi and fantasy were everywhere. Much was laid at the feet of *Lost*'s mystery-box storytelling after the show became a phenomenon for the questions it raised and rarely answered. *Heroes*, an NBC show about people with unexpected superpowers saving the cheerleader to save the world, was highly regarded as a success thanks to the appetites *Lost* awakened, although that 2007 strike cut the second series of the show so short that interest waned and ratings plummeted. Amidst that storm, while *Supernatural* didn't manage massive ratings – partly due to its audience watching online and partly because it was on a smaller network – it became an absolute mainstay of The CW. On a larger network like NBC, who famously looked for big numbers or bust for their shows – *Supernatural* might never have been allowed to last so long.

Fifteen seasons is an astonishingly good run for a show. It's the longest any show lasted on The CW and one of the longest runs for any genre show on American television. It was also far, far longer than Eric Kripke envisioned the show lasting. Throughout *Supernatural*'s first few seasons on the air, Kripke was vocal about having a five-year roadmap for the brother's story. Kripke himself was only contracted for a five-year period, although Jensen Ackles and Jared Padalecki were signed on for six seasons.

Eclipse Magazine reported on Kripke answering fan questions at a 2008 convention. When asked about that five-year plan, he joked that a sixth season would be the one with 'all the weddings' and where 'Dean literally gets on a motorcycle and jumps the shark tank.' Lasting five years at all was far from guaranteed for any show on network television. When answering fan questions for *TV Guide* in 2007, as the second season of the show was airing, Kripke made an impassioned plea to fans of the show, asking them to spread the word and let their friends know that 'there's a smart genre show on The CW, a show for people who dig *Buffy* and *X-Files*. Drag 'em in front of the TV and make 'em watch.'

For Kripke, the five-year-plan was optimistic, although it proved to be about a decade less optimistic than necessary. In 2024 when asked about a similar plan for his Amazon Prime show *The Boys*, Kripke said 'No one was more wrong in all of human history about how many more seasons their show was going to go than this guy.'[5]

5. At the time of writing, Kripke has since announced that the fifth season of *The Boys* will indeed be its last.Not only that, but both Jared Padalecki and Misha Collins have announced that they will be starring in the final season of The Boys, joining a cast already stuffed with Supernatural alum (including Jensen Ackles).

There were new additions to the cast as the show went along, although some were more short-lived than others. Jim Beaver joined the show at the end of the first season as Bobby Singer (named for Robert Singer), an old family friend and a surrogate father figure to the brothers. Samantha Harris and Alona Tal became part of the show in the second season as Ellen and Jo Harvelle – a mother and daughter running a roadhouse for hunters like Sam and Dean. Genevieve Cortese appeared as the demon Ruby in 2008, hitting it off with Jared Padalecki during her time on the show and eventually becoming Genevieve Padalecki. A key point, among all of these side characters, was expendability. With the focus of the show always on the brothers and their transient lifestyles first, other characters were written to appear sporadically and ultimately be removable.

Almost every season of *Supernatural* ended (or, in the case of the second season, began) with the untimely demise of one of the brothers, but those deaths held little weight when the show was already expected to return with the pair intact the next season – Sam and Dean were clad in solid plot armour. The side characters and guest stars became the ones that could upset the audience with impactful deaths. One of the most upsetting, and smartest, things the show did was killing off Bobby Singer in the seventh season. The character had been part of the show for long enough that his death seemed as impossible as one of the brothers staying dead. Then, suddenly, it wasn't impossible at all. Through flashbacks and parallel universes and visits to the afterlife, however, the writers found a way to bring back Jim Beaver at least once per season after his character's death.

The expendability of secondary characters really changed in the fourth season with the introduction of angels. The first three seasons had added demons to the lore of the show, and while angels hadn't been in Kripke's original plan, they were the next logical step. As writing on the fourth season began Kripke realised that his idea of an impending cosmic conflict needed an opposing side. Stepping into overtly Christian mythology was a risk, and not a universally liked decision at first. In a 2014 *New York Times* interview, Jared Padalecki remembered his annoyance at the angel's introduction, thinking 'We didn't sign up for a religious show. I don't want to make a statement on angels. I came to do X-Files.' Padalecki was proved wrong, in the end, and the angels became essential – especially one of them.

After the fourth season of *Supernatural* ended with Dean, in hell, suffering unknowable torture, the fourth season opened with him alive and unharmed, crawling out of his own grave. The reveal at the end of the episode and the introduction of Misha Collins as the angel Castiel, changed the trajectory of the show for good. Castiel stalks through the barn coated in anti-demon graffiti that Dean and Bobby have taken refuge in, lightbulbs popping at his sheer power, and he tells Dean that 'I'm the one who gripped you tight and raised you from perdition.' Revealing himself as an angel of the lord and demonstrating his shadowed wings, Castiel and the complexities of heaven and hell became an integral part of the show.

Those first five seasons of *Supernatural* told a fairly contained story. The end goal of the writers was the apocalypse, and the angels got them there. There are some obvious similarities to other works in those five seasons. It was a similar arc to *Buffy*, the fifth season finale functioning so well as an end to the show (including the death of a major character) that continuing seemed almost impossible. Obviously, *Supernatural* owed plenty to *Buffy* and shared a large fanbase with the show; various *Buffy* actors turned up on *Supernatural* through the years as a nod to those fans. Both Amber Benson and Mercedes McNab appeared as vampires, Julie Benz appeared in the first season as a woman hoping for treatment from a faith healer, and Charisma Carpenter and James Marsters co-starred as wonderfully bitchy divorcing witches in a seventh season episode.

There were also a number of references to the work of fantasy author Neil Gaiman. Eric Kripke had, in his pre-Supernatural days, pitched an adaptation of Gaiman's Sandman comics to networks, although it never came to fruition. Kripke nodded to Gaiman's work throughout

Supernatural; Castiel's main outfit on the show – a trench coat over a suit – was inspired by John Constantine, a DC comics anti-hero created by Alan Moore and Stephen R. Bisette who turned up in the Sandman comics, and the fifth season episode 'Hammer of the Gods' – which showed a gathering of gods from various pantheons at an Indiana hotel (and revealed that the wonderful trickster god played by Richard Speight Jr. who had plagued Sam and Dean in earlier episodes was actually the Archangel Gabriel in witness protection) was an homage to Gaiman's American Gods. Alongside that, there were nods to Good Omens – the comedic apocalypse novel written by Terry Pratchett and Neil Gaiman – in the fourth and fifth seasons of the show. Crowley, the demonic and deliciously camp 'King of the Crossroads' played by Mark Sheppard, was named after the demon Crowley from Good Omens (himself named for the infamous occultist Aleister Crowley).

Good Omens itself was later adapted for screen, premiering on Amazon Prime in 2019. Although the first season covered the events of the book from start to finish, a second season was released in 2023. Season Two was designed to bridge the gap between the existing story and the unrealised Good Omens sequel – reportedly planned out, but never written, by Terry Pratchett and Neil Gaiman. A third season based on that plot was announced but, after several allegations of sexual misconduct were publicly levied at Neil Gaiman in 2024, Amazon reduced that third season to just a single ninety-minute episode.

At the centre of Good Omens is the friendship between the demon Crowley and the angel Aziraphale (played by David Tennant and Michael Sheen, respectively). When the first six-episode season dropped, fans were fascinated by the pair's obvious chemistry. When angel and demon kissed and then separated at the end of the second season, viewers were both vindicated and distraught.

The Venn diagram of Good Omens and Supernatural fans had a large overlap. Those fans care deeply about the relationships on the shows – both the canonical ones and those that exist only in fan fiction. Buffy and Faith might have been the ship that launched a thousand fics, but Dean and Castiel sailed ahead a long time ago. The difference between the Dean/Castiel ship and the Aziraphale and Crowley relationship is that the former pairing never really got to become canonical. The closest it came was a tearful confession of love from Castiel that was immediately followed by being yanked into 'turbo hell' (as the fans call it) just two episodes before the end of the show. Dean's response was to stand still, speechless and sad. The intensity of the relationship between the pair, without quite crossing the border into explicit romance, has led to *Supernatural* being a show that's regularly accused of 'queerbaiting' its audience.

Queerbaiting is, in media terms, a show hinting at a relationship between a same-sex couple to attract viewers, but never allowing the couple to have an explicit relationship so as not to turn off a more conservative audience or, more importantly, advertisers. Misha Collins himself has been vocal about the obvious love between Castiel and Dean. After the Crossroads 8 Convention that took place in Birmingham in 2024, multiple fans took to social media claiming that Collins had stated on a panel that 'if The CW hadn't been so homophobic, Dean and Cas would've been balls deep.' People involved with *Supernatural* at every level were fully aware that the show had amassed a large LGBTQ+ fan base, and that the audience wanted to see their ship fully realised. The cast even appeared in anti-bullying campaigns on The CW for pride month.

That awareness of the audience did little for representation on the show. Homosexuality was often reduced to a punchline; in the fifth season episode 'The Real Ghostbusters', the final joke of the episode was that two men were in a relationship. In the seventh season, the show introduced Charlie Bradbury, played by Felicia Day. She was a rare queer character on the show, one that appeared for multiple episodes over multiple seasons. Charlie wasn't, however, given a chance on the show to be in a happy, settled relationship of any kind before being graphically murdered (dismembered by Nazis and left in a bathtub) towards the end of the tenth season.

Supernatural's treatment of women does, as I said, bear scrutiny. Many, many female characters were killed off in an effort to motivate the brothers (a media trope commonly known as 'fridging'). Even female characters that got to be on the show for a while, such as the wonderfully evil Rowena MacLeod (played by Ruth Connel) had to suffer horrific amounts of violence. Charlie Bradbury's death was no exception, and also supplied another example of the all-too-common 'Bury Your Gays' trope. Felicia Day did, admittedly, later return to the show as an alternate universe version of the character. Not long after getting the opportunity to settle down together, Charlie's new girlfriend was killed off. It was less than ideal representation.

It's possible, though it would take a better data analyst than myself to check, that a correlation could be drawn between the lack of overt queerness in a piece of media and the number of queer ships popular in fan fiction. *Supernatural* was not, in the classic sense, a teen drama. The main characters are both in their early twenties at the beginning of the story and the show wasn't following the trials and tribulations of high school. *Supernatural* was, however, a CW show – the network known for its teen audiences – and it amassed a large teen fanbase right from the beginning. That teen audience was largely (although not entirely) responsible for the massive amounts of fan fiction written about the show. These were the days of LiveJournal, and then Tumblr, blogging sites that allowed fans to gather in droves – the successors to early internet forums. The most popular romantic pairings in *Supernatural* fan fiction were all queer. Alongside 'Destiel' (Dean and Castiel), 'Wincest' – the romantic pairing of Sam and Dean – became popular. *Supernatural* fan fiction was such a large part of the fandom eco-system that an entire genre of pornographic fiction – 'Omegaverse', featuring wolf-inspired sexual relationships – sprang from a *Supernatural* fan fiction prompt on LiveJournal in 2010.

The very first *Supernatural* LiveJournal community formed on 1 July 2005, two months before the show began. It was a network creation, another attempt at viral marketing. Within twenty-four hours of the show's premiere, communities free of network influence began to spring up on the site. The first ever *Supernatural* convention, organised entirely by fans, took place on 13 October 2006, just a few weeks after season two began. In February 2007, the blogging platform Tumblr went live. A slow transition took place over the following years as fans made their way to the new site, finding communities and sharing fics and fan art via tags on the site.

The *Supernatural* fandom was huge, and loud, and became infamous on Tumblr. Around 2011, the tag 'SuperWhoLock' was born. Referring to the crossover fandoms of *Supernatural*, *Doctor Who* and *Sherlock* (the modern-day adaptation of the Sherlock Holmes novels created by Stephen Moffat and starring Benedict Cumberbatch), 'SuperWhoLock' became synonymous with online fandom. Posts both connected and completely unrelated to these shows would have replies swallowed up with SuperWhoLock memes and references. This era, around 2011 and 2012, was a unique and also strangely familiar time on the internet. It was a time when being part of a fandom could become one of the most prominent parts of a person's online identity. None of this was a phenomenon totally unique to *Supernatural*, but the show was famous at its peak for having some of the most vocally passionate fans.

By 2020, as the final season was airing, Tumblr had grown a little quieter. That was, at least, until 5 November. That was the night the eighteenth episode of the final season aired – the one with Castiel's confession of love for Dean. The debatable canonisation of the relationship caused widespread Tumblr excitement and beyond, and 'Destiel' began to trend worldwide on multiple social media platforms.

Around the same time, a rumour (later proved to be false) that Russian President Vladimir Putin was about to resign was spreading like wildfire. It was also the night that the results of the 2020 US Presidential election were being determined, and people across the world (and the internet) were waiting to find out if Joe Biden had won or Donald Trump was going to get a second term. It was a wild night on the internet – the kind of totally organic social media engagement that a network could never dream of. One Tumblr user summed up the sheer ridiculousness of the night, saying 'no one had a "memes for if putin resigns during supernatural canon gays during the us presidential election" folder prepped ahead of time.' In a reference to the bygone days of SuperWhoLock, the tag 'SuperPutinElection' began trending. Fifteen years after the show began, the *Supernatural* fandom was still dominating the internet.

The show very much existed in conversation with its audience, referring to the fandom in lovingly mocking ways. In the eighteenth episode of the fourth season – 'The Monster at the End of this Book' – the brothers discovered a book series that accurately detailed every aspect of their lives to date written by 'Carver Edlund' (a reference to Jeremy Carver and Ben Edlund – executive producers on the show). Carver turned out to be Chuck Shurley, apparently a prophet receiving visions of the brother's lives and writing them down for a profit. (He was later revealed to be God.) The *Supernatural* books in-universe allowed for meta-commentary on the show's audience. 'The Real Ghostbusters' saw the brothers tricked into attending a fan convention for the books and finding themselves caught up in a mystery while dealing with fans roleplaying as Sam and Dean – the punchline gay couple mentioned earlier were two of those role players. It was almost a mean-spirited episode that mocked the more intense viewers of the show, but it was well-received by a self-aware fandom.

The show was referential from its early days. An episode in the second season – 'Hollywood Babylon' – put the brothers in 'L.A.' (with strangely Canadian weather), trying to end a haunting on the set of a horror movie. Early in the episode, as the brothers are on a studio tour, a guide points out that they're going past the set of Stars Hollow, and the camera zooms in on Jared Padalecki as the guide tells tourists to keep an eye out for one of the stars of *Gilmore Girls*. A fictionalised version of McG played by Regan Burns directs the cursed movie in question, and McG himself appeared in a small cameo. 'Hollywood Babylon' seemed to be forty minutes of television written to mock the worst Hollywood experiences of the *Supernatural* writers.

Later episodes like 'Ghostfacers!' toyed with the format of the show, in that particular case referencing ghost-hunting shows from the real world by filming an episode entirely with handheld cameras. Immediately after 'The Monster at the End of this Book' came 'Jump the Shark'; there were no weddings and no motorcycle, but a secret third Winchester brother was introduced and immediately killed off in a soapy plot twist. In the fifth season episode 'Changing Channels', the previously-introduced trickster god trapped Dean and Sam in an endless parade of fictional TV shows. In Kripke's words in 'The Long Road Home' (a retrospective documentary that aired immediately before the final episode of the show in 2020), the episode was 'us trying to give a little bit of crap to our competition that night.' The episode parodied *Grey's Anatomy*, which was airing at the same time as *Supernatural* on ABC, and *CSI: Crime Scene Investigation* which had a matching time slot on CBS. Alongside these, the episode had a classic eighties sitcom, a Japanese game show and a tribute to *Knight Rider* that saw Sam giving voice to the Impala. It was a remarkable remix of the show's usual form as Jensen Ackles and Jared Padalecki leapt from genre to genre.

Supernatural got even more meta in the sixth season with 'The French Mistake' – widely considered one of the best episodes of the show. In the episode, Sam and Dean were transported to an alternate reality; one in which they were actors named Jared Padalecki and Jensen Ackles, starring in a TV show called *Supernatural*. Genevieve Padalecki appeared as Jared's wife, leading to a great moment of confusion as the brothers assume they're facing the demon Ruby again. Misha Collins played a fictionalised version of himself, tweeting from the set to his 'Mishamigos' before being brutally killed by an angel. The episode was self-referential, ridiculous, and a reminder to the audience that *Supernatural* was just a TV show, albeit a clever one willing to kick the fourth wall on a regular basis.

Kripke, Padalecki and Collins have all cited it as one of their favourite episodes.

Throughout the fifteen years that *Supernatural* was on, the writers kept on finding ways to break away from the show's standard structure. These were some of the most memorable episodes, like the thirteenth season episode 'Scoobynatural', an almost completely animated episode which put the Winchesters and Castiel into an episode of *Scooby Doo*. There was the third season episode 'Mystery Spot' that saw Sam stuck in a time loop, forced to watch Dean die in a number of creative ways.[6] There was a black and white episode that paid homage to classic monster movies, a Quentin Tarantino episode and an episode shot entirely from Baby's point of view. Making these clever episodes and breaking from form requires having an established form to begin with – that's something that comes with the luxury of a show getting to run for a long time.

It's rare for shows to reach 100 episodes, let alone the 200- or 300-episode milestone, but *Supernatural* did it. The 200th episode – 'Fan Fiction' – was a love letter to the fandom. There was a monster storyline in the episode – the brothers investigate mysterious disappearances at an all-girls school – but the real focus was the brothers being forced to contend with a musical based on the in-universe *Supernatural* books, and the fan-fiction version of their lives after the end of the fifth season. There were jokes about romantic subtext, with the brothers being introduced to the phrase 'Destiel', there were tongue-in-cheek references to past and forgotten characters, and the episode proved that *Supernatural* had gone way past taking itself seriously. There was even winking acknowledgement to the 'subtext' in the brother's relationship.

6. The town used to film 'Mystery Spot' would later become Storybrooke – the home of *Once Upon a Time*.

'Fan Fiction' was a celebration of the fans that loved the show enough to create their own narrative around it. When Dean, at the end of the episode, told Marie – the writer of the *Supernatural* musical – to keep writing because 'I have my version and you have yours', it was a seal of approval for all of the fans of the show. Then, finally, Chuck appeared at the end, with Rob Benedict appearing on the show for the first time since his character had disappeared at the end of the fifth season finale, to congratulate Marie on her work in a brief appearance that turned out to be setting up much of the show's final seasons.

Supernatural had to successfully raise the stakes, season after season, making the threats to the brothers and to human existence more and more grandiose. The limitations of a CW budget greatly affected what could be done on screen. At the end of the second season, armies of demons were let loose on the earth. Actually showing demon armies was far too expensive, so the show depicted the demonic incursion as small, guerilla, terroristic cells. The end of the world was often shown in hints and pieces, building up antagonists across the seasons by putting existential threats into human bodies, and it worked.

Two of the best human castings in that first block of five seasons were Mark Pellegrino and Julian Richings. Pellegrino, best known at the time for his work on *Lost*, joined the show in the fifth season as Lucifer. He went on to appear regularly over the next ten seasons, playing chillingly evil and incredibly normal all at once. The fifth season also introduced the four horsemen of the apocalypse, most notably casting Julian Richings as Death. His was a fantastic portrayal of a psychopomp. A chilling conversation between Death and Dean in a Chicago pizza parlour that set in motion the brothers circumventing the end of the world was an incredibly memorable part of what Kripke imagined might have been the show's final season.

As the show went on far past those five seasons that Kripke had first envisioned, the lore grew and the villains escalated. Castiel briefly became a godlike figure before horrifically dying (for the second time) as a precursor to the introduction of the Leviathans in the seventh season. While the Leviathans were supposed to be some of the worst creatures imaginable, dragged out from purgatory, they were widely considered to be some of the dullest villains on the show. As *Supernatural* continued there were attempts to close off hell, a redemption arc for Crowley, the Metatron – the voice of God, played by Curtis Armstrong – attempted a coup in heaven, Lucifer fathered a child – Jack, played by Alex Calvert, who eventually became a younger brother to the Winchester siblings despite accidentally killing their resurrected mother, angels fell, demons ascended, writers rose up to become showrunners and the fans stayed compelled throughout.

There were attempts, of course, at spin-offs. Two backdoor pilots aired during the show's run, but neither was picked up for series. 'Bloodlines', which aired in the ninth season, contained the set-up for a show about supernatural politics in Chicago. 'Wayward Sisters', in the thirteenth season, pulled almost all of the surviving female characters of the show together; Sherrif Jody Mills, Claire Novak and Alex Jones (the three of whom already had a family dynamic) alongside Sheriff Donna Hanscum and Patience Turner. Unlike the first backdoor pilot attempt, 'Wayward Sisters' did feel like a pilot that still really connected to the main story of the show, but it wasn't quite enough for the network. It was a pilot and potential spin-off that had been two years in the making, and when The CW announced their decision not to pick it up there was even an online fan campaign to get the show made, although it was ultimately unsuccessful.

While spin-off attempts were unsuccessful, *Supernatural* got to continue on. It was the eleventh season that revealed in no uncertain terms that Chuck was really *the* God, but it wasn't until the end of the fourteenth season that the ultimate plot twist came about – God was revealed to be the ultimate villain. When a show has run for that long, and escalated its own mythology so thoroughly, how else to cap things off?

The announcement that the fifteenth season of *Supernatural* would be its last came on 22 March 2019. Jared Padalecki, Jensen Ackles and Misha Collins filmed a teary video to release the news on social media, calling the final season 'the big, grand finale of an institution.' A final Comic-Con panel for the show in 2019 saw more tears as the actors struggled with questions about the show coming to an end. Meanwhile, co-showrunner Andrew Dabb joked that the final season was going to be 'twenty episodes of clip shows.'

Back when Eric Kripke was the showrunner, he pointed at that five-season figure being a good one to reach, saying that if the show could get that far it would be nice to bow out on his own terms rather than being cancelled. Cancellation was never truly a threat for *Supernatural*. Robert Singer in 'The End of the Road' – a documentary about the making of the final episodes – talked about wanting 'to go out while we still had our fastball…not get cancelled but pick our own exit date.' When the decision came to end *Supernatural*, it was on their terms, not the network's.

The plan for the final season was that the penultimate episode would end the mythology with the defeat of God, allowing the final episode to wrap up the emotional storyline of the brothers. Then came the second major production interruption in the show's history with the Covid-19 pandemic. In March 2020, filming began on that penultimate episode, but production was shut down after just a day's work. Unlike a lot of other shows affected by the pandemic, the network reassured audiences that *Supernatural* would still get to finish on its own terms, when possible. After the thirteenth episode of the season aired on 23 March the show went on hiatus and didn't return to screens until 8 October, allowing post-production to be completed on the rest of the season and allowing for those final episodes to be shot.

The final episode – 'Carry On' aired on 19 November 2020 (forty-four years to the day after the release of 'Carry on Wayward Son'). The episode showed Sam and Dean living their approximation of a 'normal life', still hunting monsters, but without the threat of an apocalypse on the side. The brothers destroy a nest of vampires – one of which was first introduced in a season one episode – and just as the day seems saved, Dean is impaled on a metal spike. What followed was an incredible speech from Jensen Ackles, an emotional goodbye not just to Sam but to the show itself. It was a fantastic performance in an episode that was a tad over-indulgent, although that was certainly earned after fifteen years on the air.

What followed was Dean in heaven, reunited with Bobby and opting to take Baby for a long drive. 'Carry on Wayward Son', of course, played over a montage of Dean driving while back on earth Sam got married, had a child, raised him to be a hunter and apparently acquired an atrocious grey wig before dying and being reunited with Dean on a bridge identical to the one used in the pilot episode.

The final script had to be rewritten to account for Covid restrictions. The original version of the finale had a huge gathering in heaven, in a reconstruction of the road house from the second season, with as many familiar faces as possible crammed in. Kansas even agreed to appear in the episode, performing that unofficial theme tune. By the time it came to shoot, however, it wasn't safe or reasonable to ask that many people to travel and then gather in such a small space. One thing about the script didn't change from the original draft; the previous 326 episode scripts had all ended with 'To Be Continued', but for the final script the last words were 'The End'.

At the end of 'Swan Song', the fifth season finale that was almost a series finale, Chuck says 'Endings are hard... You try to tie up every loose end, but you never can. The fans are always going to bitch.' The *Supernatural* finale proved that point. It was divisive, both among critics and fans, with many of the latter feeling that Dean deserved a better end. The *New York Times* called the episode 'an odd, awkward, maudlin and, in keeping with the show's habits, self-referential exercise.' Emily Tennenbaum at *IGN*, on the other hand, called the finale 'an episode of television that could rival the best of them.'

For a lot of shows, their legacy depends on how well they stick the landing. For *Supernatural*, those final forty minutes weren't so important in the grand scheme of fifteen years. It feels impossible that a show could begin now, in a time of rapid cancellation and short, eight-episode seasons, and go on until 2040, airing over 300 episodes. The television landscape that *Supernatural* ended in is wildly different from the one where it began.

Supernatural was able to last so long, when so many other shows couldn't, because a myriad of things came together. The large fan base obviously contributed to the show's longevity, but it was more than just that. It was the lightning in a bottle chemistry between Jensen Ackles and Jared Padalecki. It was the network that didn't care enough to cancel it, then really cared enough to keep it. It was the family of it all. In the various retrospectives created to go with the finale, the cast and crew repeatedly come back to the show feeling like a family. A show getting to run for that long doesn't just mean joy for the fans, it means consistent work in an industry fraught with risk. It means writers like Andrew Dabb getting to work up to showrunner positions. In that 2019 Comic-Con panel, Dabb admitted that 'we'll never experience this again.' *Supernatural* was a miracle unlikely to be repeated.

Family was obviously the core of the show. 'Saving people. Hunting things. The family business.' That theme carried over to the cast and crew, and to the fans as well. In that video announcement about the end of the show, Ackles passed on a message from Eric Kripke to the fans: 'In a show about family, it is amazing, and it is the pride of his life that it became family.' At the end of the final episode, after the brothers reunited on the bridge, the fourth wall smashed for good as Ackles and Padalecki thanked the fans one last time: 'Through blood, sweat, laughter and tears, you've kept us on for fifteen years.' A final zoom out saw the brothers, the crew and the car, gathered on the bridge for one final 'Cut.'

There is an incredible power to fandom, to loving something and finding a tribe of people who share that love. No show embodied that power like *Supernatural*.

Chapter 6

Glee

Welcome to William McKinley High School

Lima is a small city in the state of Ohio, in the American Midwest. Lima's William McKinley high school is an entirely fictional invention of *Glee* – the musical teen dramedy that ran for six years on the Fox network between 2009 and 2015. *Glee* worked on the premise that the high school, Lima and Ohio itself are not places to be loved for what they are; they're places to escape from, places that it's downright unfortunate to come from. *Glee* wasn't just a story set in a small town; it was a story about getting out.

Glee was a musical, set in a high school, that shared absolutely no DNA with Disney's *High School Musical* franchise. In fact, the inspiration for the show came from Ian Brennan – one of *Glee*'s creators, writers and executive producers – and his own experiences in high school show choir. In the early 2000's Brennan was making a living as an actor, not a writer, but the idea of a movie about a high school show choir wouldn't leave him alone. He bought a copy of *Screenwriting for Dummies* and some writing software, and finished his first draft of the movie script in 2005. Brennan began to shop his script around with zero success, until it landed in the hands of Ryan Murphy.

Ryan Murphy was no stranger to writing for teens having created *Popular* – a short-lived teen comedy/drama series – for The WB in 1999. When Ian Brennan's script came to him, Murphy was working on the final season of his hit Fox drama *Nip/Tuck* and debating where to go next; all he knew was that he wanted to make something comparatively light in tone. Murphy told the *LA Times* in 2009 that *Nip/Tuck* was 'a show that we jokingly say was set over the gates of hell' and that he wanted to make something feel-good instead. Along with his *Nip/Tuck* co-writer and executive producer Brad Falchuk, Murphy immediately pitched Brennan's idea back to him as a television series instead of movie. So, *Glee* was born.

Fox picked up *Glee* just fifteen minutes after receiving the pilot. The network was on the rise, with shows like *American Idol* adding to reality television's dominance of the entertainment landscape. Peter Liguori's short tenure had ended in 2007, and his successor Kevin Reilly was championing new, interesting dramas that could hold on to the viewers turning up in droves for the network's output of competition shows. *Glee* was a perfect fit, and the show was fast-tracked for the beginning of the 2009/2010 season.

Casting began immediately. Ryan Murphy chose to look outside of the traditional LA resources to find his glee club. One of the first places he began his search was Broadway; he wanted actors who understood the rush of live performance. Lea Michele and Jonathan Groff were co-starring in *Spring Awakening* at the time, and when Groff went out to L.A. to audition for a different Ryan Murphy pilot (one that never made it as an actual show), Michele came out to visit. Groff introduced the two of them, and Murphy immediately realised that Lea Michele was perfect for *Glee*. The role of Rachel Berry, the high maintenance centre of the glee club's attention, ended up being written with her in mind, and Lea Michele became the star of the show.

Murphy also found Matthew Morrison, who had originated roles in *Hairspray* and *The Light in the Piazza* and cast him as Will Schuester – Spanish teacher, leader of the glee club and occasionally far too friendly with his students. Morrison and Lea Michele were old friends, and had even briefly dated before being cast together on

Glee. Jenna Ushkowitz came from live theatre as well, having starred in the acclaimed revival of *The King and I* before being cast as Tina Cohen-Chang. Kevin McHale came from a boy band background to the role of Artie, Canadian actor Cory Monteith auditioned with an REO Speedwagon song and scored the part of Finn, and Jayma Mays found herself having to sing despite auditioning for the non-singing role of the school guidance counsellor Emma Pilsbury. She delivered a version of 'Toucha-Touch Me' from *Rocky Horror* that was so good Murphy eventually found a reason to do a whole *Rocky Horror* episode.

Chris Colfer auditioned to play Artie, and Ryan Murphy liked him so much he created the character of Kurt just for him. *Glee* was also a huge breakthrough for Amber Riley, who had auditioned unsuccessfully for *American Idol* six years before but was perfect for the role of Mercedes Jones. One of the most inspired casting decisions was to bring in comedy actress Jane Lynch to play Sue Sylvester, the fury-filled cheerleading coach who consistently delivered some of *Glee*'s best lines.

The vision for *Glee* was a musical, but one with a vague grounding in reality; in an interview with the *LA Times* Ryan Murphy called *Glee* 'a postmodern musical.' It wasn't a show about spontaneously bursting into song to move the plot along. The songs in *Glee* weren't originals written for the show (with a few exceptions), but a mixture of rearranged pop songs, classic numbers from musicals and any other genre that fit comfortably with the emotional needs of a moment. The musical numbers took place as in-show performances, or occasionally fantasies, or sometimes a surreal blend of both. This wasn't the sparkling, synchronised world of *High School Musical*, as the show's creators consistently pointed out in interviews. It was, however, a world where a handy, mute and always available pianist (named Brad for Brad Falchuk) could happily play any song on demand, and the denizens of the glee club could pick up a synchronised dance routine with no rehearsal. *Glee* was the perfect show for a network already making its money from covers of popular songs being performed on television.

When the time came to launch *Glee*, Fox tried a similar approach to the debut of *The O.C.* and tried to pull audiences in by launching the show outside of the beginning of the television season. The pilot episode of *Glee* aired on 19 May 2009, immediately after the finale of the eighth season of *American Idol*. The rest of the first season was still held back for September, making the pilot effectively into a forty-minute trailer for the rest of the show. That first episode was watched in almost ten million homes. Fox followed the examples of other networks at the time, making the pilot streamable online for free in the four-month gap between that first airing and the rest of the series coming out. Fox took things a step further by also releasing the songs from the episode to download on iTunes, in a marketing move that proved to be part of the show's biggest impact.

The pilot itself was well-received. The *New York Times* questioned that early premiere date in 'an age of Twitter-length attention spans,' wondering if the show would still be remembered come September, but the review of the episode itself compared the show to classic teen movies like *Bring it On* and *Election* and called it 'blissfully unoriginal in a witty, unimaginative way.' When the show did return to the air in September 2009, it turned out that the *New York Times* needn't have worried; there was a fan base already in place ready and willing to get obsessed with *Glee*.

The marketing that created that fan base was extensive. In those four months after the pilot episode aired, the *Glee* cast toured malls across America, appearing at Hot Topic stores (the go-to place for teens shopping for anything fandom-related) across the country on the 'Gleek' tour. 'Gleek', a portmanteau of 'Glee' and 'geek', became the catch-all name for fans of the show. A fandom named for a marketing phrase sums up a lot of *Glee*'s popularity. While the show certainly earned its fans, there was more than a hint of manufacturing around the public enjoyment of *Glee*.

There was genuine critical acclaim amongst the mass-marketing. Emily St. James of the *AV Club* gave the pilot an 'A-grade', calling the episode 'the best network pilot in a good long while.' St. James, who deservedly had a cult following of her own for her television reviewing, went on to recap the first three seasons of *Glee* as they aired for the *A.V. Club*. The conversations online about television had moved from forums, to broader home-grown sites like *Television Without Pity*, to the comment sections of more established publications. Fandoms and followings built up around reviewers themselves as much as the shows being reviewed, and *Glee* was one of the first big shows of that shift.

Alongside the reviews and the tours was a healthy amount of traction on social media. Myspace, the first major global social network, was heavily referenced in the first few episodes of *Glee*, but the site was already falling in relevance by 2009. Twitter, on the other hand, was in its infancy, and the short-form site became one of the major homes of viral TV discussion. According to an article in the *Vancouver Sun* in 2009, just a couple of months after *Glee* properly began it had become the most-discussed series on Twitter, by a wide margin.

Technology had hit a point in 2009 where it had become easy for fans to create and upload their own videos recreating performances from the show. *Glee* executive producer told the *Vancouver Sun* that there were plans in place to add karaoke versions of the songs to the soon-to-be-released soundtrack albums, making those fan videos even easier to create. *Glee* didn't so much spread by fandom word of mouth as by fans unwittingly doing the work of network marketing departments for free.

The show itself, outside of the songs, had the tone of a cartoonish soap opera. The colours were incessantly bright, from the vivid red of the cheerleader's uniforms to the sharp tones of the outfits worn by performing show choirs. The storylines were darker than the colour palette, but almost always had an undertone of comedy. Where shows like *One Tree Hill* would treat both the intense and the frivolous with equally heavy dramatic weight, *Glee* would often treat the heavier stories with the same lightness as the show's funnier moments. When *Glee* did get serious, sometimes via song, those moments stood out so far from the rest of the show that they managed to land with thudding impacts.

The first season had both a teen pregnancy and a fake pregnancy storyline. The teen pregnancy storyline was fraught with real fear; the palpable upset at being trapped in small-town Ohio by an unwanted child was a huge presence in 'Preggers', the fourth episode of the show. Emily St James pointed out in her recap of the episode that *Glee* took place in an 'essentially sad world', one where people covered up dissatisfaction with their lives 'via forced jollity.' She called the episode 'the perfect expression of its Midwestern locale' and she was right; there again was that forced sense of entrapment in this small town.

There was real depth in that storyline. The head cheerleader and president of the school's celibacy club not only going through an unwanted pregnancy but hiding the truth of the real father was performed masterfully by Dianna Agron as Quinn Fabray. Then, also, there were the depths of absurdity that kept up the show's real tone. Will Schuester's wife Terri (played by Jessalyn Gilsig with hilarious shrewishness) faking her own pregnancy and planning secretly to adopt the unwanted baby was so ridiculous it was hilarious, until it wasn't. Will's entire early storyline of feeling stuck in a relationship with his high school sweetheart only to find himself a miserable adult, was a perfect warning for the younger characters of the show: not getting out might end up being incredibly depressing. The eventual birth of Quinn's baby was set to a performance of Queen's 'Bohemian Rhapsody' by rival show choir Vocal Adrenaline – with Jonathan Groff taking centre stage as antagonist Jesse St James. It was overwrought, insane and perfectly *Glee*.

Glee was an 'issues' show. Like *Party of Five* before it, some episodes acted like public service announcements about the risks teens are facing – teen pregnancy, drinking, queerness – but with a touch of lightness absent from the shows that came before. The way *Glee* tackled the stories of its queer characters was a fantastic demonstration of how far television had come in just a decade. Queerness in earlier teen dramas had been a punchline, a phase, or a challenging exploration that had to take place almost entirely off screen to avoid offending the delicate sensibilities of the audience. In *Glee*, queerness was safe enough that Kurt, the young gay high school student played by Chris Colfer, could be both a raging stereotype and a deep and compelling character. Camp, Beyoncé-obsessed and feather-boa-wearing Kurt could have just been Jack from *Will and Grace* for a new generation but underneath that casual stereotyping that makes the early episodes of *Glee* look borderline homophobic was a real character fighting for acceptance. *Glee* also didn't shy away from depicting the (admittedly heightened) reality of what it meant to be a gay kid in small-town America. Kurt was an outcast looking for a tribe, just like all of the misfits in *Glee*.

Chris Colfer was advised not to come out as gay himself while filming the first season of the show. Speaking on *The View* in 2024, Colfer explained that while he was worried he couldn't hide it, he was told 'don't address it and you'll be rewarded in the end.' Late in 2009, however, Colfer ignored the advice and came out publicly. Discussing that decision, Colfer explained on *The View* that 'I may never win a major award. I may never get to play a superhero. But I think being a beacon of positivity and providing that comfort for people is way more important than attention.' Colfer did, in the end, win multiple awards, including a Golden Globe for 'Best Performance by an Actor in a Supporting Role in a Series' in 2011.

Ryan Murphy often used the real lives of the actors on *Glee* as inspiration for the show. When Colfer told Murphy about the time he wasn't allowed to perform 'Defying Gravity' – the big act one closer from the hit musical *Wicked* – at a school talent show because the song was written for a woman, that became a contest on *Glee* between Kurt and Rachel as the pair fought for the opportunity to perform the song. The resulting fallout of the contest – Kurt's blue-collar father Burt (played by Mike O'Malley) not just accepting his son's queerness but fighting for his right to perform a song written for a woman – started a long-running story of eventual queer acceptance on *Glee*. This was a show about outsiders and popular kids, but it was also about finding understanding, a middle ground. That soapy humour prevented the show from becoming just a depressing, finger-wagging public service announcement. The 'very special episodes' became technicolour parodies of the genre.

There were still the darker moments. Kurt was on the receiving end of some of the most challenging stuff *Glee* produced. The second season saw Chris Colfer's character bullied out of William McKinley high school (and into Dalton Academy, rival show choir The Warblers and eventually the arms of Blaine – played by Darren Kriss). The storyline continued into the third season with the bully Dave Karofsky (played by Maz Adler) being outed at *his* new school and attempting suicide in the fourteenth episode of the season. It was an incredible fifteen minutes of television; well-written and heartbreakingly performed. Sadly, it was followed by another twenty minutes of lacklustre music, before a mid-season cliffhanger finale as Quinn gets hit by a truck while driving and texting at the same time.

That episode – 'On My Way' demonstrated what *Glee* could do well, and what it did terribly. The attempted suicide storyline was an emotional gut-punch set to Darren Kriss's performance of 'Cough Syrup' by Young the Giant. The producers worked with the Trevor Project – a non-profit suicide prevention organisation for LGBTQ+ youth – and a PSA for the charity was broadcast during the episode, resulting in record amounts of traffic for the organisation and some much-needed raised awareness. This wasn't a 'very special episode', this was storytelling that made an effort. Then, there were a few bright songs and a blackmail subplot that lasted almost a full five minutes. Finally, there was that texting-while-driving ending which dripped

Right: Kristy Swanson and Luke Perry in the original poster for the 1992 *Buffy the Vampire Slayer* movie. (*Everett Collection Inc./ Alamy Stock Photo*)

Below: She may be dead, but she's still pretty. Buffy rises from her prophesied death to fight The Master in the season one *Buffy* finale – 'Prophecy Girl'. (*Everett Collection Inc./Alamy*)

'It's about power.' Buffy addresses her troops in the final episode of *Buffy the Vampire Slayer* – 'Chosen'. (*Everett Collection Inc./Alamy*)

First female Secretary of State, Madeleine Albright cosies up with Alexis Bledel on Rory's 21st birthday in the *Gilmore Girls* episode 'Twenty-One is the Loneliest Number'. (*Everett Collection Inc./Alamy*)

Above: Rory takes a leap of faith and starts her journey to rebellion alongside Matt Czuchry as Logan Huntzberger in the iconic *Gilmore Girls* season five episode 'You Jump, I Jump, Jack'. (*Photo 12/Alamy*)

Right: Always dressed to impress – Amy Sherman-Palladino and Daniel Palladino at the premiere for Netflix's *Gilmore Girls: A Year in the Life* in 2016. (*Zuma Press Inc./Alamy*)

Above: Posing for Prom; the cast of *The O.C.* pose for iconic high school dance episode 'The Party Favour'. L-R: Chase Kim, Autumn Reeser, Samaire Armstrong, Justin Chon, Adam Brody, Rachel Bilson, Navi Rawat, Mischa Barton, Benjamin McKenzie. (*Universal Images Group North America LLC/Alamy*)

Left: It's a truth, universally acknowledged, that stars of a teen drama in the 00's had to pose on a bed. The stars of *One Tree Hill* in a promotional shoot from 2003. T-B: James Lafferty, Hilarie Burton, Chad Michael Murray, Bethany Joy Lenz, Sophia Bush. (*Album/Alamy*)

See? The cast of *Gossip Girl*, The CW's most *scandalous* (according to the promos) teen drama, pose on a bed. L-R: Ed Westwick, Chace Crawford, Blake Lively, Jessica Szohr, Penn Badgley, Taylor Momsen, Leighton Meester. (*Landmark Media/Alamy*)

Penn Badgley, Lady Gaga and Leighton Meester pose together on the set of the third season *Gossip Girl* episode 'The Last Days of Disco Stick'. (*Landmark Media/Alamy*)

Above: The Museum of the City of New York, one of the many real New York locations used in *Gossip Girl*, in this case as Constance Billard High School. (*Author's Own*)

Left: Paying tribute - Blake Lively as Marilyn Monroe in *Gossip Girl*'s 100th episode 'G.G.' (*Landmark Media/Alamy*)

Jared Padalecki, Misha Collins and Jensen Ackles pose with Scooby-Doo to greet fans before a screening of 'Scoobynatural' during the 35th annual PaleyFest. (*Associated Press/Alamy*)

Misha Collins, Jensen Ackles, Jared Padalecki and Alex Calvert try not to get emotional at that final Comic-Con panel in 2019. (*Associated Press/Alamy*)

Call her 'Baby' – One of the many screen-used 1967 Chevy Impalas from *Supernatural*, on display at a fan convention in 2016. (*Laurie Goldfarb/Alamy*)

Jeffrey Dean Morgan (who was also in *The O.C.*) guest stars in *Supernatural*'s 300th episode – 'Lebanon'. (*Everett Collection Inc/Alamy*)

Making a fandom - *Glee* stars perform at the 'Gleek Tour' in 2009, ahead of the show's first season. L-R: Kevin McHale, Jenna Ushkowitz, Amber Riley, Dianna Agron, Chris Colfer, Lea Michele, Cory Monteith and Mark Sailing. (*Associated Press/Alamy*)

Promotional still for *Glee*, keeping up the 'Gleek' name. L-R: Mark Sailing, Dianna Agron, Kevin McHale, Jenna Ushkowitz, Heather Morris, Chris Colfer, Naya Rivera, Cory Monteith, Lea Michele, Amber Riley, Jane Lynch, Matthew Morrison. (*Landmark Media/Alamy*)

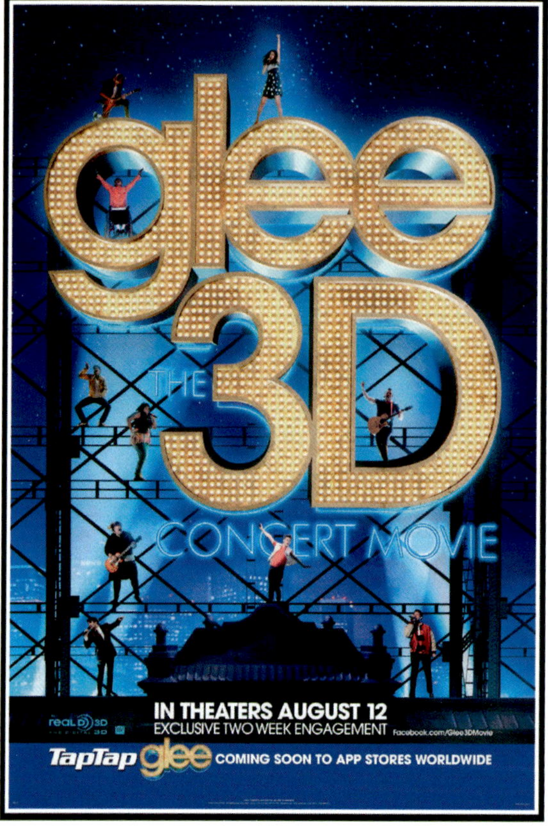

Above: Like mother, like daughter. Idina Menzel guest stars in the *Glee* season one episode 'Theatricality'. (*Everett Collection Inc/Alamy*)

Left: Poster for the *Glee 3D Concert Movie*, released in 2011. (*TCD/Prod.DB/Alamy*)

The cast of *The Vampire Diaries* make an appearance at Comic-Con in 2012. (*Everett Collection Inc/Alamy*)

'The simple intimacy of the near touch' - Damon and Elena dance for the first time and the fandom begins war over the love triangle in *The Vampire Diaries* season one episode 'Miss Mystic Falls'. (*Everett Collection Inc/Alamy*)

Posing on something other than a bed - *The Vampire Diaries* season five promotional poster. L-R: Ian Somerhalder, Paul Wesley, Nina Dobrev, Zach Roerig, Kat Graham, Seven R. McQueen, Candice Accola, Michael Trevino. (*Landmark Media/Alamy*)

Nina Dobrev appears as Elena's vampire doppelganger Katherine during a *Vampire Diaries* season one flashback. (*Cinematic/Alamy*)

The cast and creator of *The Originals* in 2013, speaking on a panel at the CW Television Critics Association Press Tour. L-R: Phoebe Tonkin, Charles Michael Davis, Julie Plec, Joseph Morgan, Claire Holt. (*Associated Press/Alamy*)

Not your average princess – Jennifer Morrison in a 2011 promo image for *Once Upon a Time*. (*Album/Alamy*)

The cast of the short-lived *Once Upon a Time in Wonderland* spin-off take part in a panel at ABC's 2013 Television Critics Association press tour. L-R: Emma Rigby, Naveen Andrews, Michael Socha, Sophie Lowe, Peter Gadiot. (*Associated Press/Alamy*)

A few years later, the creators and cast of the 'rebooted' final season of *Once Upon a Time* speak at the Television Critics Association press tour in 2017. L-R: Adam Horowitz, Edward Kitsis, David H. Goodman, Lana Parilla, Colin O'Donoghue, Andrew J. West, Dania Ramirez and Gabrielle Anwar. (*Associated Press/Alamy*)

Luke Perry and Molly Ringwald revisit their teen star pasts in *Riverdale*'s eleventh episode 'To Riverdale and Back Again.' (*Everett Collection Inc/Alamy*)

The cast and producers of *Riverdale* at the CW Winter 2017 Television Critics Association Press Tour. L-R: Top: Jon Goldwater, Roberto Aguirre-Sacasa, Marisol Nichols, Luke Perry, Mädchen Amick, Greg Berlanti, Sarah Schecter, Front: Ashleigh Murray, Madelaine Petsch, Camila Mendes, KJ Apa, Lili Reinhart, Cole Sprouse, Casey Cott. (*Sipa US/Alamy*)

Roberto Aguirre-Sacasa appears at the *Chilling Adventures of Sabrina* premiere in 2018. (*Associated Press/Alamy*)

The morning after – Jenny Owen Youngs and Kristin Russo of *Buffering the Vampire Slayer*, in shared yummy sushi pyjamas, host a *Buffy* live watch after their 2024 Buffy Prom. (*Author's Own*)

with the 'very special episode' tone – don't do this kids, or you'll get hit by a truck. The *Glee* cast even appeared on *The Oprah Winfrey Show* earlier that month and signed contracts pledging not to text while driving. Both the bullying storyline and the final car accident were attempts at sharing important messages, but while the former was an important reminder to struggling viewers that they weren't alone, the latter was cringy and contrived.

Even the episodes focused on the work of specific artists became an opportunity for 'special episode' storytelling, with varying degrees of effectiveness. In the first season, an episode exploring the work of Madonna became a story about losing virginity (featuring a montage set, obviously, to 'Like a Virgin'). The first of two Lady Gaga-centric episodes managed to continue the homophobic bullying storyline while revealing that Vocal Adrenaline coach Shelby, played by Broadway star Idina Menzel[1], was Rachel's long-lost mother. An episode exploring Fleetwood Mac's 'Rumours' album allowed the relationship between cheerleaders Santana and Brittany (played by Naya Rivera and Heather Morris) to become more than just a side joke, with the help of recurring guest star Gwyneth Paltrow (one of the greatest bits of stunt casting on television). The second of the Lady Gaga episodes incorporated even more bullying storylines, along with the various glee club members confronting their insecurities and Emma Pilsbury's severe OCD finally being a storyline, not just a punchline. For an episode, at least.

That OCD story was never really handled well on the show. It was a terrible depiction of the disorder to begin with, and it was largely mocked rather than dealt with in any meaningful way. It was briefly taken seriously in the third season episode 'Asian F'. In the episode, after

1. Both Idina Menzel and Kristen Chenoweth appeared as fictional characters in *Glee*. The two actresses originated the lead roles in *Wicked*, which also exists in the *Glee* universe. This raises a few existential questions, if you like to think about that kind of thing.

Emma's struggles resurface thanks to a visit from her parents, Will prays beside her while singing Coldplay's 'Fix You'. It was a song choice that highlights the massive difference between *Glee* and the shows that came before. 'Fix You' was only released as a single and became a hit thanks to its inclusion in *The O.C.* By contrast, it took three years of *Glee* being on the air for Coldplay to give the show permission to use one of their songs at all. Being on *The O.C.* was potentially cool, not to mention good business sense. Being on *Glee* just wasn't.[2]

Coldplay weren't the only act to turn the show down. In 2011, Dave Grohl of Foo Fighters fame went on a profanity-filled rant about *Glee* during an interview with the *Hollywood Reported*, complaining not just about the show itself but about Ryan Murphy's attitude to the bands that said no. Grohl claimed 'it's every bands right, you shouldn't have to do fucking *Glee*…And then the guy who created *Glee* is so offended that we're not, like, begging to be on his fucking show.' Feelings about being on *Glee* and what it meant for an artist ran strong, with Grohl claiming that both Slash and Kings of Leon had also turned Ryan Murphy down.

Despite those refusals, *Glee* had a stunning impact on the music industry, although it was a very different kind of taste-making compared to other shows. A 2010 *Rolling Stone* article compared *Glee* to 'MTV in its prime', explaining that '*Glee* has taken its place at the heart of pop culture, where radio and MTV used to rule supreme.' For a time, *Glee* was a dominant force. Nowhere was this more obvious than in the Billboard charts – the most popular metric for tracking music sales in America. Before *Glee*, the Journey song 'Don't Stop Believin' was already iconic – cemented in the public consciousness as the song playing when Tony Soprano (maybe) died

2. Alright, this link's tenuous. But *Buffy* writer Marti Noxon also worked on *Glee*, and *Buffy* writer Jane Espenson also worked on *The O.C*, so we can still get there in two steps.

in the final moments of *The Sopranos*, which aired in 2007. Just two years later, the *Glee* version of the song was top of the charts. In the week following the song's debut on *Glee*, performed by Rachel and Finn, that version entered the Billboard Hot 100 chart at number four; higher than the original Journey song had ever managed.

Fox partnered with Columbia records to distribute the music from *Glee*; a lucrative partnership that saw millions of digital downloads and revenue dollars. This was a time when iTunes and digital downloads weren't exactly new, but hadn't yet overtaken CDs as the dominant method of purchasing music. The dramatic download sales of *Glee* covers and soundtrack albums were some of the earliest warning signs of the approaching industry shift. In October 2010, just as the second season of *Glee* began, the cast of the show overtook The Beatles for most songs placed on the Billboard Hot 100. While musical theatre standards and classic rock still formed much of *Glee*'s soundtracks, it was the modern pop recreations that kept viewers downloading.

The turnaround for music on the show became tighter and tighter as *Glee* went on, with songs showing up on the show while the originals were still in the charts. Often the rights to use these songs would clear just weeks or days before an episode was filmed. In some cases, Adam Anders – the producer behind the majority of *Glee*'s covers – would begin working on and arranging songs before the rights were cleared, taking a gamble that the original artists would say yes. In a 2010 *Reuters* article, *Glee*'s music supervisor Adam Bloom was quoted as saying 'Now that *Glee* is *Glee* [a massive hit popular with the desirable demographic of women aged 18-49], we have the latitude to explore newer songs on their way to becoming hits and the ability to add to the hit-making machinery.'

Glee became a machine itself, churning out much more than just the requisite twenty-odd episodes a season. In May 2010, the first *Glee* concert tour began, running through the summer between the first and second seasons of the show. Fans came out in droves to watch the stars of *Glee* perform the most popular covers from the show live, or mostly live. A second tour took place during the summer of 2011, attended by even bigger numbers of Gleeks delighted to receive souvenir Sue Sylvester Barf Bags. Professional reviews of the live shows were mixed; a *Yahoo* review called the *Glee* tour 'a glorified high school talent show.' Plenty of reviewers noted the discrepancies between the live vocals and the professionally tuned, pre-recorded performances used in the TV show.

This wasn't, however, a show for reviewers. It was something else for fans to spend money on, and they did. In total, the two tours brought in over $45 million dollars in revenue. That figure doesn't include ticket or DVD sales for *Glee: The 3D Concert Movie*, a film based on the second tour that received a limited theatrical release. Alongside the DVD of the film of the tour based on the show, there was also a concert movie soundtrack album that debuted at fifteen on the Billboard 200 album chart. *Glee* was more than just a show, it was an industry.

Considering *Glee* began at a time when reality television, especially musical talent shows, was dominant on prime time, it's not surprising that the show eventually got its own reality spin-off. *The Glee Project* premiered on the Oxygen network (a cable network owned by NBC) in June 2011, during the gap between the second and third seasons of the show. Effectively, the show was a televised audition process, with a seven-episode arc on *Glee* as the prize at the end. In the first series, Samuel Larsen and Damian McGinty Jr. both won those coveted seven episodes. Both actors remained on the show beyond those seven episodes after turning up in *Glee*'s third season as Joe Hart and Rory Flanagan, before being not so much written off as left to fade away. *Glee* was not a show that concerned itself with clear continuity. Often, non-main characters would simply disappear, occasionally acknowledged in fourth-wall breaking lines of dialogue.

The two runners-up from the first season of *The Glee Project* won two-episode arcs on *Glee*. Alex Newell appeared late in the third season as transgender character Wade Adams, and their performance both as Wade and as Wade's alter ego Unique was such a hit, with the character proving so compelling to write for, that they eventually became a regular cast member. Lindsay Pearce appeared in just her two allotted episodes, and went on to a successful Broadway career that included starring as Elphaba in *Wicked*. In 2022, Pearce spoke about her time on *The Glee Project* to *Business Insider* as part of a larger oral history of the show. She claimed that the show was an environment of abuse, and said that her appearance on the show was heavily edited to make her seem like a monster. This was part of the darker side of the *Glee* machinery. It's a well-known fact that reality television can often be edited to create storylines, but the idea of a nineteen-year-old girl's self-esteem being ripped apart by the public for the sake of entertainment is hard to reconcile with the bright, surreal comedy of *Glee*.

The Glee Project was made in chaotic conditions, having been thrown together with very little planning. The Oxygen network had scored the show thanks to a deal that also allowed them to air reruns of *Glee*; an unprecedented arrangement considering Oxygen belonged to one of Fox's rivals. The deal was done so quickly, however, that the actual details and structure of the show were haphazard, to say the least. With a small budget and short time frame, most of the first season of the show was shot at an empty summer camp, with contestants sleeping in cabins in the words. They had roofless outhouses, mosquitoes everywhere and no source of entertainment beyond MP3 players full of songs to practice. In that *Business Insider* oral history, Cameron Mitchell – a first season contestant who eventually quit the show – said that 'it felt like half we were being detained against our will, and half "This is TV".' Over both the first and second seasons, contestants were encouraged to reveal deep personal details, including some clarifications about their gender identity and sexual orientation that they might not have been ready to share, in the hopes of making compelling television.

In the first season of *The Glee Project*, Lindsay Pearce was told to kiss Cameron Mitchell while recording a music video. Mitchell hadn't given his consent prior to shooting, which Pearce wasn't aware of. The producers noticed that this was an issue for Mitchell, and instead of his boundaries being respected, he was pushed in a later episode to kiss another contestant. Realising that the show didn't have his best interests at heart, he opted to quit the show. The final edit attributed his decision to 'religious values'. While *The Glee Project* became a hit, and incredibly popular on Tumblr (fanfiction about the contestants on the show was huge in 2012 and 2013, as it was about the characters on *Glee*; it's almost as if the show didn't work to distinguish between real human beings and fictional characters), the downside to fandom on social media reared its ugly head. Lindsay Pearce bore the brunt of online abuse; she was attacked repeatedly online for being a sexual predator after the incident with Cameron Mitchell, despite the fault lying with the show's producers.

The second, and final, season of *The Glee Project* aired in the summer of 2012 and had just one winner – Blake Jenner, who started on *Glee* during the fourth season during what was definitely the beginning of the show's awkward college years.[3] The end of *Glee*'s third season saw at least half of the show's leads graduating high school, with Rachel sent off to New York (and Kurt following close behind). That awkward fourth season split its time between New York and Lima, with a new crop of New Directions filling out the high school cast. The show began to be less focused on getting out, and looked more at the idea of the grass not always being greener. The new characters' motivations were murkier than the original cast, and the result was a show that looked like it had lost its way.

---

3. The second season runner-up Ali Stroker did appear in a single episode of *Glee*'s fourth season in a non-singing role, and has since gone on to become one of the many *Glee* alumni to win a Tony award.

Alongside Jenner – who played Ryder Lynn, a dyslexic footballer – Melissa Benoist joined the cast as new girl Marley.[4] Alongside Jenner and Benoist, Jacob Artist joined the cast as Jake Puckerman, Puck's until now unheard-of little brother. This wasn't presented as any kind of soapy plot twist, but was just something the audience happened to be unaware of. The character was simply there to make up for the fact that Puck had left high school. Becky Tobin joined the cast as Kitty Wilde – a cheerleader proud to be a nastier version of Quinn Fabray. The show wasn't subtle about the need for the new characters to be mirror images of those that had moved on to colleges, new story arcs or guest stardom – the first episode of the fourth season was titled 'The New Rachel'.

The fourth season of *Glee* saw a downturn in the show's critical success and viewing figures. Slowly, *Glee* stopped being a money-making machine. Those hard storylines were still there, but they were being drowned in meaningless fluff. Rachel's college boyfriend resorting to sex work to pay his way through university could have been an interesting look at the financial challenges forced on American college students; instead, it was just a way to shoehorn in the latest Marina & the Diamonds hit. The divide between New York and Ohio made the show disjointed, and forced in storylines in which every character seemed to be able to travel between the two places on a whim (which, considering the quickest method would have been by plane, must have been terrible for the fictional environment). There were some big-name additions to the New York side of the cast which sparked brief interest in the show; Sarah Jessica Parker appeared as

---

4. Jenner and Benoist began a relationship, eventually got married, and divorced in 2016. Later, in 2019, Benoist came forward to speak on her experiences of domestic violence during the marriage, and in 2020 Jenner admitted to abusive behaviour throughout their relationship. It's an upsetting story, one of many that mars *Glee*'s legacy, although the show itself did nothing more than bring those two people together.

Isabelle Wright, a character not a million miles away from Carrie Bradshaw – the role that made her famous. Kate Hudson appeared as Cassie July – a harsh dance teacher who eventually turned out to have a heart of gold in a plot twist so predictable it might as well have been written on the wall of the NYADA dance studio that Rachel suffered in. Later, former Disney star Demi Lovato joined the cast as a love interest for Santana, and things came full circle when Adam Lambert – who originally came to fame as a runner-up on the eighth season of *American Idol*, the show that launched *Glee* – joined the show as Elliot 'Starchild' Gilbert.

It was towards the end of the fourth season, and the subsequent opening episodes of the fifth, that *Glee* changed direction in a way no one could have predicted. Finn, played by Cory Monteith, spent most of that fourth season in an aimless character arc, intermittently assisting the glee club while he worked out what he wanted for his future, only finding purpose in the season's later episodes. Finn had to be written out of the last two episodes of the season, as Monteith needed to enter a rehabilitation programme for his ongoing addiction issues. In July 2013, just a few weeks before filming was due to begin on the show's fifth season, Cory Monteith was found dead in his Vancouver hotel room. He was just thirty-one years old.

Production on the fifth season was halted. The creators of the show even considered ending *Glee* entirely. Ryan Murphy and the rest of the team were sincere in their efforts to make sure the whole cast were able to take the time they needed to process things. Ultimately it was Lea Michele – who had been in a relationship with Cory Monteith for some time before his death – who was given the responsibility of deciding if, when and how the show would come back. The opening two episodes of the fifth season were already written – the two-part Beatles tribute had in fact been in the works for a few years. Those episodes went ahead as planned, with Finn written out. The third episode of the season was written as a tribute to Cory Monteith. Those first three episodes of the fifth season aired in September 2012 before the show went on hiatus as the writers worked out how to continue without one of *Glee*'s most important leading men.

That third season episode – 'The Quarterback' – was a genuine outpouring of grief from the stars of the show. Finn died off-screen, and the show never gave a reason for his passing; instead, Kurt had a few lines of dialogue about the 'how' not being important. The episode was set a few weeks after Finn's funeral, and showed various members of the glee club past and present memorialising Finn and, in the process, Cory Monteith in the choir room that served as the beating heart of the show.

It was a touching episode, a stunning memorial and a tribute to a character, and actor, who had been at the centre of the show from its beginning. Ryan Murphy told the *Hollywood Reporter* that almost everything in the episode was 'from the first take of every performance because the actors and the crew had a really hard time shooting it.' Lea Michele's tear-filled performance of Adele's 'Make You Feel My Love' makes for a sad and sweet moment in the episode, and Romy Rosemont's performance as Finn's mother Carol was deservedly celebrated by critics as a particularly heartbreaking depiction of parental grief.

One of the hardest performances from the episode to watch is, in retrospect, Naya Rivera as Santana singing The Band Perry's 'If I Die Young'. With no context other than the show it's one of the toughest moments of the episode as Santana breaks down, unable to finish the song, and runs away from the comfort of her peers. Sadly, in July 2020, Rivera died due to a boating accident, at the age of thirty-three. It was a tragedy under any circumstances, and simply unlucky that two talented performers who happened to star in the same show passed away before their time, but it's particularly hard to listen to Rivera sing about leaving too early considering she could have gone on to do so much more.

After the loss of Cory Monteith, it was clear that *Glee* was beginning to wind down. The high school structure of the show, even with the New York storylines, didn't have longevity built in. Very few shows at the time were built to last, as very few shows at the time got to last. The fifth season took place largely in Ohio for the first half. At the mid-way point another high school graduation took place; the New Directions were disbanded and as many characters as conceivably possible were sent to find new storylines in New York. Chord Overstreet's Sam suddenly decided to become a model, Mercedes went to record an album, and many of the rest were just intermittently there. *Glee* itself managed to make it out of Ohio, but the show wasn't better off for it.

One of those New York storylines eventually came full circle in real life. The show's fifth season had Rachel make her Broadway debut as Fanny Brice in a revival of the Barbara Streisand classic *Funny Girl*. It was a musical near and dear to the character, who delivered multiple excellent performances of the show's act one closer 'Don't Rain on My Parade' during *Glee*'s run. It was also a show close to Lea Michele's heart. Beanie Feldstein originally took the lead role when *Funny Girl* was revived on Broadway in 2022, but after a few months Lea Michele replaced her in a run that at least lasted longer than Rachel's – having a character achieve their dream before the end of the show leads to some poor writing choices.

Before Lea Michele could get back to Broadway, however, *Glee* had to end. In October 2013, after the hiatus following Cory Monteith's passing, Ryan Murphy announced that the sixth season of *Glee* would be the show's last. The final season was a short one, just fourteen episodes which ran from January to March 2015. It was fairly clear that *Glee*'s shelf life had been shortened by the unexpected loss, and the final season looked to be nothing more than a slow limp across the finish line. It was saved, in part, by a handful of new cast members and a return to Ohio. The new New Directions included Noah Guthrie as Roderick, a shy kid with a fantastic voice; Marshall Williams as Spencer, a footballer and 'postmodern gay' who could have had the potential to be an interesting character that didn't play to stereotypes if not for periodic reminders in the script that the character wasn't playing to stereotypes; and Samantha Marie Ware as Jane, a character who starts out attending Dalton Academy and attempting to become the first female Warbler.

The critical response to the later seasons of *Glee* had been lacklustre, and the short final season didn't have much time to perk things up, but the two-part finale was a brighter spot in a couple of difficult years of television. It wasn't necessarily better, but it was a good enough ending for the show. The first part of the finale was a flashback, showing the pilot episode from the perspective of other characters, while the second episode was less a coherent storyline and more a series of flash forwards – mostly to the year 2020. Luckily, *Glee* didn't predict the Covid-19 pandemic five years early and spend the finale with various characters experiencing lockdown-induced mania. Instead, it saw Rachel winning a Tony award and Sue Sylvester becoming the American Vice President. It was, at least, as coherent as the rest of the show.

Brandon Nowalk's review of the finale for the *AV Club* summed the episode up best, saying 'it plays like bad fan fic.' The final moments of the episode were a touching tribute to Cory Monteith, as Sue rededicated the high school auditorium to Finn, before cast members past and present in the bright red tones that became part of *Glee*'s gloriously technicolour palette turn up for a final, joyful song (a cover of 'I Lived' by OneRepublic). Absent from the gathering was Melissa Benoist, who was busy shooting *Supergirl* for The CW. Lauren Hoffman, reviewing the episode for *Vulture*, called it 'a truly lovely send-off.'

Ultimately, *Glee*'s ending was good enough not to tarnish the rest of the show's legacy. It was a hit when it began for good reason, and over the time the show developed an almost cult status for being, to put it simply, absolutely batshit (as all the best teen dramas are). Understandably, however, the show reads differently when revisited through a modern lens, and it's worth casting a critical eye over storylines that were groundbreaking at the time but handled poorly. The problem with a show doing a good job with, for example, queer representation, is that the poorer parts of that representation (in *Glee*'s case the casual use of the word 'tranny', having a cis woman play a trans man, the overt stereotyping of gay men) are all the more obvious. 'It was a different time' isn't a great excuse, but it's worth thinking about just how different times were when the show aired. A particular quote from a 2013 *New York Times* article sums up just how quietly *Glee* was putting its head above the parapet: '*Glee* is famous for addressing all kinds of issues related to tolerance; there is even a transgender character.' It's a sentence that implies, with a tone of surprise, that even more boxes have been ticked than usual.

Glee was no stranger to controversy, and that didn't go away when the show ended. Throughout *Glee*'s run there were dramas; it was accused of being anti-Christian, Lea Michele and Dianna Agron were heavily criticised for taking part in a 'racy' cover shoot for *GQ Magazine*, and fractured relationships and feuds between the cast members were widely reported on in the tabloid press. Ryan Murphy later admitted in an interview with the *Hollywood Reporter* that he had misgivings about his role in the lives of the cast members, saying that 'I was there with them all day long, and then we'd finish work and we'd go out and have fun all night, and I guess in a weird, twisted way I was trying to relive the childhood I never had.' He was another showrunner in the vein of Josh Schwartz, who became too close to his charges to be able to provide them with the best working environment.

In 2020, Samantha Marie Ware responded to Lea Michele tweeting about the 'Black Lives Matter' movement by calling her out for microaggressions on set, claiming that Michele made her first television gig 'a living hell'. Multiple people came forward to share stories of Michele's problematic conduct on set, leading to Michele losing an endorsement deal with HelloFresh. This wasn't a long-term cancellation, but a reveal that there had been issues on the *Glee* set that hadn't been discussed in the open.

Despite the controversies, the drama and the genuine problems with the show, *Glee* has remained...*remembered.* It's not a show with a current, active fandom as such, but it was so new, so different and so oddly, wonderfully terrible that the show has stayed with people. Whether it's remembered fondly or not is another matter.

Matthew Gilbert at the *Boston Globe* caught the problem with *Glee* early on. Writing about the second season he said that '*Glee* is now a phenomenon more than a TV high school story, and I'm sorry for that. It has become a powerful, promotional machine, long on hype and short on the human feeling – the glee – that once made it so addictive.' This only became truer as the show went on. The bane and boon of *Glee* was the big network that played home to the show. It wasn't just a show on Fox, it was a show on a Fox network that had unprecedented viewing figures thanks to the talent show boom and a deal to air after the Superbowl.[5] *Glee* benefited from its big network, but it also faced a lot more scrutiny, and far more network involvement than the shows on The CW quietly gathering hordes of fans on Tumblr.

Glee's fandom was manufactured from the beginning with the 'Gleek' tour. The music on the show was pre-recorded, auto-tuned and made to sell. The download sales created by the show were sales of the show's (sometimes, admittedly, excellent) cover versions, not original music being discovered by new listeners. Almost everything about the show fell deep into the uncanny valley; it was all a little too shiny, a little too bright, a little off. Where shows like *Supernatural* or *Buffy* have fandoms that have continued on way past the end of the shows themselves, *Glee* had a fandom bought and paid for, who in

5. The second season episode 'The Sue Sylvester Shuffle', which aired after the Superbowl in 2011, is one of the most expensive post-Superbowl episodes of television ever produced, coming in at around $3 million. It was watched by 26.8 million people, making it the highest rated scripted TV episode in three years.

return spent their money on merch and music and concert tickets in huge numbers. The fandom was massive compared to those smaller CW shows, but much shorter-lived.

The controversy surrounding the show is a contributing factor to its odd legacy. Newer viewers learning the history surrounding the show joke that it's cursed, especially considering three of its stars are no longer alive.[6] TikTok is full of reactions from people incredulous at everything about the show after watching it for the first time. Kevin McHale and Jenna Ushkowitz have recently released a *Glee* recap podcast, *So That's What You Really Missed*; a warts-and-all breakdown of the show that doesn't shy away from what really happened on set.

Glee was a bright, sunny, occasionally dark and heart-wrenching show. Its legacy is understandably mixed. The story of *Glee* is not one of a beloved show or a long-lasting fandom. It's a messy mixture of good and bad, groundbreaking ideas and terrible attempts. It was a show about leaving a small town behind that lost its way. Perhaps being on a big, invested network isn't the best way to make television that stays beloved. Perhaps, some shows shouldn't even last six seasons. Possibly, *Glee* is best forgotten. What's clear, however, is that it never will be.

6. As well as Cory Monteith and Naya Rivera, Mark Sailing (who played Puck) died by suicide in 2019 after pleading guilty to possession of child pornography.

Chapter 7

The Vampire Diaries

Welcome to Mystic Falls

Mystic Falls is a fictional small town in Virginia. It's home to roughly 7000 residents, depending on the week's body count on *The Vampire Diaries*. Those residents include werewolves, witches, women who exist purely to get into a romantic relationship with an alcoholic history teacher before being brutally murdered and, of course, vampires. There's a high school, a bar with an incredibly lax policy when it comes to checking ID's, a sheriff's department that's all too aware of the supernatural and a rich history centred on the town's five founding families. Well, technically six. Or seven. The phrase 'it's complicated' will be a common refrain in this chapter.

The Vampire Diaries was a show built on that small town setting above all else. Adapted by Kevin Williamson and Julie Plec from a series of popular vampire novels by L. J. Smith, this was a teen show that cared very little for high school and coming-of-age narratives. *The Vampire Diaries* was a show about a dark little town. Williamson, speaking at the Television Critics Association summer press tour in 2009, talked about how much he loved the focus on the town in L. J. Smith's books: this evil, this darkness, that lies underneath the town and how this vampire comes to stir it all up. We're diving right in.'

After diving in, and not taking long at all to swim away from the source material's story, *The Vampire Diaries* didn't come up for air for eight years, becoming one of the signature hits of The CW. The show began at a time when vampires were the in-thing, and deftly outlasted the trend by refusing to let its mythology grow stale. *The Vampire*

Diaries burned through plot at an outlandish pace, never letting up, and attracted a crowd of adoring fans. The extended universe – the show had two spin-offs – kept telling stories about Mystic Falls and the characters that got their start there for fourteen years. No show matched *Supernatural* for longest-running on The CW, but the world of *The Vampire Diaries* came the closest.

In 2009, when the show began, The CW was still finding its identity after the WB/UPN merger. The network had eliminated its comedy department in the wake of the WGA strike in 2007, and with the contract to air WWE wrestling coming to an end, The CW had nothing but scripted dramas and reality television. The CW had put all of its eggs into one demographical basket, making the most out of *America's Next Top Model* and *90210* (a reboot/sequel of the original *Beverly Hills*), as well as leftovers from The WB like *One Tree Hill*, *Supernatural* and *Smallville*. The glossy soap-opera worlds of *Gossip Girl* and *Melrose Place* (another reboot/sequel in Aaron Spelling's cinematic universe) were a draw for viewers, but overall, the network was struggling, consistently landing bottom in the ratings.

Along came *The Vampire Diaries*. On the one hand, the show was something new and different; it was driven by female characters who were much more relatable than their aspirational soap opera counterparts, set in the accessible world of small town American, and it was sexy but not overly smutty. For a show focused on the supernatural, parts of it were surprisingly realistic. On the other hand, *The Vampire Diaries* was old-hat; the show invoked one of The WB's foundational hits – *Buffy* – and one of the most popular properties around. These were the days of peak *Twilight*, the vampire romance novels-turned-movies that had become a deep obsession of teenagers everywhere.

Kevin Williamson wasn't interested at first in developing a series based on L. J. Smith's books – he didn't want to make another *Twilight*. Ignoring his unwillingness, he was the perfect person for the job. Between *Scream* and *Dawson's Creek* – his first two major creations –

Williamson had the ideal background of both horror and teen dramas. He was the perfect man for the job. Williamson had more concerns than just *Twilight* comparisons, however. It was getting harder to grab audiences in this new age of television. In 2007 Williamson had created *Hidden Palms* – a soapy teen melodrama – for The CW, and the show had performed incredibly poorly. He had expressed worries about finding an audience before the show even began during a *New York Times* interview in which he cited the recently-ended *The O.C.* as 'a show that didn't even make it to a hundred episodes, and it should have.' *Hidden Palms* didn't even make it to ten.

It was Julie Plec that successfully got Williamson on board *The Vampire Diaries*. The pair had known each other a long time; Plec was director Wes Craven's assistant on the first *Scream* movie and an executive on the second. She also helped out on *Dawson's Creek*; although Plec was only credited on a single episode of the show, Williamson admitted in a 2010 *Deadline* interview that she was more heavily involved than that single credit implied. Plec acknowledged that she learned to write for television thanks to Williamson, and he insisted on giving her proper credit for co-writing multiple episodes of *Dawson's* during a busy time in his life. Plec was the one to insist that Williamson actually give the *Vampire Diaries* books a try, in the process showing him that the small-town horror in the story was much more compelling than the *Twilight* of it all.

The books themselves far predated the *Twilight* phenomenon. The first books in L.J. Smith's series came out in 1991 and 1992. The rights to her books belonged to Alloy entertainment – the same company responsible for bringing *Gossip Girl*, among others, to the screen. It was Leslie Morgenstein – Alloy's Chief Executive – who revived the books during the height of *Twilight* mania. When vampires became trendy, Morgenstein suggested that Harper-Collins should re-release the books with new covers. L.J. Smith subsequently returned to write a few new books set in the *Vampire Diaries* universe – the *Return* trilogy.[1] Suddenly, *The Vampire Diaries* had a whole new audience, and they were more than ready to sit down in front of the television.

The impact that Stephenie Meyer's *Twilight* books, and the movie adaptations, had on the entertainment industry shouldn't be underestimated. The first book was an immediate hit when it was released in 2005. When the third book in the four-book series – *Eclipse* – came out, those first three books had spent a combined 143 weeks on the *New York Times* bestseller list. *Twilight* was everywhere, and the fans were intense, divided up sharply into 'Team Edward' or 'Team Jacob' – the male protagonists that, along with Bella, formed the love triangle that dominated the books. When the first *Twilight* film came out in 2008, it grossed $37.5 million at the box office on its opening day alone. The second film, *New Moon*, broke records for cinema ticket pre-sales. *Twilight* was a phenomenon, one that couldn't be recreated.

Of course, vampires have always been compelling on both the big and small screen. Bram Stoker's novel *Dracula* has inspired countless adaptations, cult-classic movie *The Lost Boys* from 1987 gave vampires cool hair and great taste in music, 1998's *Blade* starring Wesley Snipes wasn't just a vampire movie but one of Marvel Comics' first successful forays onto the big screen, *Interview with the Vampire* – the film adaptation of Anne Rice's book starring Tom Cruise and Brad Pitt – was a hit in 1994 and *Buffy* broke amazing ground later that same decade. With *Twilight*, however, the phenomenon was concentrated into just one set of books and movies – and the popularity came with immediate backlash. Even *Buffy* fans sneered at the sparkling vampire heroes of Meyer's novels. The movies had far too much brooding from Robert Pattinson and Kristen Stewart, and nowhere near sharp enough fangs.

1. Sadly, L.J. Smith's contract meant that she didn't hold any rights to the world she had created. She was fired after the release of the final book in the *Return* trilogy and the rest of the *Vampire Diaries* books were ghostwritten.

Then, in 2008, just as the last *Twilight* book and first movie in the franchise was coming out, *True Blood* began on HBO. The series was based on the *Southern Vampire Mystery* books by Charlaine Harris, the first of which came out in 2001. *True Blood* was, in many ways, the anti-*Twilight*. It was adult, it was full of blood and sex and drugs and gore; it gave the world the phrase 'fangbanger' and helped launch Alexander Skarsgård's career. It broadened the current vampire trend, and proved there was room for more in vampire stories than just angsty teen romance. Alan Ball, who created *True Blood*, told *Rolling Stone* in an interview (published in an issue with the three leads of the show – Skarsgård, Stephen Moyer and Anna Paquin – naked and splattered with blood on the cover) that 'to me, vampires are sex. I don't get a vampire story about abstinence.'

Vampires have long been used in fiction as a metaphor for repressed desires. *Buffy* went a step further, using all sorts of horror to represent the hell of high school. *Twilight* and *True Blood* sat at opposite ends of the popular vampire spectrum; the first was a thinly-veiled abstinence metaphor, while the other was as filthy as possible in every sense of the word.

The Vampire Diaries managed to land firmly in the middle of that spectrum. The students (and supernatural creatures posing as students) that made up the core cast didn't shy away from alcohol, sex or the gorier side of life. The sex, however, was largely off screen. Elena, the main character, clearly frowned upon her younger brother Jeremy's drug use. Things were just clean enough for the show to be a hit on The CW as the network was trying to drive up its teen and young adult audiences.

The show came together quickly after Kevin Williamson came on board. The first script was handed in to Warner Brothers in January 2009 and *The Vampire Diaries* was ordered to pilot within a week. When the pilot was shown, The CW picked up the show within a week. Clearly, the network had found what it thought it needed to boost floundering ratings. Of all the shows debuting on The CW in the 2009/2010 season,

The Vampire Diaries was the one most clearly poised to succeed. It wasn't going to be a trendsetting show – that work had already been done. Instead, mass appeal was built into the show's DNA.

Casting took place over just a few months. Canadian actress Nina Dobrev left her role on *Degrassi: The Next Generation* to play Elena Gilbert, as well as Katherine Pierce and a few others – thanks to the concept of doppelgangers on the show, Dobrev would go on to play four (arguably five) different characters during her six years on the show. Dobrev was often playing more than one of these characters in the same scene, and the work she put in during those six years to make these characters unique and different was an incredible feat.

Paul Wesley was cast as Stefan Salvatore, the brooding romantic hero who had more than the tiniest bit in common with *Buffy*'s Angel. A few years before, Wesley had appeared in an early episode of *The O.C.* and when Melinda Clarke appeared on the *Vampire Diaries* for a handful of season one episodes, she was glad to see a friendly face in the cast.[2] Michael Trevino joined the cast as Tyler Lockwood, high school jock and eventual werewolf, and Zach Roerig was cast as Matt – Elena's ex-boyfriend, Melinda Clarke's son and the most consistently human character on the show. Wesley, Trevino and Roerig all, however, auditioned for another character first: Damon Salvatore, Stefan's bad-boy older brother.

Ian Somerhalder was already well-known before auditioning for Damon thanks to his appearance in the first season of ABC's *Lost*. Kevin Williamson loved him for the part of the evil older brother described in a *New York Times* review of the *Vampire Diaries* pilot as someone 'who looks like the kind of person who would steal mittens from an eight-year-old.' The character was there to be the third point in two love triangles – one with Stefan and Elena, and one with Stefan and Katherine – their long-lost vampire lover who happened to be the

2. There you go, two links.

spitting image of Elena. Damon was the juiciest role on the show; the bad boy with a heart of gold buried very deep who, continuing the *Buffy* comparison, had more than a whiff of Spike to him (minus the British accent).

Rounding out the cast were Steve R. McQueen as Jeremy, Elena's stoner brother; Candice Accola (who had previously appeared in an episode of *Supernatural*) as Caroline, Elena's best frenemy whose character rapidly became something far more interesting than the standard high school mean girl; and Kat Graham as Bonnie, Elena's best friend and fledgeling witch.[3]

There's a commonly misunderstood story about a legal incident involving a few of the women newly cast on the show, early in the days of *The Vampire Diaries* filming in Georgia. It's generally understood that Nina Dobrev, Candice Accola, Sara Canning (who played Aunt Jenna – Elena and Jeremy's guardian and the first of many dead ex-girlfriends for history teacher Alaric) and Kayla Ewell (who played Vicky – Matt's sister and a love interest for both Jeremy and Tyler) were arrested for flashing on a bridge over the interstate. The story is far less salacious than it seems. The actresses were doing an impromptu (fully-clothed) photoshoot, and drivers had called the police to complain about camera flashes on the bridge. The fact that the actress's tops were on the whole time didn't make it into press coverage of the incident. That coverage was at its most rampant just as the show was about to debut on The CW. As marketing campaigns go, releasing genuine mugshots of the cast to the press was a unique one.

Whether thanks to the misunderstood flashing incident, the numerous trailers and billboards of the promotional blood drives held in the ramp up to the show debuting, *The Vampire Diaries* was an immediate hit when the pilot aired on 10 September 2009. The episode was watched by 4.8 million people at 8pm that Thursday

3. Graham also previously appeared in an episode of *The O.C.*

evening (the episode aired in the hour before the fifth season premiere of *Supernatural*). It was the largest audience ever for a premiere of a new series on The CW. Thursdays had remained a contentious evening for networks. NBC's sitcom popularity had dwindled but *Survivor* on CBS was still going strong. Now, with *The Vampire Diaries*, The CW was putting up a fight for the first time.

The critical response to the show was solid, but there was a wealth of *Twilight* comparisons to wade through. The *New York Times* pointed to the success of *Twilight* as the gateway for shows like *The Vampire Diaries* to make it to screen, but called the show 'slickly produced.' An *Entertainment Weekly* review of the pilot celebrated Kevin Williamson's knack for dialogue and pop culture references, saying that his take on L. J. Smith's books 'dares to have the kind of flip poor taste that high schoolers such as these characters would engage in.' By the end of 2009, the *New York Post* had released a listicle headlined '5 Reasons *Vampire Diaries* is Better Than Twilight' and multiple outlets were lauding November's mid-season finale and its cliffhanger car crash. *TV Fanatic* called the episode 'an outstanding instalment' and *The Vampire Diaries* 'the best new show on television.' The show remained on top of The CW's ratings for its entire first season, and for much of its eight-year run. An *IGN* review of the season finale – 'Founders Day', which finally saw the introduction of Katherine Piece in something other than flashbacks – called the show 'one of the better guilty pleasures on television' and rated the episode nine out of ten.

How, exactly, did a show that – on the surface – lacked any kind of originality, become one of The CW's cornerstones? *The Vampire Diaries* was a stew of things that had all been done before. The show was, by all appearances, just a mash-up of *Buffy* and *Dawson's Creek* (as multiple reviewers pointed out) and *True Blood* had gone much further in the race to be the anti-*Twilight*. The short answer is that the show was genuinely very good. It was well-written, pacy, and subverted just about all of the tropes established by the shows that came before to become a worthwhile watch in its own right.

On top of that, everything about the show managed to land just on the right side of relatability; no mean feat considering the supernatural side to the story. The metaphors weren't laid on as heavily as in the high school seasons of *Buffy*, but the idea of vampires representing various kinds of lust, of the inherent risks of getting carried away (whether it be with booze or blood or something else) worked for the audience that The CW wanted to cultivate. Where the language in *Dawson's Creek* had often been overtly ridiculous, even the centuries-old creatures in *The Vampire Diaries* were relatably chatty, with only the oldest of the old vampires using particularly dramatic language. All of this was done to a soundtrack that wasn't quite as trendsetting as some shows but was a hit with the viewers, with a sense of fashion that felt appropriate for teenagers in a small Virginia town, and with a horror aesthetic laid over everything by creators who knew exactly what they were doing.

That soundtrack was, as with pretty much every show in this book, an essential part of the success of *The Vampire Diaries*. The show wasn't launching new artists every week but the music was still influential, mixing still-emerging artists and well-established musicians. The pilot episode alone featured Placebo (covering Kate Bush), Bat for Lashes, one of the latest songs from The Raconteurs and Katy Perry. The show wasn't afraid to use music that might not have been on the target audience's iPods, either because it was too new or too retro. Psycho Killer by The Talking Heads underwrote a flashback to 1970's New York, Sara Bareilles appeared on the soundtrack multiple times – her song 'Gravity' scored Elena and Stefan's first kiss – and 'A Drop in the Ocean' by Ron Pope brought tears to viewers eyes in the closing moments of the third season's first episode.

The music supervisor on *The Vampire Diaries* was Chris Mollere, who was also working on *Pretty Little Liars* at the time. *Liars* was another book-turned-show from Alloy entertainment – a hit teen drama on the Freeform cable network. A mystery minus the supernatural, *Liars* was otherwise a twin to *The Vampire Diaries* when it came to aesthetics, fashion, off-the-wall storylines and music. Mollere took inspiration from *The O.C.*[4] He told *Rolling Stone* in a 2013 interview that '*The O.C.* was the show that changed the format on television…a placement on that show took bands to another level.' Mollere wanted to be doing the same thing. He featured Florence and the Machine long before they'd broken America or become stadium-fillers, featuring the song 'Never Let Me Go' in a memorable scene from the third season, timing the crescendo of the chorus with Damon and Elena's first kiss.

That kiss between Elena and her vampire boyfriend's older brother sums up so much of what made *The Vampire Diaries* a hit in its earlier seasons. This was a show that was never short on story. Love triangles, werewolves, vampire-werewolf hybrids, vampire-witch hybrids, eventually a vampire-werewolf-witch tribrid, doppelgangers, ghosts, witch covens galore; *The Vampire Diaries* wasn't afraid to expand its mythology, sometimes rapidly in the space of a single episode. It burned through story after story at an incredible pace.

Some of this wasn't entirely by choice on the part of the writers, but down to how television was being made at the time. In that 2010 *Deadline* interview, Julie Plec took the opportunity to rant about the requirements of a six-act structure on network television. That structure was a business decision – it was all about how many advert breaks could conceivably fit into a single hour time slot, reducing the run times of the episodes themselves in the process. As Plec put it, shows would 'live and die by those moments at the end, right before the commercial break, when something happens and everyone gasps.' With a run-time of just forty or so minutes, and the need for seven of those 'Wow' moments per episode including the pre-credits scene, burning through plot became the only way to do it. Plec asked, rhetorically, in the interview, 'When everything has to be leading to

4. Where else?

the “Wow” every five and a half or six minutes, how do you actually let a story unfold naturally from a human place, an emotional place, and give it air and room to breathe?’ Plec and Williamson both blamed that network push towards extra ad breaks for viewers looking at alternative ways to watch TV, eschewing live network television for cable and online viewing platforms.

The Vampire Diaries managed to keep burning without running out of steam. It came as no surprise when werewolves were added to the mythology – they always seem to run alongside vampires – and thanks to Bonnie Bennet witches had been part of the show from the beginning. The second and third seasons brought in the Original vampire family and some fantastic casting (including Joseph Morgan, Rebecca Holt and Daniel Gillies), eventually leading to the show’s first spin-off. A potential cure for vampirism dominated at least half a season of the show, causing multiple deaths (much like in *Supernatural,* deaths in *The Vampire Diaries* were commonplace and rarely permanent) and introducing pre-vampire immortal doppelgangers[5]. By the time high school graduation was approaching at the end of the fourth season, hordes of murderous supernatural ghosts were descending on Mystic Falls.

Amongst all of this was the ‘Event/Monster of the Week’ structure that had worked so well for so many shows. *Buffy* and *Supernatural* were definitely more monster of the week, but *The Vampire Diaries* took after shows like *Gossip Girl* and *The O.C.* with a weekly event that manoeuvred all of the characters into one place – whether it be the local ‘Miss Mystic Falls’ pageant that included the iconic first dance between Damon and Elena, or the high school ‘decade dances’ that put the characters into an array of period costumes.

There was a problematic element to all of this. The history of Mystic Falls was deeply tied to the American Civil War. It was a small

5. It’s complicated.

town in the south. One of the wealthier (secretly werewolf) families had what were clearly old slave cells on their land. While plenty of the 'events of the week' were centred around historical reenactments in the town, the show rarely spent time grappling with this aspect of small-town American history, even via supernatural allegory. Still, the long history of the town allowed for almost any episode to be an event episode, usually with the word 'founders' shoehorned in as much as possible. This kind of weekly structure had been thoroughly established by many of the show's predecessors, and despite the question of how everyone in town afforded such extensive costume wardrobes, it worked just as well for *The Vampire Diaries* as it did on *Gossip Girl*.

It was this constant racing plot and the necessary mythological expansion that helped *the Vampire Diaries* stand out from its vampiric counterparts. The show fit perfectly into teen drama tropes, but just as with *Buffy*, the supernatural elements gave it an edge over shows that focused more on the tribulations of high school. It was a unique show in a broader cultural landscape dominated by teen books being adapted for screen.

Twilight wasn't the first big publishing phenomenon turned box office success, of course. Less than a decade before, the *Harry Potter* franchise had been an immeasurable hit. *Twilight*, however, was the epitome of a new kind of phenomenon; one where a single element would be focused on and endlessly repeated. After the story of Edward and Bella came vampires everywhere. There was a theme emerging. All it took was a single Young Adult bestseller with a successful adaptation to spawn a plethora of copy-cat creations.

These things weren't always successful. *Vampire Diaries* doing so well led to, in 2011, another of L. J. Smith's series being adapted for television. Kevin Williamson took the lead on *The Secret Circle* – a modern-day witch story – but the show was cancelled after just one season, despite being the third most popular show on The CW. The cancellation was partly down to budget – *The Secret Circle* – had high special-effects demands, but it was also a sad sign of things to come; not every show was getting the chance to grow and become a hit.

After the vampire trend came teen dystopias. The first book in Suzanne Collins' acclaimed *Hunger Games* trilogy came out in 2008. By 2012, when the first movie adaptation (starring Jennifer Lawrence) came out and *The Vampire Diaries* was in its third season, vampires were out and tales of dystopian futures were in. Stories with vaguely similar premises to *The Hunger Games* filled the Young Adult shelves in bookshops; almost all of them featured a Strong Female Protagonist inadvertently leading a revolution while feeling torn between two men. Even *Twilight* author Stephenie Meyer was involved. Her dystopian alien invasion romance *The Host* came out in 2008, and a movie adaptation starring Saoirse Ronan was released in 2013 only to bomb at the box office and be widely panned by critics.

This was the problem with the Young Adult book-to-screen pipeline. *The Hunger Games* was a genuinely good story being told by a talented writer with something important to say. The imitators, especially those that made it to screen, were hollow cash-grabs by comparison. Veronica Roth's *Divergent*, the first book in a dystopian trilogy set in the ruins of America, came out in 2011 when the book trend was at its peak. A film followed in 2014, making a star out of Shailene Woodley[6] in the process. The book was well-reviewed, the critical response to the first film was mixed and, in the end, the trend had fizzled out before the final film in the series could even be made. These trends came in short bursts that couldn't necessarily accommodate a full movie-making cycle, but that didn't stop studios and writers from jumping on bandwagons.

The current trend in the pipeline is 'Romantasy' – once again brooding heroes form points on a love triangle with 'chosen one' heroines; only now there's dragons, or fairies, or both in the

---

6. The first Kaitlyn Cooper in *The O.C.*

background. The bestselling *Fourth Wing* by Rebecca Yarros has, at the time of writing, an adaptation in the works at Amazon. Sarah J. Mass's *A Court of Thorns and Roses* series has been in development at Disney-owned streamer Hulu since 2021 and the adaptation of Leigh Bardugo's hit 'Grishaverse' books – *Shadow and Bone* – has already been cancelled after two seasons on Netflix. Whether this trend will burn out or be replaced so quickly is yet to be seen.

In the time that *The Vampire Diaries* was airing, a mixture of supernatural stories and book adaptations were making waves. *Pretty Little Liars* ran for seven seasons, wandering away from its source material to a truly baffling ending. *Teen Wolf* – a reimagining of the 1985 film starring Michael J. Fox – ran for six years on MTV beginning in 2011, and *The 100*, a post-apocalyptic sci-fi teen drama based on a series of novels by Kass Morgan ran on The CW from 2014 to 2020.

Amongst this world of adaptations and young adult trends, *The Vampire Diaries* universe managed to run for fourteen years in total and maintain an active and engaged fan base – a rare feat. By being willing to push (and sometimes completely ignore) its own boundaries in favour of ramping up the stakes[7] episode-to-episode, the show managed to outlive the trend cycles that devoured so many others.

That extended universe was a huge part of the show's success – beginning with *The Originals.* The first spin-off focused on Klaus (played by Joseph Morgan), one of the members of the fearsome Original family, returning to New Orleans to claim his rightful place as supernatural leader of the city. It was a rarity right from its very beginning – a spin-off successfully making it to air from a backdoor pilot. Many backdoor pilots now exist only as odd aberrations in other shows. That *Gilmore Girls* episode that focused on Jess in California, the eighties flashbacks in the *Gossip Girl* prom episode, the multiple

7. Sorry.

attempts to launch new shows from *Supernatural*, all failed to become series. *The Originals* began with a single episode in the fourth season of *The Vampire Diaries* as Klaus and his brother Elijah (played by Daniel Gillies) visit New Orleans and discover that a werewolf Klaus had a one-night stand with back in Mystic Falls is now pregnant with his child.[8] The resulting show had to suffer through a few inevitable comparisons to *Angel*, and it did seem to have a similar intent behind it in the first few episodes. *The Originals* was darker, more violent and less female-focused than *The Vampire Diaries.*

Despite an apparent lack of originality[9] the show rapidly found its footing and a bit of critical acclaim. Some of that was down to the stellar, charismatic performance from Charles Michael Davis as Marcel – the show's sometime hero, sometime antagonist. Some of it was *The Originals*' willingness, once past the exposition-heavy opening episodes, to stand apart from its teen counterpart. *The Originals* was fairly criticised for leaning into New Orleans cliches – gumbo gets mentioned early and often, jazz musicians are ubiquitous and the opening episodes featured a French Quarter funeral – but it was another story-rich show in a well-loved universe, and it didn't take much to get the audience on board.

The spin-off also came at a perfect time for *The Vampire Diaries* – the awkward college transition. *The Vampire Diaries* had, by focusing on the town rather than high school, managed to sidestep many of the problems that arose on shows that focus too much on school as a defining part of the character's lives. Instead of three seasons of high school culminating in a graduation episode, followed by an awkward college season, *The Vampire Diaries* waited until its fifth season to send the characters to college. Instead, the big transition at the end of the third season was Elena becoming a vampire. This wasn't planned

8. The tribrid. It's complicated.
9. I'm really sorry.

on the character's part, it was down to an accident and some poor choices by Doctor Meredith Fell[10], who probably should have been fired for medical malpractice. Elena's transition to vampire adjusted the dynamic of the show and prevented it from getting stale, as well as giving Nina Dobrev the chance to play yet another character – Humanity-Off Elena.

When the awkward college years did happen, they didn't stay awkward for long before the show pushed education right to the back burner in favour of a mysterious anti-vampire society and some trauma for Stefan after he spent a summer locked in a safe. The fifth season also saw the show reach 100 episodes – that big syndication milestone – celebrated on *The Vampire Diaries* with cameos from a few of the Originals, and the death (sort-of) of Katherine Pierce.

The prison worlds[11] of the sixth season brought in Kai Parker as a deliciously psychotic new villain – a witch determined to kill as many members of his 'Gemini' coven as possible. Kai, played by Chris Wood, provided the solution to a tricky story dilemma. By the end of the season Nina Dobrev, and therefore Elena and all of her associated doppelgangers, needed to be written off the show.

As was standard at the time, most of the stars of *The Vampire Diaries* had signed on for six-year contracts. Of the cast members still actively appearing on the show, only Nina Dobrev and Michael Trevino didn't want to continue once those six years were up. For Trevino, it was unsurprising and not really an issue in the narrative of the show – sadly, his character had already been sidelined. For Dobrev, on the other hand, it was both an understandable decision and a huge challenge for the creators of the show. Playing multiple characters, often having to be in scenes with herself and therefore shooting things many times over as

10. Played by Paul Wesley's then-wife Torrey DeVitto, who also starred in both *One Tree Hill and Pretty Little Liars*.
11. Again, it's complicated, don't worry about it.

she assumed different personalities and delivered half of a conversation to body doubles, was obviously exhausting work for Dobrev. But how to continue a show without its main character?

There are some fans of *The Vampire Diaries* who believed that the show couldn't continue without Elena Gilbert, or at least shouldn't, but continue it did. After, of course, the villainous Kai placed a sleeping curse on Elena that left her not dead, but unconscious while her best friend Bonnie remains alive.

By the time Nina Dobrev chose to leave *The Vampire Diaries*, the audience had begun to wane and television had changed a lot. The show had gone from just one of many during the height of the vampire trend, to a well-respected teen drama in its own right, to slightly dipping under the radar. A 2015 *Den of Geek* piece pointed out that '*The Vampire Diaries* is now practically an anomaly on a channel stuffed with superheroes and dystopian sci-fi.' Thanks to the new influx of superhero enthusiasm, The CW had shifted towards the next big thing, and *The Vampire Diaries* had become an afterthought. The show needed reinvigorating, and with Dobrev's planned exit at the end of the sixth season, there was new energy in Mystic Falls. *Den of Geek* acknowledged that some of this new energy came from the need to get all of the pieces in place for Elena's departure, and said that 'if that's what it takes for the show to refocus and discover its mojo, then I'll take it in a heartbeat.'

The upheaval worked, and *The Vampire Diaries* managed to get more daring with its storytelling in the final two seasons. A three-year time jump was deftly introduced, first in flash-forwards before eventually moving the whole narrative into the future. That jump was even incorporated in the story on *The Originals*, allowing the two shows to continue in tandem and keeping space for crossovers that managed to enhance both shows rather than feeling like a pointless visit from old friends for the sake of drawing ratings.

There were some storylines less popular than others. Candice Accola's real-life pregnancy meant that the show needed to fabricate a way for a vampire to get pregnant despite being technically dead – rather than hiding Accola behind large props and only shooting her from the neck up for half a season. The resulting story – Caroline mystically pregnant with Alaric's children, transferred into her womb (without her consent) by the Gemini coven after Alaric's fiancé, Jo, was murdered during their wedding by her psychotic twin brother Kai, could have worked. Unfortunately, the show added a romance between Caroline and Alaric in the future timeline. *The Vampire Diaries* fandom engaged in shipping wars as much as any other, but Caroline and Alaric's relationship was no one's OTP (One True Pairing – a popular acronym in online fan spaces). Possibly, this was because he had previously been her high school history teacher, and his partners tended to die tragically.[12] Even the viewers who hated the idea of 'Steroline' (the eventual relationship between Stefan and Caroline) weren't too unhappy when Caroline left Alaric for Stefan.

Then, there was Bonnie. With Nina Dobrev off the show and Elena unconscious in a coffin for the rest of Bonnie's life, Kat Graham should have been at the forefront of *The Vampire Diaries* for the show's final two seasons. Graham had been working hard on the show from the very beginning, and Bonnie was often the character who drew the shortest straw; technically dying multiple times, at one point having to be a mystical anchor that kept all of supernatural purgatory in existence, and with a terrible romantic life, it's common consensus among the fandom that Bonnie deserved better.

The final season did see Bonnie in a spectacular, if ill-fated, romance with recurring character Enzo – played charmingly by Michael Malarkey. There was a tragic end to the love story as Bonnie was forced to witness her lover's heart ripped from his chest by a

12. It also might have been because Alaric was played by Matt Davis, better known as Warner Huntingdon III in *Legally Blonde*, or for sharing so many controversial views on Twitter that the *Vampire Diaries* fandom got the hashtag '#MattDavisIsOverParty' trending.

temporarily humanity-less Stefan – not exactly a fairytale ending. Bonnie herself survived until the end of the show, but her journey throughout raised a lot of questions about the writers and creators of *The Vampire Diaries* and their attitudes towards race. Bonnie was the only black main character on the show. Almost all of the other people of colour on the show died horrible deaths, and many of them were also witches. Some of that was intentional – Bonnie came from a long line of witches and many of the black women dying on screen were her ancestors.[13]

The high death toll of African-American characters wasn't the only issue. There was, after all, a high death toll across the board in *The Vampire Diaries*. The problem was with the writing of Bonnie herself. In the original L. J. Smith books, Bonnie was white and her powers originated with Celtic druids. By changing the character's race and then sidelining her for much of the show by making her more an emotional support witch for Elena and Caroline than anything else, *The Vampire Diaries* was contributing to the 'Magical Negro' trope. *TV Tropes* explains this one as 'A minority character will step forward to help the protagonist with their pure heart…and possibly magic.' Bonnie was, throughout the first few seasons of *The Vampire Diaries*, a witch-on-tap and often-ignored moral compass, solving the problems of her white friends and losing more than any of them in the process. Somewhere between prison world entrapment and Elena's curse, she also became Damon's best friend – although this was more told than shown – and became *his* emotional support witch in the process. Bonnie had very little agency, and when she *did* the choices she made for herself almost universally led to untold

13. Notable among those ancestors is Emily Bennet – who appeared in multiple flashbacks throughout the early seasons of the show – played by Bianca Lawson. Over a decade after *Buffy*, Lawson was still convincingly playing teenagers on both *The Vampire Diaries* and *Pretty Little Liars*.

heartbreak. She was the clearest example of *The Vampire Diaries* handling race poorly.

The show also struggled with its queer characters – the few, at least, that appeared throughout the eight-year run. The first openly gay recurring character on the show was Luke Parker, who wasn't introduced until the fifth season, died tragically in the sixth season, and at no point had an actual romantic storyline. Before Luke, the only gay character had been Caroline's father who had appeared in just two episodes, one of which was largely spent torturing his vampire daughter while using language straight out of conversion therapy. In the seventh season, the show had an actual queer couple in Nora and Mary-Louise – two seemingly immortal Heretics (vampire-witches) – but the pair were killed off in a fiery car crash before the end of the season. This led to *The Vampire Diaries* catching criticism from the 'LGBT Fans Deserve Better' movement, for playing into the 'Bury Your Gays' trope.

That movement began as a fan campaign in response to another queer character being killed off on a CW show – Lexa on *The 100*. In 2016, Tumblr user 'girlfriendluvr-remade' posted a list of all of the lesbian and bisexual women killed off on American television in the first three months of the year. Lexa was the sixth, and Nora and Mary-Louise were nine and ten. There were twelve women total on the list. A 2016 article from *Pink News* calculated that forty-two lesbian and bisexual women were killed off on American television in the 2015/2016 season. The fiery deaths of Nora and Mary-Louise were part of a much bigger and more systemic issue.

The Originals managed more diversity, by comparison. The show was lauded, when compared to *The Vampire Diaries*, both for its treatment of non-white characters and its queer characters, at least in later seasons of the show; early episodes had trodden some well-worn tropes of black women as witches. By the end of *The Originals*, at least one pairing between two women (Freya and Keelin, played by Riley Voelkel and Christina Moses), had ended happily, with the pair getting married and trying for their first child. *The Vampire Diaries* had set the bar very low, but *The Originals* did at least manage to clear it. Some of this was down to setting – the show took place in a famously diverse and cosmopolitan city, as opposed to the small southern town of Mystic Falls. The more mature tone of the show, along with a comparative lack of network oversight, were also factors that allowed more diverse storytelling to slip through the cracks.

Although the spin-off's future was in jeopardy more than once, *The Originals* did outlast *The Vampire Diaries* by a single season. The end of *The Vampire Diaries* came in March 2017, after a final eighth season in which each episode was named with a quote from the first. It was a truncated season, just sixteen episodes, and it thankfully didn't fall headfirst into the 'oh-god-it's-ending' nostalgia that some finale seasons can be guilty of, at least until the final few episodes. The ninth episode of the season, however, did its best to dredge up memories of the first with one last Miss Mystic Falls pageant and the title 'The Simple Intimacy of the Near Touch' recalling Damon and Elena's first dance.

The plot of the final season was as chaotic as the rest of the show's run. There was angst, sirens, gore galore, a visit from the man who invented hell and finally the reveal that Katherine – the woman who started it all by turning the Salvatore brothers into vampires – had become queen of hell and was going to burn Mystic Falls to the ground. Nina Dobrev returned for the final episode, both as Katherine and Elena – freed from her mystical slumber. Stefan died tragically, sacrificing himself for the good of Mystic Falls, and the final moments of the show established that everyone was smiling in the afterlife.

It was a well-received finale. *Collider* called the episode 'messy, plot-churning and emotionally resonant', congratulating the show on being 'itself to the very end'. *Vulture* called the show 'far better than it needed to be' in a recap from Rebecca Serle that celebrated the fandom of the show that had become a family, and called the finale 'a perfect ending.' *Entertainment Weekly* celebrated the closure found for almost every love story on the show. As finales go, few have been so un-divisive.

The Vampire Diaries obviously didn't end when the show itself did. The fourth season of *The Originals* had been pushed back to mid-season, and it wasn't renewed for a fifth and final season until May 2017. That fifth season, while shorter than standard network length, managed to satisfyingly tie up every narrative and finally redeem the villainous Klaus, all while being an extended backdoor pilot for the next show in the *Vampire Diaries* universe – *Legacies*. At the end of *The Vampire Diaries,* Caroline and Alaric set up 'The Salvatore School for Gifted [Supernatural] Children.' The final season of *The Originals* saw Klaus's daughter Hope (now a teenager thanks to a second time jump) attending the school. While Hope spent much of the season in New Orleans dealing with relentless plot chaos, parts of the season did take place at the school, and Hope was clearly being set up to carry the torch for the franchise.

The continuation of the universe has kept the *Vampire Diaries* fandom active and engaged, even after *Legacies* came to an end in 2022. The final (for now) entry into the *Vampire Diaries* universe had survived the major production interruptions of the Covid-19 pandemic, only for the show to be part of a wave of cancellations from The CW just as the network was about to be sold off.[14] The fandom, however, remains alive and well, multi-generational thanks to the extended universe of the show. The various relationships on the show are endlessly rehashed on Tumblr and Reddit, fanfiction abounds (the current most popular pairing on *Archive of Our Own* is 'Klaroline' – Klaus and Caroline) and viewers – many of whom have been fans since 2009 when *The Vampire Diaries* began – can't help but speculate about what Julie Plec might do next with the universe. There's even a popular recap podcast – *The Ampire Diaries* – hosted

14. We'll get there.

by renowned critic and writer LaToya Ferguson, alongside Morgan Lutich and Jill Defiel.[15]

In the last minutes of *The Vampire Diaries*, Damon and Elena find peace, making it to an afterlife that looks just like Mystic Falls after living long and happy human lives. Elena reunites with her family, and Damon reunites with his. The final words of the show bring things full circle, with a 'Hello Brother' from Damon. However, this wasn't the ending Julie Plec and Kevin Williamson had originally planned. During the second season, the pair came up with what they thought would be the perfect ending for the show: both brothers sacrificing themselves for Elena and watching over her from the afterlife as she goes on to live a normal human life. When Dobrev left the show there was no way that ending could still work – taking out Elena destroyed the love triangle for good, cementing her and Damon as the show's endgame. In an interview with *Entertainment Weekly*, Julie Plec pointed out that in the moment of Elena's departure 'the show ceased to be about a love triangle and became a show about the power of these brothers and their love for each other.' It was Stefan and Damon's reunion in the finale that was the tearjerker, not Elena and Damon.

The originally planned ending wouldn't have worked because the show outgrew it, because the show *got* to outgrow it. As Kevin Williamson told *Entertainment Weekly*, 'The big finale episode that we had always planned did not happen because the show was successful and lasted eight years.' Television is not the place to make predictions. For every eight years of *The Vampire Diaries*, there are plenty of forgotten shows cancelled after just a handful of episodes.[16] While The CW is no longer home to the universe of the show, Plec

15. Ferguson and Lutich also co-hosted four seasons of *Angel on Top – Buffering*'s sister podcast.
16. Like *Beautiful Life*, a CW show that began the same week as *The Vampire Diaries* and lasted just four episodes. It starred Mischa Barton. From *The O.C.*

insists that 'There's absolutely hope for the future' of *The Vampire Diaries*, as she told *TV Line* in 2022.

Adaptation is a unique art form. Adapting a book, or a comic, staying close to the text and creating compelling television, happens rarely. It didn't happen with *The Vampire Diaries*. Instead, Plec and Williamson took Smith's universe and ran away with the plot for eight years, plus another six of spin-offs. It worked. *The Vampire Diaries* is another success story of a show that got to last, and got to grow and change along with its audience. It got to be about family, and redemption, and guilt, as well as vampires, witches and werewolves. Through it, another fandom came together. There's overlap, of course. Fans of *The Vampire Diaries* are often also fans of *Buffy*, or *Supernatural*, or *Gilmore Girls* or *Gossip Girl*. Those people, however, might not have found each other, formed friendships, found their own ways to be a family, without the Salvatore Brothers and Elena Gilbert. A show getting to last, to run, means the world to some viewers. *The Vampire Diaries* was a lot of things to a lot of people. It was, to quote the show, 'epic'.

Chapter 8

Once Upon a Time

Welcome to Storybrooke

Storybrooke is a small town in Maine. It boasts a diner, a school with a birdhouse-focused curriculum, a bar or two, a closed library, some abandoned mines, some lush surrounding forest that looks like the outskirts of Vancouver and a clocktower that doesn't tick. Storybrooke isn't just a fictional town; it's a fictional town home to fictional characters you might already be familiar with, characters like Snow White, Prince Charming and several dwarfs. They don't know, however, that they're fictional. They don't know who they are at all. Storybrooke is the home of *Once Upon a Time*, the ABC drama that ran for seven seasons beginning in 2011, putting twist after twist on familiar fairy tales as it went.

Much like *Supernatural*, *Once Upon a Time* wasn't a teen drama, but a drama with a huge teenage fan base. It's a question that surrounds the show – who exactly is this for? The premise of the show was that fairy tale characters were trapped, unaware of their true stories, in mundane small-town America. The Evil Queen is the mayor, and the one responsible for cursing away the Storybrooke residents' happy ending. In the opening episode the mayor's adopted son seeks out his birth mother Emma – the lost daughter of Snow White and Prince Charming – and brings her to town in the hope that she can break the Evil Queen's curse. Simple enough to start with and then, as the show went on and more fairy tales were introduced, as curses broke and were cast anew, things got incredibly complicated.

The creators of the show, Edward Kitsis and Adam Horowitz, were no strangers to complicated stories after their tenure on the hit sci-fi mystery show *Lost*. The pair met at an 'Intro to Film Studies' class at university in the early nineties, and joined forces as a writing duo, heading to LA after graduation and getting work on shows like *Felicity* and *Popular*, and even writing an early episode of *One Tree Hill*. It was through *Felicity* that the pair met J. J. Abrams and began their journey to the *Lost* writer's room.

Lost was a television phenomenon. The show, created by J. J. Abrams and Damon Lindelof, ran on ABC from 2004 to 2010. It was by far the biggest hit ABC had managed since the *Who Wants to Be a Millionaire* craze in the late nineties. As previously mentioned, the show reminded networks that audiences were willing to embrace weird genre storytelling. Millions upon millions of viewers tuned in to *Lost* every week, and while the finale remains one of the most polarising endings in television history, the show itself is still celebrated as one of the greats. Kitsis and Horowitz joined the *Lost* writer's room in the first season, eventually becoming executive producers on the show and signing a longer-term deal that tied them to ABC in 2007.

In 2011, when *Once Upon a Time* began, ABC wasn't the most popular of the 'big four' networks, regularly coming behind NBC, CBS and occasionally Fox in the ratings. The network had long standing ties to the Disney corporation going back to the fifties, and Disney had bought the network outright in 1996. While working on *Lost*, Kitsis and Horowitz signed a deal that kept them both on *Lost* and available for other projects. That deal brought them to Disney's attention and led to the pair writing the screenplay for *TRON: Legacy*, a sequel to the classic 1982 film *TRON*. When *Lost* came to an end, ABC wanted to see what else the pair had to offer, and Kitsis and Horowitz brought forward an idea that they'd been toying with for a long time.

Kitsis and Horowitz first came up with the fairy tale concept of *Once Upon a Time* not long after finishing their work on *Felicity*. Horowitz told *Collider* in 2011 that 'The seed of it was that we were trying to find out what it is about storytelling that we really love…Fairy tales clicked with us because they were so much in the DNA of what made us storytellers, to begin with.' The duo began pitching the bare bones of what would become *Once Upon a Time* to networks, with no success. The lessons they had learned working together on *Lost*, however, showed them a different way to tell the story. When the time came to pitch the show to ABC, they were ready. ABC, the network able to access some of Disney's fairy tale canon, gave *Once* the green light.

Casting *Once Upon a Time* was surprisingly easy. As Kitsis and Horowitz put the pilot script together, they had clear mental images of who they wanted for each character, and most of the actors they had in mind were happy to jump into the fairy tale world. Ginnifer Goodwin, best known at the time for HBO's *Big Love*, was their perfect Snow White, and she loved the idea of playing a sword-wielding princess. Josh Dallas, who had previously worked for Disney via Marvel by appearing as Fandral in the first *Thor* movie, made a handsome enough Prince Charming that his and Goodwin's relationship developed off screen as well. The pair met on set and were married a few years later.

Kitsis and Horowitz were big fans of British actor Robert Carlyle and his work on the cult-classic movie *Trainspotting*, and had tried (unsuccessfully) to get him on *Lost* on multiple occasions. They created the character of Rumplestiltskin with him in mind, and while the idea of *Trainspotting*'s psychopathic Begbie being transformed into a glittering, giggling villain sounds absurd, Carlyle was game and the result was a resounding success. Jennifer Morrison was cast as the show's hero Emma Swan. Morrison was best known at the time for her years on the medical drama *House* as Allison Cameron, as well as a brief stint on the CBS sitcom *How I Met Your Mother*.[1]

1. Morrison was also one of the producers that brought Ian Brennan's *Glee* concept to Ryan Murphy.

Emma's plucky son Henry was played by Jared Gilmore, who was fresh off playing Don Draper's plucky son Bobby on *Mad Men*.

During a presentation about *Once Upon a Time* at Disney's D23 expo in 2011, Kitsis and Horowitz were asked if any *Lost* alumni would be appearing on the show, and they teased a 'we'll see.' And it would transpire that a former Lost cast member, Lana Parilla, would become possibly the most important part of *Once Upon a Time*: The Evil Queen. Throughout the show she was Henry's adoptive mother, Snow White's tormenter and eventually a redeemed hero. As *Once* went on, more actors from *Lost* joined the cast. Emilie De Ravin appeared late in the first season as Belle, putting the Beauty in *Beauty and the Beast* (the beast being Rumplestiltskin). Jorge Garcia played a giant named Tiny and both Rebecca Mader and Elizabeth Mitchell appeared in later seasons as the Wicked Witch of the West and the Snow Queen, respectively. Alan Dale turned up in the first season as an antagonistic, disapproving father figure to Prince Charming; he had previously appeared as an antagonistic, disapproving father figure on *Lost*[2]. *Once Upon a Time* wasn't short on *Lost* stars.

Neither was the rest of the production team short on pedigree. Jane Espenson – whose previous work included five years on *Buffy*, episodes of *Gilmore Girls* and *The O.C.* and a season working on *Torchwood* (*Doctor Who*'s answer to *Angel*) – signed on as a writer and co-executive producer. Espenson's input was clear from the outset of *Once Upon a Time* and her experience in the extensive landscape of teen dramas worked perfectly for the fantastical soap opera of Storybrooke. Then, there was Damon Lindelof. While Lindelof never directly worked on *Once Upon a Time*, his encouragement and tutelage were instrumental for Kitsis and Horowitz as they pulled the show together. The pair told the Television Critics Association that Lindelof has been a 'godfather', both to them and the show. As

2. After appearing on *The O.C.* as an antagonistic, disapproving father figure.

a result, *Once Upon a Time* was filled with little references and *Lost* easter eggs, including Apollo chocolate bars, Oceanic Airways planes and references to fictional show-within-a-show *Exposé*.

Lost and *Once Upon a Time* also shared a similar structure. The two shows had very different motivations, but there was a similar feeling in both of mysteries to be tugged at. *Once* also used a similar flashback structure to *Lost*. Where *Lost* used the flashbacks to focus each episode on a single character and show their lives pre-island, *Once Upon a Time* used flashbacks to the Enchanted Forest (the fairy tale character's real home) to show their pre-Storybrooke lives, and how the Evil Queen's curse had come to pass.

The first episode of *Once Upon a Time* aired on 23 October 2011 – a Sunday night a month after the first wave of new shows for the season had debuted. It was watched by almost 13 million people, making it the season's highest rated new drama. Putting the show on Sunday nights in the line-up was a key decision; Sundays had long been dominated by sports and reality television, not dramas, on network television. For drama on Sunday nights, viewers turned religiously to HBO, whose Sunday night schedules were iconic – the home of *The Sopranos, Six Feet Under* and *Game of Thrones*, to name just a few.

Disney, however, had a much stronger hold on Sunday nights. For years the company had aired variations of *The Wonderful World of Disney* – a variety program consisting of behind-the-scenes content, interviews and edited-for-TV versions of popular (and not-so-popular) movies – on Sunday nights. A review of the *Once Upon a Time* pilot in the *Washington Post* called the show 'an elegant surprise that stirs fond memories of Sunday-night Disney TV shows of yore.' While *Once* wasn't directly a Disney production, the ties to the corporation helped the show find nostalgic viewers. *Once* was a rare show that could find success on a Sunday night; the audience was there, waiting for it.

Other reviews of the pilot were more mixed. While *IGN* called the show 'a fairy tale worth watching', Alan Sepinwall wrote for *Hitfix* that 'If I stick with *Once Upon a Time* it'll be more out of potential…

than anything that's in these early episodes.' The *New York Times* was eager to compare *Once* to NBC's new drama *Grimm* – a police procedural take on fairy tale characters in the real world with a distinctly darker tone – and pointed out how the differences between the shows were 'demographic and conceptual,' going on to explain that in *Grimm*, where the stars were mostly male, the world needs protection from supernatural forces, while in *Once* 'our world is a frightening prison from which the mostly innocent supernatural characters must escape; the stars are women.'

The tonal difference of a woman-driven show was a key part of *Once*'s success. Shows heavily featuring women in starring roles weren't new at this point, but they were still rarer – especially in the genre space. *Once* was almost entirely focused not just on the women from these familiar stories, but on empowering those women. Kitsis and Horowitz took great joy in the almost sacrilegious act of taking Snow White – one of the Disney princesses with the least agency – and putting a weapon in her hand.

In an interview with *Entertainment Weekly* ahead of the final episodes of the show airing in 2018, Edward Kitsis recalled that many critics hadn't been enthusiastic at the beginning about the show's chance of success, especially considering the Sunday time slot. He and Horowitz had accepted that things sometimes just don't pan out in this industry, and were determined to make the best episodes of television they could no matter how short their run ended up being. Then, after the first episode aired, they discovered that 'Rumplestiltskin' was the number two Google search of the night. It turned out to be more than just pilot hype surrounding the show. The viewers kept coming back, week after week. They were still there after *Once* went on a six-week winter hiatus. That was when Kitsis and Horowitz realised that they needed to start thinking a bit longer term about the show.

Belief was the big theme in the first season of the show. Aside from Regina – the Evil-Queen-turned-Mayor – and Rumplestiltskin, minus the body glitter and running a pawn shop under his new name of 'Mr

Gold', the residents of Storybrooke had no recollection of their fairy tale lives. Only Henry was aware of the curse, thanks to a storybook given to him by Mary Margaret (his teacher, also Snow White, also technically his grandmother), and he was sure that his birth mother Emma was going to save them all. Emma herself was sceptical in the opening season, as many of us would be in this situation. Incredibly, she remains sceptical even when confronted with the mayor handing out shiny red apples while giving her best villain glare.

Without the flashback structure, viewers might have been just as sceptical, wondering if the kid clutching a storybook actually needed psychiatric help. Handily, Storybrooke did also have a mental hospital – one staffed by a handful of references to *Once Flew Over the Cuckoo's Nest*. Those flashback stories set in the Enchanted Forest showed the fairy tales in all their glory, with some fantastic costuming and CGI that hasn't aged well. It took all twenty-two episodes of that first season, but eventually Emma came around to the truth – thanks to a poisoned apple turnover and a dragon – and broke the curse.

By the time the season one finale of *Once Upon a Time* came around, the show had found a consistent viewership. *Once* was averaging between ten and fifteen million viewers per episode; not quite as many as *Lost* in its heyday, but excellent numbers in a time when streaming and cable were taking so many viewers from network television, and it was definitely a bigger audience than any of the shows on The CW. An *Entertainment Weekly* review of the finale expressed hopes going into the episode that the show would 'let Emma finally drop her Scully act and start believing,' and delighted that the reviewer's 'deepest desires had been granted' at the end of that successful first season.

The second season saw the characters on the show adjusting to their newly-returned memories of the Enchanted Forest while still residing in the real world, and introduced new familiar characters like Captain Hook, Aurora and Prince Phillip of *Sleeping Beauty* fame and Mulan (the show's token yearning lesbian). *Once* also began to expand the incredibly convoluted family tree on the show – an aspect of *Once Upon a Time* that owed more to soap operas than fairy tales. Rumplestiltskin's back story and the pursuit of his long-lost son led to the reveal that he was actually Henry's grandfather – and things only got more complicated from there.

The third, fourth and fifth seasons of the show had a two-volume structure. Each season, the first half would air between September and December, with the narrative resolved in time for the winter hiatus, and then the show would return in March with a new antagonist at play. Splitting each season into eleven- or twelve-episode stories worked well in a world of network television where cancellation could come at any moment, keeping the risk of the show ending without a satisfying conclusion to a minimum. When Kitsis and Horowitz came to create the spin-off *Once Upon a Time in Wonderland*, they only planned a thirteen-episode story for just that reason – and thirteen episodes proved to be all the spin-off got.

The third season, the first to use the two-volume structure, was split up into a visit to Neverland (including the revelation that Peter Pan was Rumplestiltskin's father), followed by a second curse that temporarily sent the residents of Storybrooke back to the Enchanted Forest, with the Wicked Witch of the West (of *Wizard of Oz* fame, played by Rebecca Mader, and eventually revealed to be Regina's long-lost half-sister) as the primary antagonist. A cliffhanger at the end of the third season set up something that viewers had long-suspected might be coming to *Once Upon a Time* as a mysterious blue liquid spilled from a time-travel portal and coalesced into a familiar blonde figure in a dramatic blue dress.

Once Upon a Time, up to that point, hadn't made much of its ties to Disney. There were subtle nods in the background, but the majority of the fairy tale characters that were a part of the show had existed for far longer than the animated versions of their stories. All of that changed in the divisive first half of the fourth season with a story that took more than just inspiration from the 2013 Disney hit *Frozen*. The characters of the film were well-represented in live action; Georgina Haig and Elizabeth Lail played Elsa and Anna respectively, Scott Michael

Foster (who would go on to star in the CW's *Crazy Ex-Girlfriend*) played Kristoff, Anna's fiancé, and there was a real-life reindeer cast as Kristoff's best friend Sven. There was, however, no talking snowman.

While the storyline of 'The *Frozen* season' did well to stay away from recreating the events of the movie – instead taking place after the main story – and the introduction of Elizabeth Mitchell as the Snow Queen made for one of the best villain arcs on the show, *Once Upon a Time* was still criticised for cashing in on one of Disney's most successful properties. It was assumed that Disney had asked Kitsis and Horowitz to use their show to promote *Frozen*, but that wasn't the case. The pair had seen *Frozen* when the movie came out and, in Kitsis's words to *eOnline*, 'there was the story we wanted to play with right away.' According the writers it wasn't easy to get Disney to agree to their use of the characters, but they loved the story and managed to make it work despite a sceptical audience.

Once Upon a Time was a completely ridiculous show that told laughably odd stories with a straight face. Within that *Frozen* season was an episode that featured Little Bo Peep (played by Robin Weigert, who previously starred as Calamity Jane in *Deadwood*) as a cockney-accented mob boss. The second half of the season had the Author of all the stories as an antagonist (played by the fantastic character actor Patrick Fischler, who had also previously starred on *Lost*), along with Rumplestiltskin and 'The Queens of Darkness' – an evil triad consisting of Maleficent, Ursula the Sea Witch and Cruella de Vil – all trying to achieve their own happy endings while *Fantasia* references ran rampant.

Then, as previously mentioned, there were those family trees. The Snow Queen being Emma's former foster mother was only saved from being laughable by the sad, calm villainy at the heart of Elizabeth Mitchell's performance. Then there was Henry, Emma's son. He had Snow White and Prince Charming as maternal grandparents and Peter Pan for a paternal great-grandfather. His adoptive mother was his grandmother's stepmother, and his adoptive grandmother was his birth grandfather Rumplestiltskin's ex (Cora, played wonderfully both by the legendary Barbara Hershey and by Rose McGowan of *Charmed* fame). There was also romantic history between Henry's deceased grandmother Milah and his new stepfather Captain Hook. Things were weird.

The multiple curses and convolutions made this weirdness work fantastically on screen. Provided, of course, the audience didn't try to think about it too deeply. The way time stopped, sort-of, during the opening season's curse meant that Emma was, at least physically, the same age as her own mother and father. There was a world of complex storytelling there, about relationships and how found and adoptive families could feel just as close as blood relations. Both her long-lost sister turning up and her relationship with Robin Hood allowed Regina the kind of lengthy redemption arc rarely seen for female villains. Then there was the delicious contrast of Cruella (played by Victoria Smurfit) in the fourth season – a completely unredeemable villain. The neat two-volume seasons didn't burn through plot at the rate of some shows, but a willingness to blow the story anywhere like an abandoned child being sent to Oz via a tornado, along with access to a treasure trove of characters that the audience already had a passing familiarity with, made for a show that stayed consistently compelling.

The same could sadly not be said of the spin-off, *Once Upon a Time in Wonderland*, which ran for thirteen episodes, beginning in 2013 and ending in April 2014. The show, which Kitsis and Horowitz co-created with Jane Espenson and producer Zack Estrin, struggled for multiple reasons. It wasn't in a favourable time slot, airing on Thursdays and going up against *The Big Bang Theory* and *American Idol*, both of which commanded massive audiences. It was running concurrently with *Once Upon a Time*, although while some familiar characters did turn up there was very little in the way of narrative crossover, and viewers didn't seem willing to keep up with both shows week-to-week. *Wonderland* was also ridiculous in a way that *Once Upon a Time* had managed to build up gradually. A *New York Times* review of the first episode of the spin-off suggested that 'If we could get high enough, maybe we could see some reason to sit through this Disneyfied pastiche of Lewis Carroll and "1001 nights". Or maybe not.'

Wonderland saw Alice, played by Sophie Lowe, begin the series locked in an asylum; a common motif in adaptations of Carroll's work. She escapes the threat of a lobotomy thanks to Michael Socha as Will Scarlet/The Knave of Hearts and the White Rabbit (voiced by John Lithgow). They return to Wonderland to hunt down Alice's missing genie lover, who is being helped captive by Jafar – the villain from *Aladdin*, played by *Lost* alum Naveen Andrews – who is working with the Red Queen (Will Scarlet's ex). Iggy Pop voiced the hookah-smoking caterpillar.

It was for the best that the story, set in a Wonderland that thanks to a limited CGI budget looked mostly like the same Vancouver forests of the parent show with a few plastic toadstools dotted about, was written as a contained thirteen episodes. While a lot of the visuals on the show were praised – there was some fantastic costuming and the CGI work on the Red Queen's castle was wonderfully stylised – the show was just too nonsensical, even for the *Once Upon a Time* audience. The Knave of Hearts character was popular enough with audiences that Michael Socha joined the cast of the main show for the fourth season, only for the writers to realise that they'd already wrapped up his story, barring some fleshing out of his relationship with Robin Hood and the Merry Men, and the character faded into the background before being written off the show.

Missing from *Wonderland* was the Mad Hatter. The character had featured in the first and second seasons of *Once Upon a Time*, played by Sebastian Stan.[3] (The character went by the name Jefferson as a nod to the band Jefferson Airplane, whose sixties hit 'White Rabbit' was inspired by *Alice's Adventures in Wonderland*.) Stan was unable to

3. Who had previously appeared a few times on *Gossip Girl*, and was almost cast on *The O.C.*

reprise his role as the Mad Hatter for the spin-off show because of his commitment to Marvel – he was starring as Bucky Barnes in *Captain America: The Winter Soldier* at the time. Kitsis and Horowitz hadn't spoken publicly about recasting the Mad Hatter, but fans online still got into an uproar at the idea that they might, and began an online campaign demanding that the role *not* be recast. They got their wish, and *Wonderland* remained Hatterless. Sadly, it also lacked an audience.

The audience for *Once Upon a Time* remained, although it waxed and waned as the show went on. The fans who were watching, however, clearly cared deeply about the show and wanted to talk about it, loudly and often. The show never had a single clear demographic. It was popular in the eighteen to forty-nine age range that advertisers like, but the show didn't have a solid, focused appeal beyond that. Although the show was about fairy tales and had a kid as a main protagonist, *Once* certainly wasn't a kids show; there weren't *Game of Thrones* levels of violence and nudity, but the show didn't shy away from swords and stabbing.

It was that eighteen to forty-nine demographic that consistently watched *Once Upon a Time* live, and the audience definitely skewed female. It was the younger end of the viewers, however, that were talking about the show the most. *Once* regularly charted as one of the most reblogged shows on Tumblr. When it was being shared, and discussed at length, it was the shipping that was most important and most vehemently argued about.

The *Once Upon a Time* fandom were constantly engaged in dedicated 'shipping wars', fighting over which preferred pairing, canon or not, was the most important. The most popular ships were the canonical 'Captain Swan', Emma's relationship with Captain Hook; 'Outlaw Queen', the canonical pairing of Regina and Robin Hood; and 'Swan Queen', the ship of Emma and Regina that never sailed. In 2015, *Once Upon a Time* was the property with the largest amount of fanfiction depicting a relationship between two women (known as 'femslash') on *Archive of Our Own*, and the majority of that was about Emma and Regina.

There were hints of the relationship in the show, but just barely. There was obvious tension between the two, there was an enemies-to-friends arc that had clear romantic potential, and thanks to Henry's adoption they technically shared a son. There were enough references to Henry's 'moms' plural that viewers couldn't help but think of *Heather Has Two Mommies* – the well-known children's book released in the late eighties that educated multiple young generations about queerness and became a shorthand for lesbian relationships. Despite the potential, Swan Queen never became canon on the show; the relationship existed purely in the fanfiction archives.

The most passionate fandoms do, of course, have some bad actors. One of the most unpleasant aspects of fandom culture is the sense of entitlement some viewers have towards 'their' show. In *Once Upon a Time*, this was apparent when it came to 'Swan Queen'. Fans would harass writers, producers and actors from the show online, furious that their hoped-for pairing wasn't going to be made canon on screen. It wasn't just the Swan Queen fandom guilty of this, fans of *Once Upon a Time* in general were very vocal when it came to what 'their' show was doing, but the shippers were often the loudest. There was some understandable frustration underlying these online campaigns. *Once Upon a Time* didn't have much in the way of queer representation. There were just a couple of relationships between women on the show, and no romantic relationships between men. This might not seem important – after all there were other shows around with queer characters – but representation means a huge amount, and can do so much in normalising queerness to general audiences. Mulan was shown to be in love with Aurora early on in the show, although it was unrequited. Then, there was Ruby.

Megan Ory's role as Ruby was a difficult part of the show. The twist that Little Red Riding Hood was really a werewolf was a predictable one – it's an aspect of the story that's been explored time and time again in twisted versions of fairy tales. Ruby was unfortunately a character that the writers struggled to find a place for, and just as she came to the forefront in the second season Megan Ory was cast on another show and had to step back. *Once*, like some of its predecessors, struggled with writing off characters, tending to let them fade away into obscurity instead. As a result, Ruby just wasn't present until suddenly, in the fifth season, she was.

It was revealed that she'd returned to the Enchanted Forest to look for her werewolf kin, having been transformed by the witch from the *Brave* subplot into a guard-wolf, and eventually regained her human form and fallen in love with Dorothy (from Kansas by way of Oz). When the pair finally kissed on screen, it was the first realisation of a queer relationship on the show, and after that Ruby was never seen again thanks to Megan Ory being cast on something else. It wasn't even originally planned for Ruby's character to be queer – the writers had planned a relationship between her and Doctor Whale (actually Frankenstein, played by David Anders, named for James Whale who directed the 1931 *Frankenstein*), only for David Anders to be cast on *iZombie* and step away from the show. It's understandable that, with representation so scant, viewers clamoured for more; even if that clamouring was unpleasant.

In the final season there was a much more established and present relationship between two women – Alice (as in Wonderland, but not the same one from the spin-off, also sort-of Rapunzel and Captain Hook's daughter but an alternative Captain Hook from another realm, not the one that Emma marries) and Robin (daughter of Robin Hood and Zelena, the Wicked Witch – who at one point spent a few months pretending to be Hood's deceased wife Marian). It was far better handled than the Ruby and Dorothy relationship; the pair got to exist on screen for more than a single episode. Many viewers hoped to see more of them in a future spin-off, but none was forthcoming. When asked about the pair by *Entertainment Weekly*, Kitsis explained that 'A fairy tale was always something that passed on from village to village, so now Robin and Alice belong to the Oncers and the fandom, and they'll live on in fanfic.' The fandom was something that the creators were well aware of, and to them there was something so meaningful and important about having told a story that could continue to live and grow long after the final episode aired.

While the fandom was an enthusiastic one, *Once Upon a Time* wasn't a particularly influential show compared to some of the more obviously teen dramas. The soundtrack wasn't exactly stuffed with new and interesting music – instead there was a more timeless approach. In the vein of classic Disney, the score was the most important part of the soundtrack – composed for all seven seasons by Mark Isham. While most of the music composed for the show was unique, Isham did incorporate a few famous Disney motifs; most notably the refrain of 'Tale as Old as Time' from *Beauty and the Beast* for key Belle and Rumplestiltskin scenes, and 'The Sorcerer's Apprentice' – used in *Fantasia* – during the Author storyline. Actual songs were used sparingly, although the writers did give Henry a particular taste for eighties synth-pop – including a scene of him introducing a girl in Camelot to the wonders of MP3 players with the song 'Only You' by Yaz.

Once Upon a Time didn't stick to the Disney tradition of its characters bursting into song, but the idea of musicals wasn't far from the writer's minds, or the viewers. In February 2017, as the sixth season was airing, the announcement came that *Once Upon a Time* was finally doing what the audience had hoped for – a musical episode.

Buffy's 'Once More with Feeling' had opened the floodgates and set the trend when it came to musical episodes. In the years since that episode aired, multiple shows had played with the idea. The *Scrubs* episode 'My Musical' aired in 2007, both *Community* and *Grey's Anatomy* aired musicals in 2011, and in the same year that *Once Upon a Time* aired its musical, the CW shows *Flash* and *Supergirl* aired a musical crossover episode that reunited *Glee* stars Grant Gustin, Melissa Benoist and Darren Kriss. *Glee* had obviously had its own influence on musical television, The CW's musical comedy drama *Crazy Ex-Girlfriend* began in 2015 and ran for four seasons, and ABC even had a short-lived musical sitcom – *Galavant* – on the air for two years. In 2015 Disney even began a series of musical TV-movies – *The Descendants* – based on the children of fairy tale characters. Between TV trends and *Once*'s relationship to Disney, a musical episode was inevitable.

The idea for the musical had floated around the *Once* writer's room for a while, but budget restraints pushed it back to the sixth season. At the beginning of 2017 Kitsis and Horowitz met up with Broadway composers Alan Zachary and Michael Weiner to discuss the episode. The plot was mostly focused on Emma and Hook's wedding, with a flashback to the Enchanted Forest that showed Snow White making a wish that made everybody start singing. Somewhere in the background lurked a new and awful curse about to be cast by the Dark Fairy (the season's antagonist and Rumplestiltskin's mother, played by Jaime Murray, who would go on to star in *The Originals* the following year). Really, the plot and the curse and the wish were irrelevant. There was something about Emma having a song in her heart all along, but what really mattered was that the characters were finally singing.

Colin O'Donoghue as Hook delivered a rousing number about revenge that was more sea shanty than breakaway pop hit, Lana Parilla did her best furious stomping as the Evil Queen, singing 'Down with Love', the musical spell inexplicably wandered over to Oz and gave Rebecca Mader a fantastic number as Zelena sang 'Wicked Always Wins', and Snow White and Prince Charming sang something sickeningly hopeful about the power of love. It was exactly what anyone would expect from a *Once Upon a Time* musical episode – slightly mad, barely logical, fun to watch and pretty to look at.

It was a well-received episode, culminating in a big song-and-dance number at Hook and Emma's wedding that led to an *AV Club* review pointing out that 'The influence of *La La Land* is prevalent here.' The costumes were wonderful and the climax of the episode had more than a hint of the old-fashioned musicals *Once* was trying to evoke. 'The Song in Your Heart' wasn't the most ground-breaking television musical episode, but it did the trend justice.

The most important of those wonderful costumes was obviously Emma's wedding dress, which was modelled after Grace Kelly's at the request of Jennifer Morrison herself. It was Eduardo Castro who actually designed the dress – as well as all of the costumes for *Once Upon a Time*. While *Once* definitely wasn't a trendsetter, stuffed to the gills with designer labels, Castro's work on the show was extensive and distinctive. The world of Storybrooke was made to look as mundane and ordinary as possible. The town itself is damp, grey and unappealing until Emma rolls into town in the first season driving a bright yellow Beetle and wearing her signature vivid red leather racket. That mundanity was contrasted by the fantastical costumes in the Enchanted Forest. There were incredible Evil Queen get-ups on Lana Parilla – sweeping trains on embroidered jackets over sensible riding trousers. There was a swan feather wedding dress on Snow White in the pilot, as well as a whole host of sensible bandit-wear for her as the show went on. There were magnificent gowns and cloaks and leather jackets everywhere. There was the alligator skin jacket that Rumplestiltskin wears, the jacket that leads to Hook dubbing him 'crocodile' (in the show it's Rumple that takes Hook's hand and begins the pirate's quest for vengeance).

As magic infiltrated Storybrooke, the costumes began to shift. Slowly, characters stepped out of the mundane, with Castro creating modernised versions of the fantastical outfits. One of the most distinct choices was made in dressing Rebecca Mader – even when out of Oz, the Wicked Witch always dressed to look just a little bit witchy, with hints everywhere of her signature green.

There were more distinct and direct references in the costumes too. Elsa and Anna, in the fourth season, were both depicted as live action versions of their animated counterparts, with costumes as close as possible to the ones they wear in the original *Frozen* movie. When Merida appears in the *Brave* subplot, it's in her distinctive blue dress. Pixar animators even supplied Castro and the costume department with the correct pattern of tartan for Merida's clan.

Emilie De Ravin as Belle suffered through wearing sky high stilettos that seemed at odds with her librarian aesthetic during much of the show's run. This was mostly because De Ravin isn't particularly tall, and needed to be visible in the same shot as Robert Carlyle without resorting to standing on a crate (as Sarah Michelle Gellar often had to do when filming scenes with David Boreanaz on *Buffy*). De Ravin did get to don Belle's iconic golden ball gown, based on the one from the 1991 animated *Beauty and the Beast*, on multiple occasions, including a honeymoon dance with Rumplestiltskin clad in the Beast's classic blue and gold courtly gear.

The Belle costume highlighted something – *Once Upon a Time* was creating live action versions of these famed characters way before Disney started their own version of the trend. *Once* wasn't recreating costumes from the Disney animation catalogue every week, but when the show did, it did it well. Arguably, in the case of Belle, *Once* had a much better version of the ball gown than the one used in the 2017 live-action *Beauty and the Beast* starring Emma Watson.

There were a few low points in the costuming, like the corseted fairies that somehow resembled jellyfish, but there was plenty of fantastic work. The various monochrome furs on Victoria Smurfit as Cruella somehow looked perfect no matter which realm she was dwelling in. There were sharply terrifying suits worn by Kirsten Bauer van Straten as Maleficent that stood in neat contrast to her dramatic, leather-clad Enchanted Forest appearance. There were occasional dresses for Emma – minor touches of femininity for the strong female hero; and intimidating mayoral pantsuits for Regina that slowly softened as the character began her redemption arc. *Once Upon a Time* had a lot to deliver when it came to retelling fairy tales, and it did some of its best work visually.

That fairy tale focus inevitably led to *Once* being held up against other works. The comparisons with NBC's *Grimm* fell off sharply once the tonal difference between the two shows became clear. Harder to shake was the comparison to *Fables*, Bill Willingham's comic book series published by Vertigo, which also featured fairy tale characters in modern day America. ABC did in fact have the rights to adapt *Fables* into a television series, but opted not to go ahead with the show, instead green-lighting *Once Upon a Time*. Kitsis and Horowitz were aware of the comic book series, which began in 2002, but insisted that they were no way inspired by them, telling *Comic Book Resources* that the two properties were drawing from the same well because 'these stories are iconic for a reason', and insisting that the similarities between *Once* and *Fables* were purely coincidental.

There were other shows airing at the same time as *Once* that drew less clear comparisons, but pointed to new trends emerging. Television was getting more eccentric, and studios and networks were starting to take a few more risks. *Galavant*, ABC's medieval-themed musical sitcom, didn't do as well in the ratings as *Once Upon a Time*, but became a cult favourite among certain audiences. It was a show that shouldn't have worked, and didn't last long, but it shared some similarities with *Once Upon a Time*, as well as a network. It was a more irreverent show, with a bit more *Monty Python* in its DNA and recurring appearances from 'Weird Al' Yankovich, but it took a similar approach to *Once* of finding a fresh take on old stories. There was also another distinct connection to Disney; the music on *Galavant* was created by Alan Menken, the renowned Disney composer responsible for the scores of films like *Beauty and the Beast*, *Aladdin* and *The Little Mermaid*.

The CW, meanwhile, was toying with historical drama for teens with *Reign*; this show that very (*very*) loosely adapted the life of Mary, Queen of Scots ran from 2013 to 2017. There was a distinct overlap in fandoms between *Reign* and *Once*; something about the ridiculousness of the shows, *Once*'s ability to tread new ground with old tales and *Reign*'s ability to ignore history completely in favour of drama written with the tonal sensibilities of *Gossip Girl*, that captured like-minded viewers. *Reign* was also a show loved for its costuming – the show ignored period-accuracy in favour of aspiration for the viewers, making the American version of high-street fashion look just old enough to work for a Tudor-era story, while staying just accessible enough to sell clothes to its teenage audience.

Looking at these odd shows and knowing that they got to not just exist but run for multiple seasons feels miraculous. It was thanks to these younger fandoms willing to talk about their excitement, especially online, about the shows in question that allowed these shows to thrive and open doors for each other. *Once Upon a Time* attracted millions weekly. It was consistently recapped on places like *AV Club* and *Entertainment Weekly*, and those recaps grew their own little fandoms of avid commenters. *Once Upon a Time* is not a show whose episodes regularly land on best-ever lists, but it was consistently good, if slightly non-sensical. It's hard now for new shows to be made at all, let alone run for multiple seasons. *Once* could, in the current landscape, get more of a chance than most new series thanks to the recognisable intellectual property at play, but it would probably be viewed with a much more cynical eye as a result. As it was, *Once* existed in a time before *everything* was based on something else, and it got to flourish.

There is a downside to shows getting to last as long as, say, seven seasons, and that's the six season contract. Signing multiple actors or writers on for five or six seasons can have a huge impact on a show that gets to last longer. There was *Buffy*'s network switch and the absence of Tony Head in the show's sixth season, there was Eric Kripke's abdication of his showrunner position on *Supernatural* and there was Nina Dobrev's exit from *The Vampire Diaries* – all brought about by shows outlasting their original contracts. Then there was the final season of *Once Upon a Time* – the reboot season.

After six years on the show, more than one actor decided to make a graceful exit. The news that *Once Upon a Time* was getting a seventh season, and the resulting contract negotiations, came early on in production for season six; the writers knew what kind of ending they needed to aim for. ABC entertainment president Channing Dungey told

Deadline that she expected Kitsis and Horowitz to 'find closure in this particular narrative' in the sixth season before resetting the world for the seventh. The resulting final season was unloved by much of the fandom.

Jennifer Morrison, Ginnifer Goodwin and Josh Dallas all chose not to sign on for another season, which took Emma and her parents off the board. Jared Gilmore also stepped away, although he agreed to a guest role. As the narrative for the final season took shape, it became clear that there was very little room for Emilie De Ravin or Rebecca Mader in the story, and so both actresses were taken off the main cast roster, although they did both make appearances. Along with the cast changes came ABC's decision to move *Once Upon a Time* to Friday nights, leaving Sunday clear for reality TV and putting *Once* in the schedule next to ABC's forays into the Marvel television universe. Friday nights weren't a popular spot – a lot of the potential audience for *Once* were less likely to be home and watching television on a Friday evening – and that scheduling decision certainly factored into the dip in *Once*'s ratings.

The reboot season saw a cursed adult Henry (played by Andrew J. West), living in Seattle having forgotten his fairy tale experiences, and struggling to write his second book after the success of his first – *Once Upon a Time*. The plucky youngster role that Henry had previously filled went to Lucy – played by Alison Fernandez – his daughter with Cinderella. The storyline was set up in the sixth season finale – compelling viewers to return next season to find out why Henry lives in Seattle and no longer believes in fairy tales. It worked, to start with, until things got even more convoluted.

Colin O'Donoghue was able to remain on the show as an alternative version of Captain Hook – one from a 'wish realm' established in the sixth season. In Seattle, he was a confused cop working with the harsh Detective Weaver (Rumplestiltskin). The villain was Cinderella's evil stepmother. Then it was revealed that said stepmother was actually Rapunzel and the evil step-sister Drizella (played by Adelaide Kane, fresh off her lead role in *Reign*) was the real villain, until she wasn't. There was a confused young girl named Alice, of Wonderland fame, who turned out to be Captain Hook's long-lost daughter with Mother Gothel – the villain from the Rapunzel story based loosely on Disney's 2010 animated hit *Tangled. Once Upon a Time* was no stranger to this kind of storytelling, but in the final season things got downright messy.

There were aspects of the season that were truly successful. Belle and Rumplestiltskin getting a happily ever after, of sorts, was one of the high points. The single episode that Emilie De Ravin returned for saw Belle and Rumple settle down at the edge of realms to await sunset so that Rumple could be free of his immortality. The story wasn't that important, what mattered was how it was told. The sequence of flashbacks in the seventh season episode 'Beauty' showed the pair building first a house and then a life together in a wordless montage that served as an extended reference to the infamous opening act of the Disney/Pixar hit *Up*, with Mark Isham's score even taking inspiration from the sequence. With this episode, *Once* successfully managed to incorporate one of the newer Disney properties outside of the world of fairy tales in a way that didn't feel like marketing for a second – it was a sweet resolution for a beloved character, and set Rumplestiltskin on a path for the rest of the season that became one of the show's best redemption stories.

There were other references, in the final season, to newer Disney works. Kitsis and Horowitz had mentioned in multiple interviews that they wanted to do something inspired by *The Princess and the Frog* – particularly the 2009 Disney version – and in the final season they managed to introduce Mekia Cox as Princess Tiana, Jeff Pierre as Prince Naveen and Daniel Francis as a deliciously wicked Doctor Facilier. There were small nods to other films that were more easter eggs than anything else; the chef at the dive bar that Regina runs is named Remy, after the rat in *Ratatouille*, and when Cinderella's stepmother wants the restaurant Cinderella works at destroyed, she orders someone named Ralph to 'wreck it.' Despite the chaos of that final season, these nods and adaptations managed to deepen the story at best, and not get in the way at worst.

The reboot season also suffered from a different kind of curse, one that so much television suffers from in an era where producers and studios seem intent on remaking anything and everything for the sake of earning the nostalgia dollar: technology is suddenly conspicuously everywhere. *Once* had, largely, stayed away from anything more complex than basic cell phones and walkie-talkies. Nothing about the use of technology in the first six seasons of the show particularly dates it. In the final season, everyone has an app for everything and finds a way to reference it. Camera phones are suddenly plot relevant.

In a lot of rebooted shows, the app usage and tech references serve as a shorthand, a patronising wink to the audience that says 'we know people do things differently now!' In *Once*, at least, following this trend served a purpose. It misdirected the audience before the show eventually revealed that the curse that transported everyone to Seattle also moved them back in time – to when younger Henry was still living in Storybrooke. It was a necessary twist that explained away the absence of certain characters on the show – the ones whose actors were no longer available. While the twist did its job, the use of the latest (at the time) technology dated the final season in a way that the rest of the show had managed to avoid. It felt, as it does in many rebooted shows, clunky and unneeded.

As mentioned, the final season of *Once Upon a Time* wasn't quite as well-received as the rest, by fans or critics. The announcement that the seventh season would be the show's last came in February 2018 and surprised no one. Kitsis and Horowitz knew they were taking a big swing by rebooting the show the way they did, and had gone into the final season well aware that it might be the show's last; as a result they had written towards an ending that could wrap everything up neatly. Neither writer was severely disappointed by the cancellation. Kitsis pointed out in an interview with *Entertainment Weekly* that the show was 'every critics prediction to be the first show cancelled' during its first season, so reaching 156 episodes wasn't particularly upsetting.

While the final season was chaotic, the last episode did at least manage to bring everything together. There were happy endings for all and the episode finished with all of the many fictional realms somehow being transplanted to a single plane of existence, with Regina crowned no-longer-Evil Queen over them all in a democratic decision, showing that a happy ending didn't need to be a romantic one. Snow White and Prince Charming returned, and even Jennifer Morrison put in an appearance in the episode's final minutes, wearing the signature red leather jacket. *Once* was almost saccharine in its resolution, but what else could you expect in a show about fairy tales?

Once Upon a Time was ridiculous. It was convoluted. It was messy. It didn't have a clear target audience, it wasn't a trendsetter, it shouldn't have worked. Yet, somehow, it did. It worked for seven years. There was a fandom that stuck with it through thick and thin, through Oz and Camelot and the Land of Untold Stories (a short subplot that allowed the show to incorporate public domain characters like Captain Nemo, the Count of Monte Cristo and Jekyll and Hyde). The show had an audience that became a point of pride for the creators of the show – Horowitz told *Entertainment Weekly* in that post-finale interview that 'it's always truly knocked me out whenever I meet them and come into contact with this incredible fandom that this show has spawned.'

This is a show that demonstrates something important. Television should be allowed to be weird, and messy, and not necessarily have the broadest of broad appeal. That fans are there, ready and willing to engage in these shows and argue passionately about who the Evil Queen should date. *Once Upon a Time* and shows like it are examples of what happens when ridiculous television gets to live, and grow. They will find audiences, and those viewers might find something that they'll fall deeply in love with. *Once Upon a Time* may not have been one of the most popular dramas on network television, but its unabashed oddness and the fans that adore it to this day make it one of the most important.

Chapter 9

Riverdale

Welcome to Riverdale

Riverdale is a small town somewhere in America. It's a town that could be anywhere in America. *Riverdale*, the teen drama that ran for seven seasons from 2017 to 2023, was the last gasp of teen dramas on The CW. The town had a high school, of course, and at various points during those seven years on television it also boasted rival biker gangs, a high-end prison facility, a vintage diner named Pop's Chock'lit Shoppe with a speakeasy hidden underneath, a brothel that became a venue for selling maple syrup-based rum, and a bounty of palladium mines. The town is the setting of the *Archie* comics, and on *Riverdale* it bore a striking resemblance to the town of Twin Peaks.

Like many of the shows I've mentioned in this book, the town of Riverdale looks like the outskirts of Vancouver. Establishing overhead shots and locations within the town itself might look familiar to viewers well-versed in the world of teen dramas; that same stock footage was used in multiple Warner Brothers-produced shows including *Gilmore Girls* and *Pretty Little Liars*. *Riverdale* itself stood out from those other shows; it paid homage to the teen dramas that had come before while also taking inspiration from David Lynch, Stephen King, Ray Bradbury, classic cinema and so much more.

The *Archie* comic books have a lengthy history, and in 2017 they were ripe for adaptation. The character of Archie Andrews was first introduced in Pep Comics issue #22 in 1942, and became the star of his own comic book. *Archie* the comic went on to run up until

2020, with a brief three-year reboot taking place between 2015 and 2018. Along the way, various characters were introduced, spun-off and crossed-over, including Josie & the Pussycats and Sabrina the Teenage Witch. Almost a century of storytelling, various animated adaptations throughout the years and occasional visits to live action made the *Archie* comics a ubiquitous part of American culture.

At the time *Riverdale* began, comic book adaptations were everywhere. The Marvel Cinematic Universe had begun in earnest in 2008 with the release of *Iron Man*, and by 2017 the MCU was in its 'phase three', building up to the massive cinematic event of *Avengers: Endgame*. Alongside the films, various Marvel television shows had turned up on both ABC and Netflix during the previous five years, and more were to come with the approaching launch of the Disney+ streaming service. DC Comics had been airing projects on the small screen for a while. The WB had success with *Smallville* from 2001 onwards; the story of a young superman attending high school had been one of the network's biggest hits, with a large teen audience that skewed more masculine than many of the network's other offerings. *Smallville* ran for ten years, moving to The CW after the 2006 WB/UPN merger.

In 2012, the year after *Smallville* came to an end, Greg Berlanti (who had previously show-ran the latter three seasons of *Dawson's Creek*) brought *Arrow* to The CW and kick-started a huge extended universe of TV shows based on DC comic books. *The Flash* (starring Grant Gustin, who previously appeared on *Glee*) began in 2014, followed by *Supergirl* (starring Melissa Benoist, who also previously appeared on *Glee*) in 2015. Then came *Legends of Tomorrow*, *Black Lightning* and *Batwoman*. The 'Arrowverse' spanned multiple shows, including minor cameos and crossovers with non-CW shows, lasted eleven years in total on television, numbered around thirty-seven seasons, featured multiple universes and brought comics to the small screen in a groundbreaking fashion. The Arrowverse was also a departure for The CW – these shows weren't teen dramas focused on characters attending high school. This was a wholly new adaptation trend for television, and a more mature route for a network that had built a huge teen audience.

Into this world of adaptation came the *Archie* comics. These were, initially, a less appealing candidate for adaptation. There were no superheroes or villains, just fairly wholesome teenagers living barely eventful lives. They came to screen in a roundabout way, through a few years of development hell, largely thanks to Roberto Aguirre-Sacasa, Sarah Schecter and Greg Berlanti.

Aguirre-Sacasa was a playwright before he came to write comic books, but he was also a long-time *Archie* fan. In 2003, he debuted a play called *Weird Comic Book Fantasy*, about a character named Buddy who comes out of the closet, moves to New York and dates a would-be serial killer. The play's original title was *Archie's Weird Fantasy* and the entire show was based on characters from the *Archie* comics. Just twenty-four hours before opening night, Aguirre-Sacasa received a cease-and-desist order from the *Archie* publishing house, and was forced to change the names of the characters in his play to protect the innocent.

Through his work in theatre, Roberto Aguirre-Sacasa was hired to work as a comics writer for Marvel. He then transitioned into writing for television, and was hired to work on *Glee* in 2011. Thanks to a chance conversation at New York Comic-Con, he was then hired to write the four-part crossover comic *Archie Meets Glee*, and just two years later in 2013 he became Chief Creative Officer at Archie Comics.

Riverdale started life as a traditional teen coming-of-age movie inspired by the works of John Hughes. It was Sarah Schecter who brought Roberto Aguirre-Sacasa and his friend Jason Moore – director of *Pitch Perfect* – to pitch the project at Warner Brothers. Unfortunately, there was a Vice President in the room with a few too many ideas. Aguirre-Sacasa's story of the pitch meeting was reported by *TV Guide* in 2016; the VP first suggested adding a time travel element to the story, realised the idea hadn't gone down well in the room, then pivoted to suggesting portals to another dimension, telling the writers that 'Portals are huge right now.'[1] The film stalled there, although that didn't stop multiple outlets in 2013 announcing that an *Archie* film from Aguirre-Sacasa and Moore was coming, and speculating on whether Roberto would incorporate any of the zombie storylines from the popular *Afterlife with Archie* comics that he was working on at the time.

Sarah Schecter went on to work with Greg Berlanti (she is, at the time of writing, the chairperson and partner at Berlanti Productions), and in 2014 she contacted Roberto Aguirre-Sacasa to discuss bringing his *Archie* ideas to television instead. The untitled *Archie* project that would become *Riverdale* kicked around being almost-developed at Fox for a while before landing at The CW, who ordered a pilot in 2016.

During the development process, *Riverdale* became a much more subversive take on the *Archie* comics than the original coming-of-age idea, with a much darker tone. A murder mystery became the backbone of the season; Aguirre-Sacasa later told *Entertainment Weekly* that adding the mystery was how 'the show unlocked creatively for me.'

With the *Riverdale* pilot ordered, the core cast had to come together, and it formed largely from lesser-known actors. Camila Mendes was fresh out of college when she won the role of rich-girl Veronica Lodge. Mendes mentioned in an interview with *Glamour* that she had grown-up watching shows like *The O.C.* and *Gossip Girl*, admiring characters like Summer Roberts and Blair Waldorf and incorporating lessons from them into her performance as Veronica; the kids that had grown up watching teens on television were now joining these casts themselves. Roberto Aguirre-Sacasa had wanted to pursue Kiernan

1. Eventually, both time-travel and inter-dimensional portals were incorporated into *Riverdale*.

Shipka for the role of Betty after seeing her work on *Mad Men*, but Shipka wasn't available at the time (although she would later star in the *Riverdale* universe). Instead, the role went to Lili Reinhart – another largely unknown actress who had mostly performed in bit parts before joining the *Riverdale* cast.

Cole Sprouse, who was cast as Jughead, was probably the best known of the 'core four' having worked as a child actor; he starred in the Disney Channel sitcom *The Suite Life of Zack and Cody* and briefly appeared in *Friends* as Ross's son Ben. The last of the core group to be cast was Archie. The team behind *Riverdale* had been auditioning red-haired actors for months when KJ Apa, freshly arrived from New Zealand where he'd spent two years on the soap opera *Shortland Street*, walked through the door. He proved to be perfect for the part, once his naturally brunette hair had been dyed Archie's signature red.

Of course, there were also parents in the world of *Riverdale* to be cast. The show reached all the way back to the roots of teen soap operas by casting Luke Perry – who played Dylan on *Beverly Hills 90210* as well as starring in the original *Buffy* movie – as Archie's father Fred. Molly Ringwald, member of the eighties brat pack and star of multiple John Hughes movies, joined the cast late in the first season as Archie's mother Mary. By casting Mädchen Amick as Betty's mother Alice, the show had another connection to the world of *Twin Peaks* thanks to Amick's previous work as a 'diner girl'.[2] The first season also introduced a host of more minor *Archie* characters, including Cheryl Blossom, played by Madelaine Petsch, a member of the wealthy, red-headed Blossom family who opened the show grieving the loss of her twin brother Jason; he had apparently passed away in a boating accident on the fourth of July. That murder mystery was the driving

2. More relevantly to this book, Amick also appeared in *Gilmore Girls* and *Gossip Girl* – just like Sonic Youth.

force of the thirteen-episode first season. Along the way, as the murder was resolved, the show also featured an affair between Archie and his music teacher, aspiring pop stars Josie and the Pussycats (with the incredibly talented Ashleigh Murray as Josie McCoy), a drug-dealing biker gang (the drugs being supplied by Cheryl and Julian's father Clifford Blossom, who was using the family maple syrup business as a front), a brief and thankfully rapidly resolved love triangle between Archie, Betty and Veronica, a touch of cheerleading drama and the reveal that Betty's sister Polly (played by Tiera Skovbye, who played Robin in the final season of *Once Upon a Time*) wasn't just pregnant with twins fathered by the deceased Jason Blossom, but that she was also technically Jason's (distant) cousin. Again, this was all in thirteen episodes. The first season of *Riverdale* went at a breakneck pace, rivalling and overtaking *The Vampire Diaries* for burning through plot, and the show didn't let up from there.

As the first season screeners went out to reviewers and *Riverdale* began to air on The CW, the critical response was a mixed one with an undertone of bafflement. Jeff Jensen for *Entertainment Weekly* acknowledged that the show knew exactly what had come before, calling it 'the sum of all trends: franchise extension, comic-book adaptation, theory-baiting crypto serial, edgy YA romance, and densely ironic deconstruction.' Jensen didn't consider this a negative – *Riverdale* knew what it was and didn't try to hide it. An early *Collider* review argued 'the fact that *Riverdale* is so campy, self-aware and overwritten will be catnip to some, but it feels like a missed opportunity to tell a strong, high school set story.' It is true that high school dramas had become few and far between by 2017, but high school dramas that didn't contain either supernatural elements or camp, over-wrought soap-opera stories (or both) had been a rarity for much longer.

It can't be ignored that *Riverdale* went far beyond classic soap-opera camp into intense degrees of weirdness. The second season remained in the murder mystery/neo-noir space, featuring a serial killer named 'The Black Hood' who turned out to be Betty's father. The third season centred on a mysterious *Dungeons and Dragons*-like game called *Gryphons and Gargoyles* that lead to Jonestown-style suicides, while a mysterious cult called 'The Farm' that turned out to be a front for organ harvesting lurked in the background. The fourth season saw Jughead fake his own death after going to an elite private school, with a few mysterious video tapes adding an extra ominous tone to the season. The fifth season jumped forward seven years and had alien abductions by 'mothmen' that turned out to be an incestuous offshoot of the Blossom clan that enjoyed hunting and kidnapping people. Then the sixth season introduced an alternate universe and gave the characters superpowers, and things got really weird. *Riverdale* took to heart the idea that a show can't jump the shark if it starts in mid-air and never comes down.

These were all just the main plots, and there was plenty more insanity in the background. *Riverdale* aired towards the end of the listicle era, and the show was perfect fodder for 'The Top Ten Weirdest/Craziest/Most Ridiculous Moments on *Riverdale* This Week/Month/Season/Ever' style articles. It spawned plenty of them. One such piece published by *Rolling Stone* just before the final episode aired called *Riverdale* 'a campy, Frankensteinian mash-up of genres, pop-culture references, and pie-in-the-sky melodrama that's frankly unlike anything that came before it.' The piece referenced events like the time Archie got into a fight with a bear, the haunted doll possessed by the spirit of Julian Blossom (the triplet Cheryl absorbed in the womb) and 'Dark Betty'; Betty's occasional evil alter-ego influenced by her 'serial killer' genes (which she did *not* inherit from her serial killer father).

Riverdale didn't take itself seriously. Greg Berlanti's influence, and the experience Berlanti himself had on *Dawson's Creek*, was apparent in the over-written dialogue that at very few moments resembled actual human speech, let alone teen-speak. Jughead declared in the first season that 'In case you haven't noticed, I'm weird. I'm a weirdo. I don't fit in. And I don't want to fit in.' (He largely considered himself a weirdo for always wearing a signature beanie with a crown-shaped brim – a reference to the original design of the comic-book character.) This became a rallying cry for the show. When Archie (serving time in a juvenile detention facility for a murder he was framed for by his girlfriend's father Hiram Lodge) learns that one of his fellow inmates has never played team sports due to dropping out of school at a young age to deal drugs, he responds with the show's most infamous quote: 'That means you haven't known the triumphs and defeats, the epic highs and lows of high school football.' This line was ridiculed and memeified constantly; out of context it was an example of everything wrong with *Riverdale*. But the show was in on the joke, it mocked the line on multiple occasions and somehow the 'epic highs and lows' came to summarise one of the best things about the show – a willingness *Riverdale* had to go over the top, and then gratuitously laugh at itself.

As with the *Archie* comics, *Riverdale* also spun off into an expanded universe with two shows that were wildly different in tone, both from each other and their parent show. One of these shows, *Katy Keene*, had much more in common with the latter seasons of *Glee* than with *Riverdale*. It starred Lucy Hale, fresh from *Pretty Little Liars*[3], as the titular Katy – a would-be fashion designer living in New York. Ashleigh Murray left Riverdale for the big city, joining the cast of Katy Keene so Josie McCoy could begin her music career in earnest. The spin-off was short-lived. It ran for just one season on The CW in 2020, concurrently with the latter half of *Riverdale*'s fourth season, before being cancelled due to the Covid-19 pandemic. The show managed to gather a healthy collection of *Riverdale* fans, partly thanks to multiple crossovers, but there simply wasn't enough of an audience to justify the cost of keeping it in production.

3. Hale also, many years before, appeared in an episode of *The O.C.*

The other show in the extended universe – *Chilling Adventures of Sabrina* – technically wasn't a spin-off, and had a much looser connection to *Riverdale*. Kiernan Shipka finally became available, and starred in the show as the titular Sabrina, alongside Miranda Otto and Lucy Davis as Sabrina's aunts Zelda and Hilda. Technically, because *Sabrina* didn't air on The CW but was instead produced for Netflix, it served as a companion show rather than a direct spin-off – although locations and minor characters did overlap. Still produced by Greg Berlanti, and with Roberto Aguirre-Sacasa at the helm, the show had much more of *Riverdale*'s dark sensibility than *Katy Keene*; unlike *Riverdale* however, *Sabrina* was wholly supernatural – focused on witches and eventually featuring both the Devil and Lillith (played by Richard Coyle and Michelle Gomez respectively) as characters.

Sabrina Spellman was a character who had been brought to live action before. *Sabrina the Teenage Witch* had been a popular part of ABC's T.G.I.F lineup for four years, and when audiences for the show dwindled it moved to the newly-formed WB for its final three seasons. *Chilling Adventures of Sabrina* had a much shorter lifetime, running from 2018 to 2020 before being abruptly cancelled (due, in part, to the pandemic). The surprise cancellation left the show with storylines still to be wrapped up, and led to Sabrina finally visiting *Riverdale* in the show's sixth season.

Chilling Adventures of Sabrina landed on Netflix because of the ongoing relationship between the streamer and The CW. The network first signed a distribution deal with Netflix in 2011. In 2016, a renewal of that deal allowed Netflix to release complete seasons of shows like *Riverdale* just eight days after they wrapped on the network, as well as the streamer handling much of the international distribution of those shows. It was an unprecedented deal at the time; the commitment that Netflix was making – purchasing these shows and airing them almost immediately – was estimated to be worth around $1 billion to The CW.

This was a rapidly changing time in television. The streaming boom had come to dominate the industry, and television was adapting quickly. Live audience figures and Nielsen ratings were no longer vital to networks, especially a small network like The CW. The network's priorities shifted from gaining big live numbers that would increase ad sales, to a focus on building sizable streaming audiences. More and more people, especially the teen audience that the network had cultivated, were watching shows at their leisure rather than bothering to catch them live, and those streaming figures became increasingly valuable to the networks.

This massively changed how television was being made. It was cheaper for streamers to purchase ready-made shows from networks like The CW, rather than producing their own content, and often these shows came not just pre-prepared, but with an audience ready to sit down and binge them. From a network perspective, there was more flexibility – a show didn't need to do well in the ratings provided it could be sold to Netflix.

Other CW shows that found their audiences this way included the previously-mentioned *Crazy Ex-Girlfriend*, along with *Dynasty* and *Nancy Drew*. *Dynasty* was a remake of the classic eighties soap opera, and *Nancy Drew* was a modern, darker take on the classic kids' detective novels; both shows were developed by Josh Schwartz and Stephanie Savage. None of these shows managed significant numbers when it came to live audiences, but they were worth enough to Netflix to keep them going. They didn't exactly have *Supernatural* length runs, but in a time when it was nearly impossible to get new shows off the ground at all, it was streaming that kept these shows alive.

The eventual end to the Netflix distribution deals also, unsurprisingly, had a huge impact on The CW. Both *Katy Keene* and *Sabrina* struggled due to the pandemic, but in *Katy's* case the audience was also the issue. While *Riverdale* fans did want to watch something new set in the universe of the show, by the time *Katy Keene* was airing

The CW was no longer sending everything to Netflix. More and more streamers had emerged by 2020 as every company tried to get in on the action. As a result, after it finished its live run, *Katy Keene* was made available on new service HBOMax (since renamed to just 'Max') – owned by Warner Brothers, the production company behind the *Riverdale* universe. For fans of the show, and fans of *Riverdale*, *Katy Keene* alone wasn't worth subscribing to a new streaming service, and so the show lost much of its potential audience. More streaming platforms emerging had harmed the industry as a whole – audiences were willing to pay a monthly fee for one or two, but a large percentage of people were unwilling to shell out additional fees for every other streamer going, and it was shows like *Katy Keene* that suffered as a result.

The pandemic affected *Riverdale* directly, as well as contributing to the shortening of the show's spin-offs. The need to shut down production truncated the fourth season and created a strange timeline of events on the show. The fourth season had already gotten off to a difficult start. Late in production for season three, Luke Perry had sadly passed away from a stroke. All of the *Riverdale* episodes left that season were dedicated to Perry, but the show decided not to acknowledge his passing directly until the opening of the fourth season, to avoid cramming in the demise of Fred Andrews among the rest of the chaotic sub plots.

Instead, the fourth season opened with a touching tribute to Luke Perry. In the episode, Archie learns that his father has been killed in a car accident while helping a woman at the side of the road. Shannon Doherty, Perry's co-star from his *Beverly Hills* days, guest-starred as the woman in question, leading the core four in a prayer for Fred. The episode ended with the townspeople of Riverdale coming out in droves in an impromptu funeral procession for Perry's character. The episode, which was given to Luke Perry's closest friends and family for approval, served as a eulogy and celebration of an actor who had been part of teen television, and so much more, for over thirty years.

It stood alone at the opening of the season, not touching on any of the other plots, in a tribute to Perry that was full of the respect for his work.

When the storylines picked up again in the fourth season, it was senior year for the high schoolers on the show. Due to the pandemic, however, production had to go on hiatus with just nineteen episodes made. There were a few more planned for the end of the season, including prom night, graduation and the resolution of the 'auteur' storyline, in which someone was making creepy videos around Riverdale and eventually faking murders on camera (it turned out the culprit was Jughead's little sister Jellybean). These episodes had to move to the beginning of the fifth season.

After those awkwardly tacked on episodes, *Riverdale* took a page out of *One Tree Hill*'s book by jumping forward in time seven years; skipping both the awkward college years and the question of whether or not to directly show the pandemic on television.[4] It was a necessary move for the show that gave the main characters a reason to be in Riverdale after scattering to the winds post-graduation, while also allowing the clearly-not-teenage actors to play actual adults. The fifth season was also shortened due to pandemic restrictions, coming in at just nineteen episodes. With the end of the fourth season taking up time at the beginning, that left just fifteen episodes for the gang to fix up a dilapidated Riverdale that had been deconstructed by Veronica's villainous father (while also dealing with the mothmen.)

By the time the fifth season of *Riverdale* was airing at the beginning of 2021, the show's cultural impact couldn't be denied. It was being discussed everywhere – the good, the bad and the downright ridiculous. Unlike the teen dramas that came before, however, *Riverdale* wasn't particularly influential. The show wasn't selling

4. While the pandemic itself wasn't depicted, the episodes that took place seven years in the future did reference remote learning and social distancing.

clothes or phones or an aspirational lifestyle. In fact, the show barely used brand names at all, instead using alternate names like American Excess for American Express, Fresh-Aid for Kool-Aid and the Five Seasons instead of the Four Seasons. All of this served to heighten the show's sense of surrealism, as if it existed in a universe even farther to the left of ours than Stars Hollow. Some real brands were present in unsubtle thuds of product placement, but *Riverdale* wasn't selling anything new. The show had a wholly vintage feel, with hints of fifties wholesomeness everywhere in the aesthetics that alluded to the show's source material, along with more direct homages to the pop culture of the past.

Those pop culture references were all over the place. This was another show that didn't look down on its teenage characters or its teenage audience, instead trusting the viewers to understand the episode that paid tribute to *Citizen Kane* or the moment when Veronica announces 'Blow winds, and crack your cheeks', quoting *King Lear* while ranting about her father. The *Riverdale* kids were savvy, they knew the classics from Shakespeare to Stephen King, and the show presumed its audience could keep up.

The music of the show also spanned wide swathes of pop-culture history. *Riverdale* incorporated music from many genres into its soundtrack; plenty of songs from major artists were incorporated into the background of the show, but there were also regular musical performances from the cast. A *Paste Magazine* article about the music in the show was another piece that brought up the things that *Riverdale* borrowed from its predecessors: 'A hint of murder mystery from *Pretty Little Liars*, a dash of supernatural suspense from *Teen Wolf*, but most importantly, the frequent musical numbers featured in *Glee*.' While the *Riverdale* characters weren't in a show choir, there were still plenty of opportunities to perform. One of the earliest numbers on the show was a revamped version of 'Sugar Sugar', the bubble-gum pop song originally created for 'The Archies', performed by Josie & the Pussycats. Through cheerleading performances, the speakeasy, karaoke nights in bars and the school auditorium, there were numerous chances for the characters to sing and dance.

These performances fit perfectly into the general insanity of the show. There was 'Jailhouse Rock' – performed by the cheerleading squad outside the juvenile detention centre while Archie tries to teach his fellow inmates about the epic highs and lows of football. There was a performance of 'Mad World' based on the Gary Jules cover of the Tears for Fears song, made famous by the movie *Donnie Darko*, which began as an innocent karaoke performance at a biker bar and ended with a striptease performance from Betty that would hopefully gain her entry into her boyfriend's biker gang – with both her mother and his father in the audience. There was a performance of 'Bittersweet Symphony' sung by Veronica and Josie at Veronica's confirmation. Veronica invites Josie to duet with her by asking if she knows the song 'from the *Cruel Intentions* soundtrack,' referencing not The Verve – the band that recorded the song – but the 1999 movie starring Sarah Michelle Gellar as a wealthy catholic school girl who keeps cocaine in her crucifix.

Then there were the musical episodes. Each season of *Riverdale* apart from the first featured some kind of full musical episode. These episodes were all based around existing musicals, structured around putting on those musicals in the early high school years. The second season musical was *Carrie* – the famous flop of a musical based on the classic Stephen King novel. The school production of *Carrie* didn't actually get to go ahead – behind the scenes the minor character of Midge, who was supposed to be playing Carrie, was murdered by The Black Hood, with her corpse left on stage to horrify the audience as the curtains opened.

The third season musical was based on a production of *Heathers* – the much-more-successful-than-*Carrie* Broadway musical based on the classic eighties teen movie of the same name. In that particular episode, the show went ahead and led to a fantastic character introduction. Throughout the season, the cult called The Farm had been an ominous background presence, with its leader Edgar Evernever remaining an unseen threat. At the end of the *Heathers* performance Edgar finally revealed himself, having attended to watch his 'daughter' Evelyn (who was actually not his daughter, but his wife, posing as a high school student to recruit vulnerable teens into their cult) in the show. As the characters finished a joyous final number and took their bows, Edgar finally revealed himself, delivering an ominously rhythmic standing ovation, and the camera panned to his face to reveal none other than Chad Michael Murray – not seen on his teen television since his *One Tree Hill* days.[5]

The fourth season musical 'Wicked Little Town' had the students fighting censorship to perform songs from *Hedwig and the Angry Inch* – a cult musical that celebrates queerness in all its forms. Even into the fifth season, with high school in the rear view, *Riverdale* continued the musical tradition. The first musical episode of the fifth season – 'Return of the Pussycats' – didn't follow a particular show, instead using musical numbers to reunite Josie McCoy (fresh from *Katy Keene*) with her high school pussycats. The episode felt very much like a backdoor pilot, leading many viewers to suspect that a Pussycats spin-off was coming. No such show was ever made, with Ashleigh Murray instead taking a lead role in *Tom Swift* – a spin-off of The CW's *Nancy Drew*. Later in the fifth season, the episode 'Next to Normal' had musical numbers taking place mostly in Alice Cooper's head as she copes with the loss of her daughter Polly (murdered by the mothmen) in a surprisingly subdued depiction of grief. Well, subdued by *Riverdale* standards.

---

5. I'd be remiss if I didn't mention the ridiculous conclusion to the cult storyline. Edgar Evernever attempts to escape to space on a rocket that he built himself, before being shot by Betty's mother, who was secretly working with the FBI, who had recruited her via her long-lost son Charles, who was also a serial killer and dating the boy who had pretended to be Alice's long-lost son in the previous season.

The sixth season used a serial killer convention taking place at Veronica's newly opened casino to bring in a series of musical numbers from *American Psycho* – the musical based on the Bret Easton Ellis novel of the same name. This was a full circle moment for Roberto Aguirre-Sacasa, who wrote the book for the Broadway show. Then, in the final season (which was set in the 1950's) the show finally had a full set of original musical numbers as a part of a story that saw Kevin Keller attempt to write a musical about the life of Archie Andrews.

These big musicals and smaller numbers, the episodes named after classic movies that paid homage to said movies in the plot, and the constant broad pop-culture referencing was a big part of what made *Riverdale* so popular. There were characters twistedly named for real-life authors – Bret Weston Wallis, Donna Sweett and Brad Rayberry – who appeared in storylines based on their namesake's work. The David Lynch references were ever-present, with the show going so far as to name an episode 'Lynchian' – the episode paid even more direct homage to Lynch's work and introduced a video shop named 'Blue Velvet Video'. The audience loved it. Either they understood the references, and felt seen by writers who didn't presume that their cultural knowledge began and ended in their own lifetimes, or they wanted to understand the references and made the effort to seek out the inspiration.

The *Riverdale* fandom had a lot to contend with; this was a show that was deeply, widely mocked across the internet. Still, they persevered, fighting for their favourite ships and diving deep into the minutiae of the show. The people making *Riverdale* knew this, and were happy to acknowledge it. The ship names like 'Bughead' and 'Varchie' were introduced into the show's vocabulary in a completely unselfconscious act of self-mockery, while the show toyed with various permutations of the couples. Of course, fans were incredibly vocal and at times irritatingly so when it came to their preferred ships. Cole Sprouse was asked about the future of 'Bughead' in a 2017 interview as the second season of the show was airing. Sprouse's response was a frustrated one; he pointed out that 'Our writers are not writing as a fan service…If we were writing what the fans wanted to see, Betty and Jughead would be the most linear, monotonous narrative of all time.'

Some actors were more passionate about the fans that shipped their characters. Madeleine Petsch spoke to Roberto Aguirre-Sacasa about her character Cheryl's sexuality as early as season one – she wanted Cheryl to have a girlfriend, and Aguirre-Sacasa agreed. Petsch was also a huge cheerleader for her friend Vanessa Morgan, who joined *Riverdale* in the second season as Toni Topaz, a member of the Southside Serpents (the biker gang that Betty was trying to join). The 'Choni' pairing was by far the most popular ship on the show, and the relationship between Cheryl and Toni lasted on screen, on and off, through six seasons of the show. A ship between two women being the most popular for a TV show isn't a rarity, but that ship also being canon, and ending with a happily ever after, doesn't happen often.

Cheryl's queer narrative wasn't an easy one. The show dealt with the extremes of parental homophobia in its usual subtle, nuanced manner, with Cheryl's mother sending her to a convent (run by the Sisters of Quiet Mercy, who also used the convent as a front for drug running) for secret conversion therapy. Unfortunately, *Riverdale* fell into certain traps with its queer narratives, both by making a coming-out narrative something that had to be fraught and upsetting, and with Kevin Keller – played by Casey Scott – reducing a gay character to little more than his sexuality for much of the show. There were also criticisms of erasure in the show. Before *Riverdale* began, the Jughead of the *Archie* comics had come out as asexual in a recent storyline. Viewers hoped to see that represented in *Riverdale*, but the writers chose not to pursue it.

Morgan and Petsch were two of Choni's biggest fans; they reposted fan art, supported each other at conventions and heavily promoted episodes that focused on their relationship on their personal social media accounts. As Alex Zalben, writing for *Decider*, pointed out in a post-finale article, those two stars didn't just steer their ship: 'They were the shipyard owners, the deck hands, the galley chiefs, the whole damn crew.'

While the fans were falling in love with their ideal pairings, *Riverdale* also built what could only be described as an anti-fandom. Portions of the internet were dedicated to mocking this ridiculous show. Clips of the hammy dialogue were shared and made fun of, and for those not deeply into the intricate weekly storylines, *Riverdale* was a source of derision. The fact that it was discussed so heavily at all, however, probably contributed to keeping the show alive for so long.

By the time the sixth season of *Riverdale* came around, it was almost a miracle that the show was still on the air. Untold numbers of network television shows had been cancelled in the wake of the pandemic, but *Riverdale* was still very much alive in 2021. The CW wanted the sixth season to premiere with some kind of multi-episode special event, and *Riverdale* delivered. The opening five episodes of the season were set in an alternate universe – in a town called Rivervale – thanks to an explosive fifth season finale that careened the show into a new dimension. Rivervale was a town much like Riverdale, only darker, with the supernatural very much present. The opening episode of the Rivervale event saw Archie sacrificed by a smiling town in an attempt to revive struggling maple trees, and the show only got stranger from there.

The event gave the show the chance to bring in not just supernatural elements, but a visit from Sabrina Spellman herself, marking the first real crossover between *Riverdale* and *Chilling Adventures of Sabrina*. The later events of the season allowed for Kiernan Shipka to show up one last time, wrapping up the storylines from the cancelled-too-soon *Sabrina* and bringing a few *Riverdale* characters back from the dead into the bargain. Roberto Aguirre-Sacasa was thrilled that The CW wanted a special event for his show, and delighted at the opportunity to make *Riverdale* even weirder. He told *Entertainment Weekly* at the time that fans had been hoping for a while that the show would embrace the supernatural and go 'full horror', and with the Rivervale arc things finally 'felt really right.'

The five-episode arc culminated in *Riverdale*'s 100th episode, which had the universes clashing together before being set, sort-of, to rights. *Riverdale* was forced to go on hiatus after those five episodes due to Covid protocols, but when the show returned it was clear that the weirdness was there to stay. The aftermath of the Rivervale arc led to the core characters suddenly discovering that they'd developed superpowers, just in time for an evil immortal sorcerer to turn up hell-bent on destroying the town. Also, Cheryl was briefly possessed by her ancestor Abigail, who wanted to kill the core four for the crimes of their ancestors.

It was a season that ran at an even more breakneck pace, culminating in Cheryl (who had developed the ability to set fire to things with her mind, and raise the dead) receiving everyone's superpowers in the hopes that she could stop the comet that was heading straight for Riverdale. The show remained stupidly referential even in those last moments of chaos; when Veronica (who could now poison people with a touch and had effectively become a human dialysis machine) announced that she'd be delivering those superpowers to Cheryl with a kiss, Cheryl accused her of queerbaiting. It was a nod to the show's pilot episode, which had Betty and Veronica kissing in a cringy attempt to get on the cheerleading squad. Veronica's response – 'That's not queerbaiting, it's saving the world.' – showed that the writers were not just aware of their past failings, but willing to mock them. A *Den of Geek* review of the sixth season finale explained what the show had become: 'Riverdale is objectively not "good" television. Yet its what-the-fuck nature is so transgressive that the series is, in fact, great.'

In the last few moments of the sixth season finale, the characters were transported back to the 1950's, now looking much more like their comic book counterparts and back in their junior year of high school.

It was a hard reset for the show's final season that, surprisingly, had nothing to do with any of the actors being on six season contracts and wanting to leave the show.

Roberto Aguirre-Sacasa had long toyed with the idea of sending the show back to its vintage roots, and the supernatural ridiculousness of the sixth season allowed it to finally happen. He also needed to build towards an ending for the show. The decision that the seventh season would be *Riverdale*'s last came from The CW before the sixth season had finished airing, and knowing that the seventh season would end it all gave Aguirre-Sacasa the perfect opportunity to reset the show and explore who these characters could be in a different time. This wasn't the bright, shiny, vintage world of the *Archie* comics. By putting the characters in a time when things were far from rosy for queer characters, non-white characters and women, the show had the opportunity to explore social justice in a much more challenging way.

The *Riverdale* writers went into the final season well aware that they'd have to handle queer stories differently. Kevin Keller, while often reduced to his sexuality, had at least been able to live a multi-faceted life as a twenty-first century gay character – out of the closet and engaging in serious relationships. In the fifties setting, the character was forced into a much quieter, more fearful coming-out story. The introduction of new character Clay – played by Karl Walcott – gave Kevin a brand-new relationship on the show, one that was more challenging to get off the ground but ultimately more rewarding in the narrative. The same was true for Cheryl and Toni, who also had to find a way to be together in a much less accepting society. The show didn't shy away from the challenges that these queer interracial couples faced, but embraced them.

Alongside those couples were the relationships between the core four. As the seventh season was going to be the last, the writers chose to throw everything but the kitchen sink at the audience, using the idea of overcoming repressed sexuality in a more restrictive era to toy with a variety of pairings. Archie's character suffered the most in this situation – in trying to bring the show closer in tone to the comic books, Archie was dumbed down, his angst erased in favour of a 'gee willikers' good-boy attitude, and for much of the season he came across as an enthusiastic golden retriever just happy to be there. After playing with love triangles and partner swapping, the show settled on the reveal in the final episode, that Archie, Jughead, Veronica and Betty had spent their final year of high school in a 'quad' – a polyamorous relationship with all four dating each other. Finally introducing romance between Betty and Veronica was rewarding to an audience that had been clamouring for it for years, and for a show that had been rightfully accused of queerbaiting on multiple occasions, the relationship between the two was built slowly and carefully.

Alongside queerness and relationships, race also came to play a much bigger part in *Riverdale* during the show's final season. *Riverdale* was not a particularly diverse show, and had been criticised throughout its run for sidelining its non-white characters. Vanessa Morgan took to Twitter to express her frustrations in 2020, saying that she was 'Tired of how black people are portrayed in Media, tired of us being portrayed as thugs, dangerous or angry scary people. Tired of us also being used as sidekick non-dimensional characters to our white leads.' Morgan also stood up for her friend and co-star Ashleigh Murray after Murray had reportedly been called a 'diva', pointing out that 'diva' was a word often thrown at black women who have simply stood up for themselves. Roberto Aguirre-Sacasa's response was swift, acknowledging that Morgan wasn't wrong in her complaints. He tweeted a reply promising that 'We will do better to honor her and the character she plays. As well as all of our actors and characters of color.'

The treatment of non-white characters on television was being discussed widely in 2020, partly due to the surge of 'Black Lives Matter' protests in the wake of the murders of Breonna Taylor and George Floyd. Many writers, directors and showrunners made statements similar to Roberto Aguirre-Sacasa's, and some put their money where their mouth is. He certainly tried his best on *Riverdale*.

Tabitha Tate – played by Erinn Westbrook, another *Glee* alum – had been introduced in the fifth season, another black character that the show had sidelined. She was brought further to the forefront in season six with the reveal that she was a time traveller, as well as the town's guardian angel, in an episode that sent her through history dealing with racial injustice in *Riverdale*. Erinn Westbrooke, speaking to *W Magazine*, said that she was 'so glad that Evan Martin, an African American writer for *Riverdale*, and the writers' room as a whole, chose to confront those realities through a character like Tabitha.'

When Josie McCoy was brought back for her single season five episode, the writers didn't shy away from calling themselves out for underusing the character in past seasons. Josie gets the opportunity, in the episode, to tell all of her white school friends that they had treated her as an acquaintance, at best. This was *Riverdale* at least trying to acknowledge its more serious flaws – not just giving African American characters a more active role in the narrative, but giving one of those characters a chance to call out how she was written as a sidekick in the past.

The final season had a vague overarching narrative that the characters were in the past to try and make the world a better place, to put it on a more positive path. The characters weren't aware of this – or their past lives in the future – at all, but the story gave the writers even more of a reason to look at issues of the time. This wasn't an idyllic version of the fifties. While *Riverdale* often fell deep into surreal fantasy, the historical elements of the show's final season were grounded deeply in reality. The opening episodes of the season discussed the Emmett Till case: a black man murdered for apparently whistling at a white woman, and the subsequent acquittal of his murderers. Ironically, the show then sidelined Erinn Westbrook by sending the fifties version of Tabitha off to become a more active part of the civil rights movement in the wake of the Till case.

As the season went on, the show examined more than just racial tragedy, with Toni beginning an African American literary society alongside Clay that incorporated the work of the Harlem Renaissance poets into the show. The aftermath of the Korean war was very much felt, with Reggie (played by Charles Melton) introduced as a farm boy and basketball player with a Korean background. In *Riverdale*'s modern-day seasons, Reggie's character had been a dumb jock turned mobster, and the show hadn't engaged with his race at all. In the final season, it was a necessary part of his story.

Of course, there was the standard *Riverdale* ridiculousness in the final season as well; alongside testing out every possible relationship the show could offer there was comics censorship, McCarthyism, a serial killer dressed as a milkman and a secret Russian bomb threat. The relentless plot refused to let up as the show wound towards the end.

In the penultimate episode, guardian angel Tabitha returned to the fifties to reveal the truth to the characters, giving them back their memories but telling them they had to stay in the past. The final episode showed Betty as an old woman, revisiting her last days of high school in an extended dream sequence, escorted by a recently-deceased Jughead. It was pure fanservice from top to bottom – not a finale that would make 'best-ever' lists, but one that gave everything it could to the show's loyal audience. As Betty revisited her high school friends, watched them share memories, and listened to Archie mock his own 'highs and lows' speech, the episode delivered heartfelt conclusions for each character, explaining how almost all of them lived happily ever after.

The ending was well-received by critics – not so much for the content of the episode itself but because of what *Riverdale* had become over the seven years it was on television. It was a show that many people loved, a show that celebrated the teen dramas that had come before it and a show in a style that might not be seen again. Alex Zalben had recapped *Riverdale* religiously for *Decider*, amassing his own fans as the show went on, and he wrote of the finale that 'It wasn't about the relationships, which is why with a few exceptions the characters don't end up together. It wasn't about the mysteries, which is why the final season mostly ignored them. *Riverdale* was about the ephemeral transience of human existence.' When the final minutes of the episode showed the characters reunited as their younger selves in an endless heavenly version of the diner where they'd spent so much of their time, the audience could breathe a sigh of relief; relief both that the madness had come to an end, and that a sweet hereafter waited for all.

Many of the reviews of that final episode eulogised *Riverdale* for what it had come to represent – the show was the last bastion of teen dramas on television. *Entertainment Weekly* pointed out that 'there will never be another show like *Riverdale* again – simply because the world where a network allows a lavish, sexy teen genre drama to run off the rails for seven gloriously outlandish seasons no longer exists.'

Riverdale got to end on its own terms. Sara Schecter pointed out in a post-finale *Deadline* interview that 'I've worked on a bunch of shows where the finale was unintentional. The show just didn't get picked up. And so it was a rare privilege to be able to plan an ending in television, especially nowadays.' At the time *Riverdale* ended its seven-year run in 2022, more and more narrative shows were facing cancellation after just one or two seasons on the air, and fewer new shows were being made at all. This was no longer the heyday of television, and definitely not a time where teen dramas could thrive.

Riverdale was the last gasp of the genre. It summed up what makes these teen dramas so fantastic, and so able to build intense and adoring fandoms. It was a show that was unapologetically weird, and ridiculous. It explored teenage existence while telling insane stories about cults and serial killers. It was a miracle that *Riverdale*, that *any* of the shows in this book, got to exist at all. When *Riverdale* ended, there was no replacement. Television like this had largely stopped being made. To the industry as a whole, there's too much inherent risk to make a show like *Riverdale* viable. With the finale of *Riverdale*, what had begun in Sunnydale in 1997 had come to an end, in 2023, in a small town, on The CW.

Chapter 10

After Riverdale

Welcome to Streaming

Now, there isn't a small town. Not a diner, or a club with an impressive line-up of bands that's oddly accommodating to teenagers, or a high school, or a cemetery, or a basketball court, or a convent, or a football field, or a murder mystery in sight. There's no longer one network to look at, one place to point at on screen, no single home for teen dramas and everything that they encompass.

What do teen dramas look like in a post-Riverdale world? Television aimed at teens and shows that gather huge teen audiences haven't disappeared completely. Fandoms have moved from forums and message boards to comment sections to Twitter and Tumblr to TikTok, but they haven't gone away. People still find television to fall in love with. There's just much less of it compared to the last few decades.

Netflix boasts shows like *Sex Education*, the British teen drama starring the likes of Gillian Anderson and Ncuti Gatwa (who went on to become the Doctor in *Doctor Who*), that ran from 2019 to 2023. This was a show that celebrated identity and openness, that played with teen drama stereotypes by using American aesthetics despite its British setting, and in a rarity for Netflix, it ran for a full four seasons (totalling thirty-two episodes) and ended on the creator's terms. There are smaller teen shows on Netflix, like *Ginny and Georgia* which draws comparisons to *Gilmore Girls* for its exploration of mother-daughter relationships. Then there are the big hitters: *Stranger Things*, the eighties-set sci-fi/horror/mystery drama began on Netflix in 2016 and has not yet – at the time of writing – aired its final season. Arguably, *Stranger Things* isn't a show specifically pitched at teenagers, but it has built an audience of them nonetheless.

There are teen dramas in other places as well. HBO has *Euphoria*, a dark show driven by Zendaya's star power which has so far aired two seasons (eighteen episodes total) with a third in the works. There's *Yellowjackets* on Showtime, a story about an all-girls high school soccer team lost after a plane crash in the nineties, that also follows the teen survivor's modern-day lives. These shows are rarities, though, in the current TV landscape.

Shows both featuring and pitched at teens rely heavily on both nostalgia and familiar works now, with adaptations remaining popular. *Stranger Things* relies so heavily on eighties nostalgia that it's made a generation of fans wistful for a time before they were born. Netflix had some success with *Shadow and Bone*, which ran for a total of sixteen episodes before being cancelled and left with a cliffhanger ending. *Heartstopper*, the British coming-of-age drama created (and based on the graphic novel) by Alice Oseman, has been more successful; at the time of writing the show has aired three seasons – totalling twenty-four episodes – and is likely to be renewed for a fourth and final one.

Newer streamer Apple TV+ has taken a different approach, looking further back in history for works to adapt. *The Buccaneers* – a show based on the unfinished Edith Warton novel of the same name – with its *Gossip Girl*-but-historical feel, had a successful first season and hasn't yet been cancelled. Meanwhile *Dickinson*, a comedy-drama that put a modern twist on the life of poet Emily Dickinson (played by Hailee Steinfeld), with distinct *Dawson's Creek*-style angst, ran for a successful three seasons (thirty episodes).

There are plenty of remakes around, some more successful than others. *Bel-Air*, a dramatic reimagining of the nineties sitcom *The Fresh Prince of Bel-Air*, has lasted three seasons so far on NBC's streaming platform Peacock. *Cobra Kai* – the teen drama sequel to the *Karate Kid* movies – began on YouTube's streaming service before moving to Netflix and lasted a full six seasons. *Pretty Little Liars* had multiple sequel spin-offs: first there was *The Perfectionists* in 2019, which ran for just a single season on Freeform, followed by a two-season spin-off created by Roberto Aguirre-Sacasa that ran on HBO Max before being abruptly cancelled in 2023. HBO Max also aired a *Gossip Girl* reboot in 2021 – it also only lasted for two seasons, and was cancelled in 2023.

Teenagers have gone from a newly viable market to an in-demand audience to a far less important subset of viewers over the last twenty-five or so years. Now, as network television dwindles and streaming dominates, and fierce competition emerges from homemade media on YouTube and short-form video sites like TikTok, teen dramas are becoming a tough sell. As a result, television is growing less innovative. Teen dramas have long been trendsetters, ground-breakers and proving grounds for new ideas on television. Now there are less risks taken, less exciting new things being tried, and very few shows are lasting long enough to build devoted fandoms. Why take the risk of falling in love with something when the next six- or eight-episode drop might be its last? How can you get people discussing a show week to week when an entire season comes out at once?

The CW developed a reputation for being *the* network for teen programming soon after it emerged from what was left of The WB and UPN in 2006. That's no longer the case. In the 2024/2025 season, the network had just two original scripted dramas: *All American* – an ongoing sports drama that began in 2018 – and *Superman & Lois*, a Greg Berlanti-produced show that began in 2021, and will conclude in 2025. The rest of the network's line up is made up of reality television, sports, game shows and a couple of dramas imported from Canada. Comparatively, ten years before in the 2014/2015 season, The CW had thirteen original dramas, and the majority of them had huge teen audiences. So, what happened?

When The CW was formed, the idea was that the network could air low-cost scripted series that could be sold internationally for decent profits. With the streaming boom and that 2011 Netflix deal these shows, largely teen dramas, became even more lucrative. Things first began to shift in 2019, when the Netflix deal came to an end. Instead, CW shows were funnelled out to new streaming platforms belonging to the corporate overseers of Warner Bros TV and CBS Studios, who owned The CW. At the same time, sales to foreign markets decreased as these new streaming platforms tried to become world-wide entities.

Then, in May 2022, The CW cancelled ten of its current shows, only renewing eight. This was the highest cancellation to renewal ration from the network in years, and marked a huge slash of their scripted programming. Those cancelled shows included *Riverdale* and the *Vampire Diaries* spin-off *Legacies*. Julie Plec, who oversaw the latter, tweeted in the wake of the cancellations that 'It's the Red Wedding at WBTV/CW today,' referencing the infamous, slaughter-filled episode of *Game of Thrones*. A *Hollywood Reporter* article at the time reported that the network was in debt, and its corporate parents were looking to sell it to the Nexstar station group. The announcement came in June 2022 that the sale had gone ahead, and Nexstar promised to make the network profitable by 2025, largely by gutting the shows that were left in favour of cheaper television.

This end to scripted television on The CW was entirely financially motivated – television is a business first, after all, and the teen audiences that the network had previously cultivated were no longer a decent source of cash. Many people, however, were vocally disappointed about the change to The CW's content strategy and what it meant for television as a whole, including Jared Padalecki.

Padalecki had collectively been on The WB and The CW for twenty-four years when the announcement came that his post-*Supernatural* project *Walker* (a reboot of the nineties action series *Walker, Texas Ranger*) was ending with its fourth season. This wasn't a planned ending; the show had ended on cliffhangers that were supposed to be resolved in a planned fifth season that was also to feature James Van Der Beek of *Dawson's Creek*. Nexstar had sadly already started on their new direction for The CW. Padalecki was incredulous in a 2024 *Variety* interview that The CW would now be home to game shows like *Trivial Pursuit* and *Scrabble*, based on the popular board games. He was disappointed that the network was 'looking for really easy, cheap content that they could fill up time with', allowing himself brutal honesty and saying 'fuck it. They can't fire me again.'

It wasn't just The CW that had opted for new content strategies. All of the major networks have, in the last few years, majorly cut back on original dramas. There were around thirty dramas on network television in the 2024/2025 season, and the majority of those were either crime dramas, medical dramas or legal dramas. None of these shows are distinctly about, or loved by, teenagers. In comparison, the 2014/2015 season boasted double that number of scripted dramas, with much more variety on offer. Again, the argument can be made that teenagers are devotees of streaming, and there's no need for teen dramas on network television. However streaming services have also, in recent years, begun to devote much of their programming budgets to cheap-to-make reality television. Solid dramas do get big budgets, but they're far fewer in number.

The dwindling production of original television can be partly blamed on two recent massive interruptions to the television industry. The Covid-19 pandemic led to unprecedented production shutdowns. Many shows were cancelled rather than being put on indefinite hiatus, and the shows that were able to return-post lockdown were often cut short or struggled to re-find their audiences. Then, in 2023, the Writers Guild of America and SAG-AFTRA went on a joint strike.

Labour strikes in Hollywood are nothing new. They tend to take place every time technology for watching films and television changes, when the way writers and actors are compensated aren't adjusted accordingly. There were strikes when movies first started being shown on television, when DVD box sets became a thing and when shows first became available to download online. The 2023 strikes were focused on fair residuals being paid to actors and writers who worked on projects being streamed, and the creeping use of AI in the film and television industry. This combined strike was almost unprecedented, however. It's rare that both of the major Hollywood guilds strike simultaneously, and this particular strike was one of the longest in history.

Many of the shows that had survived the pandemic filming restrictions were now, again, on pause, alongside a large number of films in the works. Networks and production companies put planned work on hold. Warner Brothers alone suspended deals with Mindy Kaling, J. J. Abrams and Greg Berlanti. While those major names did eventually get back to work, by the time the strikes were over the television industry had changed for good.

Then again, television had been changing for a while. The streaming model that led to the strikes has rendered long-running television shows and network-length seasons of shows unsustainable. In the wake of better protections and residuals for creatives being negotiated during the strikes, major streamers are even less interested in keeping shows going for a long time. Unless a show is guaranteed to keep bringing in more subscribers, it's cheaper in the long run to cancel it than make a second season (where writers and actors might expect a pay increase), let alone let it run to five, or seven, or fifteen. Across the internet and media, television viewers are expressing constant frustration with the rapid cancellation of shows.

Netflix's *Lockwood & Co.* – a British supernatural detective show based on the Young Adult book series by Jonathan Stroud – rapidly built an enthusiastic and vocal fandom when the first season came out in 2023. Despite high viewing figures (the show reached the #1 spot globally for Netflix during its second week on the platform), excited fans spreading the word about the show and the obvious potential for multiple seasons, an announcement came in May 2023 that the show was cancelled. An article from *Mary Sue* at the time listed another twelve shows that Netflix had abruptly ended in recent months. While Netflix is the most obviously guilty party when it comes to rapid cancellation, the same thing is happening across almost all of the current big streamers. It's becoming increasingly clear, now that streaming has become the dominant way to consume television, that letting shows run for a long time and build audiences no longer seems like a viable business model.

Teen dramas have become a rarity, and when they are being made, they're often short-lived. There is just less new television being made. In July 2023, *Cosmopolitan* released a listicle: '45 Best Teen TV Shows for When You're in Need of a Binge-Watch'. Of the forty-five shows on the list, only eighteen were either ongoing or on the air in the last five years.

Does this matter? Absolutely. The words 'teen drama' encompass a wealth of storytelling. The shows in this book, and the myriad others that I didn't have the space to mention, were oddballs. They were shows that got to break new ground, and they usually did it on small budgets. With no new *Buffy*, or *Glee*, or *Riverdale*, there are untold lost opportunities to try new ways of storytelling and give people new things to connect to.

There's a reason some shows build huge fandoms. They become a place of connection, a shared language and a comfort. These stories, these ridiculous overblown stories that take real problems and throw them into fantastical technicolour, are rallying points. Those fandoms remain long after the stories themselves stop being told. How stories are told on television has changed dramatically, but these dramas remain. Hopefully, there will be more to come in the future.

Conclusion

You Are Now Leaving...

It is a Saturday night in Brooklyn. People dressed in formal wear and cosplay and fantastic combinations of both are dancing to nineties music. Outside, I speak to people who were introduced to *Buffy the Vampire Slayer* as children, by older siblings or babysitters or lenient parents. I speak to people who watched it live as teenagers and found common cause with fighting vampires, demons and the forces of darkness. I speak to people who came across the show later in life and found something they never knew they needed.

These people have travelled. Some just locally, some from across the United States and some from further afield. One man has come from Australia, timing a stop in New York on a three-month world tour around attending this prom. All of these people have been brought together by *Buffy*, and by *Buffering the Vampire Slayer*. People have become friends, become family, through a show and a podcast and a Facebook group that feels like home. Now, they are gathered, singing and dancing and communally celebrating what amounts to a TV show that many would write off as being a bit silly.

On Sunday, pyjama-clad fans assemble to watch a couple of episodes of *Buffy*. Together, we sigh at the sight of Rupert Giles in 'Band Candy' and cry as the song 'Wild Horses' plays during 'The Prom'. Many of us are tired, some hungover, all emotionally buoyed and exhausted from a weekend of celebrating a shared love.

Communities like this grow because of shows that get a chance to be loved. Maybe the celebrations aren't all inspired by a high school prom, but around the world people are finding ways to celebrate the shows they love together. Whether at conventions or online, whether via years of podcasting or writing fanfiction or creating art of just sharing stupid jokes, fans find each other, they come together, and community arises. Just like the small towns home to almost all of the shows in this book, these communities become places for everything – they're townships linked by something more than mere geography.

It's important that television like the shows I've written about in this book gets to exist. That these shows get to find their people, and those people get to find their tribes as a result. It's important that television gets to be weird, and overly-referential, and try odd new structures like musical episodes and *Citizen Kane* homages. It's important that these shows with multi-faceted characters exist, that teen audiences can discover new ways to think of their own identities. Teen dramas are shows that open minds and push new ideas.

The television landscape going forward might look bleak. There may never be another network like The CW. It may not be enough anymore for viewers to just watch a show and adore it. Then again, trends are cyclical, and this is true on television as well. Viewers' appetites change, and come around again. Television that gets to push boundaries, be different, last and create communities; this isn't lost for good. When the cycle comes around again, it will most likely be teen dramas that lead the charge in changing what television can be.

Maybe none of this seems particularly vital. This is, after all, just television, and teen television at that. That doesn't mean it's not important. Those tribes that form around shared loves, the shared sensibilities that come from loving the same show – it's essential stuff.

So, find the shows you love. Talk about them. Enjoy unabashed weirdness. Hope that more of these shows come to pass. Find communities to love them with you, to share inside jokes and art and ideas. Let television be important, not a guilty pleasure, and celebrate the stories; the good, the bad and the unhinged. Maybe you'll learn something, maybe you'll see the world in a different way. Then maybe, just maybe, you might win a themed trivia night in a Brooklyn bar.[1]

1. Just like 'The Rupert Giles Research Assistants' did.